DIARY OF A
BLACK MAN
ON
WALL STREET

Word Association Publishers
205 Fifth Avenue
Tarentum, Pennsylvania 15084
www.wordassociation.com
1.800.827.7903

ISBN: 978-1-63385-411-6

Library of Congress Control Number: 2021901678

Layout and Design by Jason Price

DIARY OF A
BLACK MAN
ON
WALL STREET

FROM YOUNGSTOWN, OHIO TO THE BIG APPLE

J. DEREK PENN

WORD ASSOCIATION PUBLISHERS
www.wordassociation.com
1.800.827.7903

CONTENTS

INTRODUCTION

Growing up in Youngstown, Ohio, in the late sixties and early seventies, Wall Street may as well have been on the moon! An industrial, soon to be *rust belt* city, tucked in the northeast corner of Ohio, about fifteen miles from the Pennsylvania state line, Youngstown rarely heard the term or place Wall Street come from the lips of its citizenry. The roughly 140,000 inhabitants of this gritty city in the sixties and seventies were inextricably tied to the steel industry, a geographic part of the Mahoning Valley, or the Steel Valley, as it was, and still is, known to locals, even though the business of making steel packed up and went to Japan in the late seventies. The architecture of steelmaking dominated the gray and sooty skyline, with gargantuan, erector-set like fiery hot and smoky companies called Republic Steel, U.S. Steel, and Youngstown Sheet and Tube. Nearly everyone's family had at least one member, if not the entire family, working in the steel industry or some related business. If one wasn't a physical participant somewhere on this occupational trail, their mind, soul, or at least the fullness of their stomach, was connected to the waxing and waning of this monolithic industry. Given the dominance of iron, carbon, and blast furnaces in the Steel Valley narrative, a reference to Wall Street was generally only heard on the evening network news, with the venerable Walter Cronkite or David Brinkley mentioning the Dow Jones, which for me and most of my contemporaries could have been the name of the latest R & B singing group.

The only juxtaposition of Youngstown and Wall Street was the founding of both entities in the 1790s. The first official trade on Wall Street happened in 1792, in lower Manhattan, at the corner of Wall Street and Water Street. The various brokers created a trading accord and called it the Buttonwood Agreement, named after the Buttonwood tree they gathered around to trade their assets. This agreement would eventually lead to the New York Stock Exchange and the physical building that was opened in 1865, which is currently the home of the largest stock transaction venue in the world. Youngstown was founded five years after the Buttonwood Agreement, in 1797, by its namesake, John Young, an American surveyor and pioneer from New York, via his birthplace in New Hampshire. Young was reportedly attracted to the iron ore and coal deposits along the Mahoning River, a central river in Youngstown. He purchased 15,560 acres from the U.S. government for $16,000, a sum today that would get you a fractional share (5/100ths) of the most expensive stock on the NYSE (i.e., Berkshire Hathaway, class A stock trades around $327,000 in the fall of 2020).

The citizens of the sixties and seventies of this blue-collar town were varied, with nearly every nationality represented in this melting pot. The steel industry of the nineteenth century and the local railroads had attracted many Polish, Italian, and Hungarian immigrants. Blacks from the South had migrated to Youngstown (a town equidistant between Cleveland and Pittsburgh, Pennsylvania—about 70 miles from each) in search of employment. A number of Puerto Ricans had also found their way to Youngstown in search of stable jobs and a better life. This midway location also was appreciated by organized crime and the Mafia, as they did their "dirty" work in Cleveland and Pittsburgh, but returned and lived in nearby centralized *bucolic* Youngstown. As a teenager, it wasn't a totally rare occurrence for me to hear a car bomb in the middle of the night, or drive by a burning porch or garage of a local mobster whose home had been firebombed due to a lack of cooperation or recognition of order.

Aside from the steel industry, there was another facet of Youngstown that knitted this Mahoning Valley community together in a positive way: sports, especially football. Other sports were popular and played, but football was, and still is, king. Friday and Saturday nights in the fall were treated like holidays, and people lived for the *big game*. No one planned anything else on these nights, with the exception of burglars. It was common knowledge that the best night to rob someone's home was on Friday or Saturday night because every member of that family who wasn't working the night shift at one of the mills or at the massive General Motors plant outside of Youngstown, in Lordstown, was at the local football stadium. As a result of this vulnerability, some families started to leave the less than ambulatory grandmother or grandfather at home with a shotgun to watch the house. It was customary to have five thousand to ten thousand fans at any given stadium in the Youngstown/Warren area, watching the fifteen or so teams in the City Series Conference or the Steel Valley Conference block and tackle their way to hopeful collegiate scholarships. I was one of those participants who had spent twelve years, starting with the

McGuffey Midgets at age six, playing football for the love of the game, for respect within the community, and for a hopeful scholarship down the line. During my adolescent years, Youngstown was a national hotbed for football talent and, to some degree, it still remains attractive for college coaches, despite the population drain and high school shrinkage. During my football years in Ohio, college coaches from all over America blanketed northeast Ohio to watch high school games in the fall and came back to recruit and hand out hundreds of scholarships in the early spring.

Like most children, my foundation was cast by my wonderful parents, William and Quincy. Early on, my older half-sister, Celeste, and my older half-brother, James, also played major roles in my early development. Celeste kept me on my toes, as she many times imparted "anti-wisdom" and got me in parental trouble, much to her delight, while James imparted the typical wisdom one gets from a big brother in trying to school me in the ways of the world. My younger brother, Karl, didn't arrive on the scene until I was nine years old, but he quickly had a major impact on me, including someone I could practice my tackling on while he hopelessly tried to run the miniature football across the couch-pillowed boundaries set up as a goal line in our living room. I owe much of my adolescent tackling proficiency, especially when the runner tried to leap over me, to my wonderful little brother, Karl.

1

MY FAMILY AND EARLY UPBRINGING

My beloved father, William Penn, spent most of his young working years toiling in the blast furnaces of Republic Steel. I can remember being a preschool kid and riding with my mother in the car to pick him up after his 7 a.m. to 3 p.m. shift, or, on a rare instance where my mom succumbed to my histrionics, the 3 p.m. to 11 p.m. shift. I stretched above the car's inner door frame, from my backseat, to see him climbing through the intricate large pipes that lined the bridge and separated the road from the sidewalk, which led to the stairs descending down to the bright orange molten blast furnaces below. I was always fascinated seeing my dad suddenly appear through the puzzling pipes, dirty and visibly tired, carrying his gray metal lunchbox, but truly happy to see Mom and me. Once, like many young kids, I said, "Dad, I

1

want to do what you do when I grow up!" The smile on my dad's face went from one of love to near contempt when he emphatically said, "I'm doing this so you never have to think of a job like this! Don't you ever lower your ambition to working in a hellhole like this!" He later lowered his voice and said, "This is good, steady, honest work, but it's not what you should strive for." I never forgot that directive.

This proclamation by my dad was consistent throughout my young days on the tough streets of Y-town. Most parents generally desire their offspring to experience better lives than them, and however you want to qualify or quantify *better*, my dad was no different. William Penn was born one year into the Great Depression in 1930, and there is no doubt that the struggles that came with that time period affected him greatly, as it did for most who endured those lean and torturous years. He grew up in a two-bedroom house, with two parents, a sister, and four brothers. When I used to visit my grandparents in the Smokey Hollow section of Youngstown, at 271 Willard Street, I used to wonder how six kids slept in one 15' by 15' bedroom, especially when one of them was a female. I usually left there feeling very fortunate that I only had to share a bedroom with my older brother James.

Despite my father raising a family, working two jobs, and going to school for his undergraduate degree at Youngstown College (it became Youngstown State University in 1967), it seemed to me that he spent the majority of his time at home with me and my family. A lot of that time was spent sleeping, understandably, but when he was awake, he spent as much time "preaching about the ways of the world" as he did anything. Preaching, for better or worse, got his messages across to me and my three siblings. His words weren't voluminous, as he was very economical with his nouns, verbs, and direct objects, but they certainly resonated and were on point the majority of the time, even if I didn't immediately embrace them all at the time. Today, my father might be considered by some as a stern disciplinarian, but I rarely saw it that way after giving his teachings and directives some thought. I was fascinated by his wisdom, experiences, and insights. Furthermore, if you wanted to stay on my father's positive and pleasant side as a child, or as a young adult, you made sure that you executed on four things, in this order: take care of the academics, or books, as he would say; be respectful of everyone you come in contact with; do what you say you are going to do, to the best of your ability; and finish what you started. If you didn't take care of the first requirement, the books, then the other three almost didn't matter in the grand scheme. My siblings can all recount countless times hearing, "You are preparing your passport for your very life. If your passport is littered with trashy grades, you can expect a trashy life!"

My father's intense focus on academic achievement for his children emanated from his numerous personal experiences, many of them negative and, unfortunately, racially tainted. For instance, my dad was acutely aware of what he thought was a systemic effort to place black children in underachieving classes, and he led with a non-acceptance stance whenever a school situation warranted it. He shared with me many situations that prevented him from achieving all he thought he could achieve or that didn't allow his capabilities to flourish. At the core of his negative academic experiences was racism, some of it just a subtle sign of the times, some of it blatant. The one story, among many, that still causes me to shed a tear to this day when I think of it, was while he was attending Youngstown College. As a junior at the College, he was doing well while majoring in business, with a double minor in history and politics. He was going to school while working in the mill, as well as occasionally at a fancy local hotel, as a white-gloved waiter in the hotel restaurant that *never saw a black face consuming food*. My dad had a solid GPA, despite his family and working situation, but was rarely on campus to fraternize with fellow students or get to know any professors or administrators. One inauspicious day, he was summoned to the dean's office. He went there thinking something was wrong with the financial billing or something related. He had never met the dean and only knew that she was female. When he walked into her office, she looked up at him and asked, "Who are you?" When my dad said, "William Penn. You wanted to see me," the dean just put her hands on her head, and with a distressed and sorrowful look on her face, put her head on the desk. After a few seconds, she raised her head and said, "Mr. Penn, I don't know how to tell you this, and I know it's not right, but based upon your academic achievement, you were selected to receive a scholarship to attend a prestigious university in a joint program with our institution; however, this scholarship was for a white person. I'm terribly sorry." My dad never told me what prestigious university it was, and perhaps he never found out himself. I never asked him what school it was or any other details because I could see the immense hurt in him, even twenty years after this offense occurred. I think this event affected my dad his entire life.

My dad relayed this story to me when I was in high school and at an age when he said he thought I could internalize it and learn from it. He relayed the unfortunate story to me with two instructive angles. First, he said, "Be involved. Ingratiate yourself with the whole 'ball of wax,'" as he would call it. Second, he said, "Don't isolate yourself, self-ostracize yourself! Perhaps if that dean had known me, she could have done something or at least not broken my heart when my heart didn't even need to know of the opportunity!" On another front, he said, "Understand that you have to be head and shoulders above the majority to maybe get the same chances and opportunities. It may not be fair, but understand that fair is only for pigs and cows!"

■ ■ ■

I spent my first six years of life living with my family in my maternal grandfather and grandmother's large house on the black, Puerto Rican, and downtrodden Caucasian east side of Youngstown. It was a great social existence, given that people were always around, coming and going, and my older brother and sister had many neighborhood friends. The first friends I had were Johnny and Ray-Ray, two white kids down the block who were brothers and about as indifferent to race as I was at the time. Just as I was hitting my stride with Johnny and Ray-Ray, my dad announced that we were looking for a home of our own on either the north or south side of town, in relatively upscale areas compared to where my grandparents' home was located. I can recall Sunday car rides after church through various neighborhoods, looking at homes from the car, wishing and hoping, along with my older brother and sister, as we passed what we thought were impressive homes. My parents seemed to love one particular home that we drove by often and were intent on placing an offer. It was on a border street of one of the largest metropolitan parks in the state, Mill Creek Park, on the largely white south side of town. It was only years after we purchased a home on the predominantly white and Jewish upper north side of town that I found out the sellers of the Mill Creek home *preferred* not to sell to a black family and refused to entertain my dad's interest in the home.

Our new home on Crandall Avenue, on the north side, was absolutely beautiful, even though I terribly missed Johnny and Ray-Ray and a few other old neighborhood friends. We were the second black family within three blocks, as far as we knew, and I felt like a fish in the proverbial fishbowl. At the grade school I attended, Harding Elementary, I was one of three blacks at the heavily Jewish-populated school. Harding had a reputation as being one of the best grade schools in town, and here is where I saw my father's first sensitivity to racial issues up close and personal, when I was in the second grade. Harding administrators, understandably, asked me to take a proficiency test in a few areas to see where I was academically after having attended an inferior school, in my father's eyes, even though I had gotten straight A's at the previous school. My father, sensing that my previous school had not prepared me for Harding's rigorous academic environment, asked if I could have the appropriate study materials for two weeks before taking any tests. I studied the materials, with my mom by my side, for what seemed like every non-sleeping moment. After each study period, I took the proficiency tests and fared reasonably well, but was given some additional materials to bolster my current and ongoing studies. My dad insisted upon me being placed in the most accelerated second-grade class and that I be included within that class's most progressive group. I can remember my dad expressly telling me, "If you get treated differently than others in your class, or you get moved from one of the accelerated groups or classes, you let me know immediately." As most any responsible parent would do with his or her child in a new school, he asked almost daily how school was going, but then he would drill down further if he heard any wavering or lack of certainty in my response or voice.

Harding Elementary proved to be an absolute home run on many fronts. First, the educational curriculum and expectations at Harding were far superior to what I had been accustomed to in my young life at my previous school. Second, I was around other students who came from households where academic achievement was paramount and other existential issues were secondary. I also made numerous friends with kids with last names like Roth, Richstone, Feuer, Cohen, Shagrin, and Solomon, who accepted me and invited me into their homes. The outgrowth of these friendships led to them inviting me to their Boy Scout meetings to see if I had any interest in joining their local troop. I was terribly intimidated at first, especially given that I would be the lone and first gentile in the troop, but I joined. Quite honestly, though, a number of the Jewish kids in Troop 19 who met at Temple Rodef Sholom on Monday nights told me months after I had joined the troop that they thought I was Jewish! When I asked one of my fellow scouts, who had previously mistaken me as Jewish, why he thought I was Jewish, he said, "Your skin is whiter than mine, your hair is coarse like mine, and you speak like me." He went on to say, "The only reason I paused a little bit (on your ethnicity) was because you were faster and stronger than any of us!" I had obviously distinguished myself in the weekly dodgeball competitions that we used to play in the bowels of Rodef Sholom at the end of our scout meetings, as I was usually the last man standing after blasting all my fellow Jewish troopers.

■ ■ ■

By the fifth grade at Harding Elementary, I had established myself. I was consistently getting straight A's academically, but every now and then, I received a "poor conduct" mark on my report card. Most of the time it was because I let my sense of humor out of the bag at an inappropriate time, or was talking too much in the back of the class, or was having a tiff about who had darker skin amongst my Jewish brethren. One of the more outrageous times was when Joel Clayman stabbed me in the arm with a number 2 lead pencil (I still have the mark) for a reason I don't remember. I do remember pulling the broken lead out of my arm, trying to choke the life out of Joel as my arm was bleeding, and chasing Joel home every night after school for what seemed to be months. I only caught Joel when I felt like really fighting. I sort of treated him like a wounded antelope on the Serengeti, where I was the lion that took out a pound of flesh whenever I felt like it but didn't want to kill him because I liked the daily, albeit, handicapped hunt. As I look back, I had him in a pretty cruel situation, but after I had caused Joel to improve his hundred-yard dash time exponentially, we became friends and ended up in the same Boy Scout troop.

I also learned one of the foundations of capitalism at Harding—supply and demand—when I charged a quarter for anyone to touch my coarse hair. Many times, my Jewish friends wanted their money back because they said my hair felt just like theirs (maybe that's why Joel stabbed me with the pencil when I wouldn't give him his quarter back)!

My relative physical prowess and larger size also exhibited itself in our daily mixed gender volleyball games in the Harding gym, where everyone wanted to be on my team, mostly because they didn't want to be on the receiving end of my powerful spikes at the net. Mr. Cioli, a very cool and physical sixth-grade teacher at Harding, would occasionally pull me aside and tell me not to spike the ball so hard because I was scaring the other kids, or causing them to visit their orthodontist to adjust their braces more often than generally scheduled. In fact, just to level the playing field, or to show me how it felt when I insisted on blasting someone, Mr. Cioli would join the opposing team and fire a few shots back in my face! I loved the senior competition from him and was proud when I beat him or was able to return his spikes.

In my latter years at Harding, at the ripe age of eight, I also joined the cross-town little league football team. I often visited my two first cousins, Keith and Kevin, on the other side of town, and during one visit, I went to their little league football practice to watch. I immediately decided I wanted to play the game. I spoke with the head coach, Ray Carter, an icon in the community and the head coach of the McGuffey Midgets. He told me to bring twenty-five dollars to the next practice, and he would buy me some cleats and get me suited up. The only problem was how was I going to get from the north side of town to the east side of town for practice every day. My dad was working at General Motors at this point and, primarily, working the 3-11p.m. shift, and my mom was a school teacher, who rarely got home before 5 p.m. How was I going to get to practice? My dad had suggested that I play for the team on my side of town, the team sponsored by an upstanding funeral home director, McCullough Williams, and I could walk to practice. I remember telling my dad that Mr. Carter had reached out to me and wanted me on his team. Not that the McCullough Williams team wouldn't have accepted me, but they hadn't reached out to me and made me feel wanted like Mr. Carter had. My dad nodded his head, and said, "Always better to go where you're wanted rather than where they don't or are indifferent." In fairness to the leadership of the McCullough Williams team, I never presented myself to them as I did to McGuffey, but many of my father's stories about being an outsider colored my decisions early in life, through today.

I managed to hook up with six other athletes on my side of town, and we all carpooled with Mr. Saunders, football player parent and assistant coach, in his Buick Electra 225 (aka deuce and a quarter). Every day in the late summer and fall, we drove through housing projects, over railroad tracks, up dusty dirt roads, and to an area of town known as the Sharon Line. There used to be a streetcar that ran along the main road (Jacobs), between Youngstown and Sharon, Pennsylvania, in the early 1900s, hence the name Sharon Line. We rode in the deuce and a quarter in our football pants and carried our cleats in our helmets, with our helmets stuck in the head hole of our shoulder pads, with the jersey over the pads, so that we could quickly jump out of the car, pull on our shoulder pads, lace up the cleats, put on the helmet, and start our warm-up laps. The thirty- minute ride to McGuffey Center, the local community center and football team sponsor, was spent razzing on anything and everything amongst the boys, with Scales (Mr. Saunders) telling us what we needed to do to improve, while also being parental in asking who was trying to be cute and not wearing all the requisite pads in their football pants. Many athletes today wear the pants without pads, in an effort to be quicker and, in some cases, snazzier without the bulging pads. Mr. Saunders didn't let us get away with that, though, and throughout my eighteen-year football career, I wore every single pad I could find. His early safety teachings probably saved me a few broken bones, and certainly some scars, even though I broke enough bones over the years (collarbone, forearm, wrist, fingers, and toes) and have at least one scar representing each of my eighteen playing years.

Our little league team was quite the prolific team, with a squad that, over a nine- year span, was 88–7, and usually ended up playing McCullough Williams or the West Side Colts for the championship. The McGuffey Midgets and McCullough Williams were the two most powerful all-black teams in the league. The all-white power team was the West Side Colts. All three teams had players that went on to play Division 1 college football, and, in a handful of instances, some went on to play in the NFL. One funny moment that comes to mind during my tenure with the McGuffey Midgets was an extremely cold December game against the West Side Colts. When my team got off the bus in the sub-zero weather, with the wind whipping, we looked like participants in the Iditarod in Alaska. We all had multiple layers of underwear, sweaters, coats, gloves, scarves, and all sorts of cold weather gear that didn't belong on any sports field. To add insult to injury, I personally had to take off my many layers to strip down to my jock strap to make the 105-pound weight limit, as did a few players on both teams. In any event, we lost the game before it even started. When we went out on the field to warm up, we looked at the other end of the field and saw that the West Side Colts had on cut-off half jerseys and were doing calisthenics! One of my teammates said, "Penn, look at that shit! Those white dudes ain't even cold!" We were psychologically done before we even started. Our head coach was telling us that the Colts weren't any tougher than we were, as he was shivering his ass off and could barely form his words, his lips sticking together in the hawk. If you could read the lips of my teammates behind their mufflers and ski masks, in their helmets, it would have been a universal, "Bullshit. They ain't tougher than we are!" I don't remember the final score, but we were only remotely competitive in the game, as the Colts won the championship in a game that we wished had been postponed, if not canceled altogether. Some of my teammates thought the whole championship game setup was a conspiracy, because the Volney Rogers League officials should have known that black people *don't do cold weather* and the schedule should be moved up to avoid the frigid field and allow our athletic talents to appropriately flourish.

One of my more memorable and satisfying athletic feats was when I played on a little league baseball all-star team. I was selected to represent my team, the Buckeye Elks, and to play third base. Unfortunately, the team was coached by a man whose son was also on the team and played the same position as I did. I had played this coach/son team during the regular season, and as soon as I heard who the coach was, and that his son had also made the team, I told my coach that I didn't want to play. My coach asked why I didn't want to represent the Elks on the all-star team, and I told him that I wouldn't get much playing time because the coach's son plays the same position. My coach said, "Get out there and TAKE your position!" Well, as I suspected, I got very little playing time during the two-week tournament. Every now and then, I got in the game during the late innings, when the game's outcome wasn't in doubt, as we were undefeated, but each game, I got more pissed, and I told my dad that I was going to quit the team. That conversation ended quickly. My dad said, "You're not a quitter. Be prepared when your opportunity arises." As we got to the semifinal round, the opposing pitcher was mowing our team down with his fastball; it was unhittable. The score was 2-0, in the opponent's favor, going into the eighth inning, and we had only gotten a few hits off this "gasser"; however, we had gotten two men on base in this inning, via two walks, and as I sat at the end of the dugout, sulking, with my feet propped up, blowing Bazooka bubbles, I heard my name. "Penn, you're up!" I only realized that I had been really called when everyone in the dugout looked at me as I squinted, looking into the infield. "Penn, get your ass in gear and get out there. You've been frowning over there for three days. Let's see what you can do!" As I jumped up, my legs were asleep from being propped up all game, and I nearly did a face-plant on the spit and pumpkin seed-laden dugout floor. All eyes were on me as I got myself together and selected my bat, put on a batting helmet, and approached the on-deck circle to get in a few practice swings. As I walked past the dugout, I heard the coach say to the assistant coach, "Watch this. Here's another strikeout." I got up to the plate, dug in my feet, took a couple practice swings, and set, ready for the pitch. The pitcher wound up, and I wound up, and the next thing I knew, the first pitched ball went over the centerfield fence! Not only did I unload on this pitch, but I hit and dented the windshield of a car in the parking lot! Thankfully, the car happened to belong to the coach, which I found out after the game. I couldn't hold in my ironic joy as my teammates laughed their asses off. The only two people not laughing were the coach and his son. We won the game, 3-2, and I never played again. We lost the next game and were eliminated from the semifinal round of the tournament, but I had gotten my pound of baseball flesh.

2

JUNIOR HIGH, HIGH SCHOOL, AND THE RAMP TO DUKE UNIVERSITY

After Harding Elementary and its Jewish-dominated student body, I enrolled at Hayes Junior High School. The transition from Harding to Hayes was considerable, given that I was going from a 2 percent gentile school to a serious melting pot at Hayes. Aside from a more diverse student body and interacting with more students that shared my place in society, I welcomed junior high school, because the school was across from my home on Crandall Avenue. Nothing was better than being able to get out of bed thirty minutes before my daily home room, put some Afro Sheen in my "natural," get a hot shower to help the Afro Sheen penetrate my hair follicles, pick out my fro into a nice round bush, and being able to run out the front door, in any weather above twenty degrees, without a coat, and be in my seat before the first bell of the school day.

One of the more interesting pursuits of junior high was my continuance of my violin lessons and playing in the school orchestra. In elementary school, I rarely stood out when I carried my violin case back and forth from school in the third through sixth grade. At Hayes, where glue sniffing, smoking marijuana (or "herb," as it was called around my neighborhood), chasing girls, and pre-publicized after-school fights were on the daily calendar along with the books, I stood out like a sore thumb carting a black violin case around. Given my living down the street from a reputed mobster, who every other summer had his garage firebombed or his car blown up, I often hoped the people who saw me with the violin case thought I was carrying a nice long gun! By living across the street, I could sometimes sneak into school unnoticed with my violin case, but every now and then I got the "WTF look" from a classmate who spotted me.

My penchant for the violin was totally revealed when the school held a much dreaded, on my part, school concert in the gymnasium. As the students filed in and saw me sitting in the first chair violinist seat with a strange bow in my hand and a brown almond-shaped instrument resting on my lap, they all took a second look. As the students got settled in their chairs, I could see out of the corner of my eye the various students careening to see me, and I could hear the detectable murmur of conversation in which the first couple sentences, I'm sure, were, "Are you kidding me? Is that Derek Penn playing the goddamn violin or whatever that instrument is?" One of my classmates, who was on the junior high basketball team with me, loudly said, "Penn, I know that isn't you with that wooden guitar!" Well, after I summoned all the intestinal fortitude I could muster, and along with my other orchestra mates, I put on a pretty good show and couldn't have been cooler. When I went out a few days later and managed to put up twenty points in a school basketball game, I became ultra-cool, at least in terms of the only demographic I cared about—the girls.

■ ■ ■

In junior high I developed a love of English composition because of two extremely good English teachers: Mr. Malone in the seventh grade and Mr. Rios in the eighth grade. Both were exceptional and helped me to become passionate about the structure of our language. Nevertheless, I continued my disruptive ways in class, as I generally finished my work before most of the other students and decided that being the class clown and causing everyone to laugh was more fun. During my junior high tenure, corporal punishment was still in vogue, and legal, in Ohio, and I took more than a few paddles on my hind parts from both Mr. Malone and Mr. Rios. I think I got paddled at least once from every single teacher I had at Hayes, but as prominent as Malone and Rios were on the English interest meter, they were equally high on my pain meter, and, if there were ever any group paddles, I was always on that list and would be out in the hallway with four or five other students, hands on the metal lockers, ass stuck out, as the teachers, with their custom-made wood paddles, went down the line inflaming a number of behinds. If you were ultra-cool, you came back to the classroom with a pleasant face and acting as if the paddle wasn't painful and that you took the teacher's best shot and it was nothing. If you came into the room wincing, limping, or holding your ass, that was fodder for instant suppressed laughing, as the students tried to hold back their humorous outcries. Given my lack of melanin and skin color, my face was as red as the white kids when I walked back in the classroom, trying to play off the pain while walking sideways, like a wounded gazelle! If you shed a tear, your machismo got taken down a number of notches. Fortunately, my external machismo stayed at a high level, despite my buttocks' blood being mechanically transferred via an oak paddle to my face, which quickly resembled a strawberry.

The biggest pain that I endured during my middle school days was outside of school and away from any ball field. One of my Jewish Boy Scout friends had invited me to his bar mitzvah, and this would be the first and last bar mitzvah I attended. It was held in the gymnasium or some large meeting room at the local YWCA on Rayen Avenue, near downtown Youngstown. As usual, I was the only person of color at this event, but I was very appreciative of my friend inviting me for this important event in his life. Upstairs we were cutting a rug, and I was one of the better dancers. A pretty young girl named Rachael noticed my dancing prowess and also thought I was quite the catch. She lured me back into the coatroom and proceeded to kiss me in ways that I had never experienced. I was clearly on the learning end of this interaction and was very concerned about us being discovered making out amidst the coats. Well, before she could nearly rip off all my clothes, and before I felt every part of her body, I suggested that maybe we should continue this at either her house or my house at a later date. So, we walked out of the coat room, clothes askew, and walked back to the dance floor. I think everyone but the DJ saw us come back to the floor all *loved up*!

There was some effort, for reasons I don't recall, to get all the boys on one side of the dance floor and all the girls on the other side of the floor. I could see Rachael's friends gathered around her, as we lustily stared at each other from opposite sides of the floor. On my side, all my buddies were patting me on the back, making complimentary and/or jealous remarks. Suddenly, from afar, I saw *my new girl* start to cry and immediately thought that we were in trouble for making out in the coatroom. Just about the time Rachael started the waterworks, the DJ instructed us to meet the girls in the middle of the floor, so I quickly walked over to her to find out why she was crying. My buddies followed me, as they also were curious about the tears. When I asked Rachael why she was crying, she said, "You didn't tell me you were a nigger!" If I could have dug a hole to China, I would have done so on the spot. The moment seemed like an eternity. One of my Jewish buddies put his arms around me and said, "Forget her, Derek. Let's go!" I didn't remember how I got outside, only that someone's dad took me home. I walked in my house and went to my basement and sat for what seemed like hours. My Jewish buddies consoled me for many days afterwards, and I never forgot their kindness, concern, and caring. They got me through that sorrowful and debilitating incident. I never mentioned what happened to my parents, but I do think someone told my dad. Smartly, rather than directly and overtly tearing off that specific bandage, my dad said, "Son, this country was founded on racism, and racism will always be here. Grow a thicker skin and try not to put yourself in situations where racism can rear its ugly head and mortally hurt you." Lesson learned the hard way!

Besides this painful social lesson, I also became aware around this time of my dad's appreciation and deep respect for Jewish people, in particular. I appreciated how they rallied around me after this awful incident, but my dad told me of one occurrence with our next-door neighbors, the Bernsteins, that stuck with me to this day. The breadwinner of the household, Mr. Bernstein, was a door-to-door rug and carpet salesman. Mr. Bernstein had a sudden heart attack, and my dad went next door to see the family and wish him a speedy recovery. Mr. Bernstein expressed his concern about being able to support his family and, most importantly, get his son Jerry through college and Rob through medical school. They were members of the Temple Rodef Sholom, where my Boy Scout troop met. My dad told me that at the very next synagogue gathering that Saturday, the congregation took up an offering for the Bernstein family and the tuition for Jerry and Rob to finish undergraduate and medical school, respectively, was paid in full. My dad was absolutely amazed at how the Jewish people came together and assisted one of their flock in need. He had tremendous respect for the Jewish people and their stick-togetherness.

Besides this social awakening and vicious learning experiences at Hayes (middle school), I was a very successful and well-rounded student. I managed straight As, rose to first chair violinist in the orchestra, and started at point guard on the basketball team. I was also a finalist in the school spelling bee, and if I had won, I would have represented the school in the Youngstown spelling bee competition. In the final round of three people, I exited in what everyone, from administrators, teachers, and fellow classmates claimed at the time, was a purposeful miss of a word on my part because I didn't want to win and appear uncool or nerdy. I can honestly say that I didn't purposely misspell *plantation*, even though a fellow classmate wearing a red, black, and green button symbolizing the black power movement said, "Good miss, Penn! Screw the white man making you have to spell that word!"

While at Hayes, I remained very involved in the Boy Scouts. I had risen through the ranks, accumulating many merit badges, and had attained the coveted Eagle Scout status. I have Dr. Seymour Feuer, our wonderful scoutmaster, to thank for my attaining the Eagle status, because he refused to allow me to quit when I wanted to exclusively pursue sports and girls, not necessarily in that order. Another reason I didn't quit the Scouts is because my always supportive mom had schlepped me for years to Cub, Webelos, and Boy Scout meetings and various scouting camps for years, and if I quit, all of that could have been construed as wasted effort and accommodation. I also couldn't fathom looking my dad in the eyes and telling him that I had quit something. That revelation could have prompted some serious dental bills or, at the very least, some psychotherapy. I should add that my dad only hit me once in my life, and that was because I pestered him at his bedside one morning, after he had worked the night shift, to have him drive me to pick up some weightlifting equipment at a Sears warehouse, in two feet of snow, so that I could have them for Christmas. After one significant audible moan on my part and a good five minutes of begging my dad to get up, he arose from the bed like a hibernating bear being disturbed in his cave and whacked the shit out of me in the torso. I took the whack like a man, despite being startled, as my dad fumed but quickly realized what he had done. On the ride to Sears, he was silent, visibly pissed, and I think slightly embarrassed, as we swerved all over Interstate 80 in our little blue Lancer. I tried to make a joke and said, "If I get these weights and work out, I'll be better able to withstand your hits!" All I got was that "William O." look that my siblings can all attest to! As they say, a look is worth a thousand hits! I never again attempted to disturb my dad when he was in his "headquarters," as my brother Karl came to call my parents' bedroom.

In the eighth grade, my scoutmaster, Dr. Feuer, encouraged me to apply for a full fellowship/scholarship to attend the Boy Scout World Jamboree in Japan. Despite being a pretty good student, especially in geography, I couldn't imagine going to a place that wasn't on my cherished wooden U.S. puzzle map that my parents had purchased for me as young child. Japan? I'd have to get on a commercial airplane, something I hadn't yet experienced. I had been in a small prop plane while working on an aviation merit badge in the Boy Scouts with my fellow scout-mate Billy Roth, with his dad as the pilot, but my closest experience to getting on a commercial plane was watching a jet land at Youngstown Municipal Airport when we used to go pick up my aunt, and my father's only sister, Mae Etta, when she'd visit Youngstown from New York for the Christmas holidays. Regardless, I applied for the scholarship and was extremely fortunate to receive it, even though I think my well-connected scoutmaster had greased the skids for me or the whole situation was outright fixed in my favor. During my scholarship interview, I remember one of the three-person decision panel members ask me, "What is the shortest distance between two points?" In my mind, I was thinking that maybe they were interviewing me to go to the special or short bus jamboree, but I answered the question, as well as a few others, and the next day I was informed that I was the "chosen one." The highlights and observations of the 1971 World Jamboree included being the only black Boy Scout in the entire United States; I didn't see one other person of color in the hundreds of scouts in the U.S. contingent. Camping at the base of Mt. Fuji was no joke, especially when Typhoon Olive swooped in, reportedly killing a scout or two and dangerously propelling bamboo, tents, pots, and pans through the air, which warranted our rescue and evacuation by the Japanese National Guard. I also remember going to Tokyo for the city part of the excursion and buying a Kobe beef hamburger in a restaurant with my fellow scout and tent mate Randy Feuer (the scoutmaster's son) and becoming googly-eyed when we did the Japanese yen currency conversion and realized we had bought, and eaten, a $40 hamburger! If we could have regurgitated that hamburger and gotten our money back, it would have been a done deal! Another food memory I have is taking the Bullet Train from Tokyo to Kyoto and getting a boxed lunch on the train. I quickly bit into the boxed lunch sandwich, without pause, and one of my molars hit something gelatinous. I peeled off the top layer of bread and saw that I had bitten into the eye of something that I think came from the sea, and belonged in the sea, not on a sandwich. That Kobe beef burger from two days prior, along with the current mouthful of eye gel, was soon on the Bullet Train window, as we sped at 200 mph to the Kyoto Imperial Palace. That experience is when I got hooked on McDonald's, Japanese style, for the balance of my trip.

When I returned to the States about ten pounds lighter, I had to immediately pick up playing little league baseball again for the Buckeye Elks. We practiced at Evans Field, deep down in the hood, near the Westlake Terrace projects. Something sinister always seemed to be going on in this sea of identical connected brick apartments, affectionately called Brick City, but on this particular day, the center of attention seemed to be on the head baseball coach, Mr. Cunningham, and me. I had missed about ten games while in Japan and, consequently, incurred the wrath of Mr. Cunningham, who claimed that he didn't know I was going to Japan and the team hadn't won a game since I left. I may have been an important part of the team, but my absence was hardly the reason they hadn't won a game during the three weeks I was gone. Nevertheless, as some sort of comedic punishment, Mr. Cunningham sent me out to my third-base position, without my fellow infield teammates, and proceeded to continuously hit ground balls to me, in rapid-fire succession. As I fielded them on the rock and glass strewn infield and threw the balls back to the catcher as another ball or two was on its way, Mr. Cunningham loudly and continually scolded me for going to Japan. "Dick (he either couldn't or wouldn't call me Derek), what in the hell are you doing in Japan? Ain't no black people over there! We ain't won a goddam game and you over there with them Japanese! Well, we gonna wake your ass up today and get that jet lag out of your ass!" My teammates, specifically Maurice Stewart, Michael Fordham, and Fred Saunders, to this day, enthusiastically tease me about this scene with Mr. Cunningham, which could have been a very entertaining comedy segment today on *Funniest Home Videos*. I'll never forget my teammates inflaming the situation even further when I reminded Mr. Cunningham that I had indeed told him and the whole team I was going to Japan for three weeks, but when asked, they said, "Mr. Cunningham, we didn't know he was going either! He just cut out on us!"

■ ■ ■

In the fall of 1971, I entered Rayen High School, made up of approximately 60 percent black, 20 percent Latino, and 20 percent white students. Rayen was located next to a large parking lot that separated my elementary school, Harding, but the two schools couldn't have been more different. Rayen also had a much bigger footprint, which included a wonderful football stadium that held approximately 8,000 to 10,000 people. Most of the Jewish kids I went to Harding with went to a high school in the suburbs, like Liberty High, or to boarding schools. If my dad had his wishes, I never would have entered Rayen, as my father preferred me going to boarding school at Deerfield Academy, in Deerfield, Massachusetts. Since early in junior high, my dad had talked to me about Deerfield, gotten other people that knew of Deerfield to talk to me, and had me read their school materials that he conveniently ordered for me. As I became a young teenager, my dad constantly worked on my psyche about being black in America. He constantly reminded me that "Mr. Charlie" (his code name for white people) had a 300-year head start. He enforced that the Civil Rights Act was bogus and had very little teeth in the legislation. He discussed that 1619 (the arrival of the first slaves) and 1776 (the year that America supposedly became a country for all) merely represented 157 years of suppression and racism. My two brothers can attest to constant reminders from my father that each and every day we were creating our *passport for life*. 'Don't hang around knuckleheads!" This applied not only to friends, but to family as well. If my dad thought that even a first cousin was a bad influence, or just a general knucklehead, steer clear. "Stand up straight and proud!"; "Dress correctly!"; "Shine your shoes!"; "Make sure your clothes fit properly!" I had constant reminders when I was fitted for clothes. My dad made sure my clothing was altered properly, and he even called out a clothing store manager and his tailor once when my suit was haphazardly altered. There was a constant reminder that "Mr. Charlie doesn't care how you look. You have to care how you look."

■ ■ ■

Despite the pressure from my dad to go to Deerfield Academy, I was able to appeal to him on two fronts. I wanted to play major high school football, and there was no better competition than the Youngstown City Series League. Every college of any consequence recruited there for some of the best football players in the nation. Of the twenty-two players in the City Series League that were voted first team All-City, normally at least half of them went to Division 1 schools on full scholarships. The second reason that surprisingly softened my dad up was the fact that Deerfield was an all-male boarding school (in 1989 the school went co-ed). I remember painfully saying, "Dad, you are going to send me up in the cold woods of Massachusetts with a bunch of hard legs?" He replied, "You'll be studying and playing ball. You won't have time for a girlfriend. You'll be working on your "passport!" My dad relented when I appealed to him and said, "Dad, I'm a straight-A student. I'm doing well playing football and my three other sports here. My friends are here. I've not gotten into an ounce of trouble despite all the craziness going on around me. Can we just not mess this up?" Thankfully, he eventually agreed without much angst and a little assistance from my ace-in-the-hole, Mom. I was actually surprised that he rolled over so easily, and his listening to my reasoning made us even closer. I started to build a nightly routine and bond with my dad when he would come home from work late at night and sometimes wake me up to watch the *Tonight Show* with Johnny Carson with him. He loved Carson, and I grew to love Carson as well. He brought my father much intellectual comedic joy and laughter, and Carson became *must-watch* TV for me as well until he left the air many years later.

■ ■ ■

My freshman year was relatively uneventful, as I once again excelled academically in a college prep curriculum and played all the three major sports that were offered at the school: football, basketball, and track. There was an effort to start a baseball team at Rayen, but that effort was short-circuited when someone, or most likely some group, stole all the new uniforms before the season even started. I wasn't sure whether I should laugh or report the individuals who were wearing the stolen orange and black Rayen baseball jerseys down at Evans Field, whether they were playing sandlot ball, driving to the hoop for a layup on the basketball courts, or were rolling dice against the walls of Brick City.

The other significant occurrence my freshman year was playing the reluctant quarterback on our freshmen football team. I clearly didn't have the best arm on the team for the position, but our freshman coach, Mr. Hunter, told me, as I sulked about being put at quarterback, that I had to play quarterback because, in his estimation, I was "the only one that could remember the goddam plays!" That isn't true, but that was how it literally played out. I threw two passes all year—one for a touchdown to the only white guy on our team and another one for an interception. The third time I tried to pass I got sacked and got a permanent scar on my elbow. From that play on, the only plays I needed to remember were ones where I either ran the ball or handed it off to running back, and lifelong friend, Gerald Price. Unfortunately, I also had to give up the violin, as I hurt my bow hand playing quarterback and couldn't play in a concert. The music teacher, Mr. Bush, told me that I needed to make a decision—violin or football. After I did a mental check for about thirty seconds and surmised there were far fewer violin scholarships than football grants, the Stradivarius was discarded. (About ten years ago, I bought a violin, and one of these days, I'm going to learn again how to play Mendelssohn's *Violin Concerto*, or at least *Pizzacato Pete*.)

My sophomore year is when I started to seriously work on getting a college football scholarship. I started at middle linebacker and played quite well until I broke my collarbone while running a kickoff back. Prior to breaking my collarbone, our team bused to Painesville, Ohio, a town about seventy miles northwest of Youngstown, near Lake Erie, to play the local team. I vividly remember some of the fans, and even some of the players, from the all-white Painesville team, calling our virtually all black team "niggers" and "jungle bunnies" as we headed to and from the locker room at the stadium and onto the playing field. One of our black assistant coaches came into the locker room at the scoreless half and was furious, throwing his clipboard, banging on the chalkboard, and loudly imploring us to go out and kick some ass in the second half. He shouted, "They're calling us niggers and jungle bunnies! I'm not taking that shit! I'm not a nigger! You guys better go out in the second half and knock that 'nigger' shit out of them!" Unfortunately, we lost the game 6-0, as we thought that not only were the Painesville people inhospitable, but that the referees shared their biased sentiment. In the locker room after the painful defeat, many members of my Rayen team raided the adjacent lockers that I think were the lockers of other Painesville students. About twenty minutes into our painful journey back to Youngstown, our bus was pulled over by two Ohio State troopers. This stoppage precipitated bus windows being quickly opened and the side of the road being littered with Painesville student gym shoes and clothing. It also caused our truly embarrassed and pissed off coach, Mr. Pat Ungaro, to cancel our stop at McDonald's to refuel some empty bellies. Needless to say, the next week of practice was borderline cruel, but well deserved. A few games later, in a game against one of our city rivals, North High, I broke my collarbone and missed the last quarter of the season. Fortunately, it healed quickly enough so that I was ready for the upcoming basketball season. I also ran track in the spring and was the biggest 440-yard dash runner (yards didn't become meters until years later) at every track meet, even though I did win a few races in what many consider the most physically demanding race in track.

During my junior year, I began taking everything more seriously. I loaded up my elective course work—Latin, advanced chemistry and biology, physics, etc.—to ready myself for a pre-med curriculum in college. I once again ran the 440-yard dash, as well as the first leg of the 4 X 110-yard and the 4 X 440-yard relay teams. I also high jumped, even as my body weight started to ease over 200 pounds. I became the high jump bar's worst nightmare when I landed *on* it rather than *over* it when the bar went above six feet. In basketball, I started at point guard. I became the ball handler and distributor while making the occasional driving layup or outside jumper; however, I really started to hit my stride in football. Our team was ranked in the state for much of the season, and despite us imploding a bit toward the end of the season, I was unanimously awarded All-City honors at linebacker.

My senior year at Rayen was about as good personally as I could have imagined, with the exception of my high school sweetheart, and cheerleader, Karen Walls and me breaking up at the beginning of the academic year, primarily due to us having different aspirational goals. My academics were solid and my efforts on the gridiron were exploding. My team didn't measure up to preseason expectations and win the City championship, but we packed the fans into our home stadium as well as at away venues to see the exciting Rayen

Tigers. The season-long highlight for me off the field was the crazed college recruiting effort. Throughout the season, and especially immediately after the season, when post-season honors like All-City, All Northeastern Ohio, and All-State recognition were granted, college coaches visited nearly daily. I received football scholarship offers from nearly one hundred schools, ranging from the University of Washington and Stanford out West, to Ohio State and Michigan in the Midwest, to Duke and Maryland on the Eastern seaboard. I took fifteen official recruiting trips and basically made decisions reflective of who had good basketball teams that would be playing home games during my recruiting visit. (Today, a high school athlete can only make five visits to Division 1 or Division 2 schools, per NCAA rules). I went to NC State when phenom David Thompson was leaping out of the gym after leading the Wolfpack to a 30-1 season and the national championship the previous season. In the NC State situation, I had another motivation to visit the university aside from their vaunted basketball team. I was recruited by Coach Lou Holtz, who was born and raised in nearby East Liverpool. He came into my life in a very inauspicious way when he was sitting in my living room with my father one day when I got home from school. He mentioned he was at my school to talk with me but never found me. I told him that I was around and not sure how he missed me. He said he had my class schedule, which he showed my dad and me, and that he went to two of my afternoon classes, but I wasn't there. My dad looked at me with that look and summoned me to the kitchen. He pushed me up and nearly through a kitchen closet coat door and said, "Don't lie to me. Where were you?" I told him that I skipped school in the afternoon, and with the car he sometimes allowed me to drive to school, went to the mall with my cheerleader friend, Francine Shon. With smoke coming out of his nostrils, he said, "Okay, I'll deal with you later. You go and apologize to Coach Holtz and tell him that this was an aberration and that you would like to visit his university. You're probably not going to his school, but you don't want a bad story like this out there." I walked back into the living room where Coach Holtz was sipping a beverage and told him I was a straight-A student and had only skipped school a few times in my life. I also asked him to please invite me for a visit. Twisting the knife even further, Coach Holtz said, "Mr. Penn, I'm not sure we want someone like your son at our university, but I'll give it some thought tonight and get back to Derek on my decision tomorrow." Well, that was a long, lonely night but, thankfully, Coach Holtz sanctioned my visit, which I took a few weeks later.

A vivid memory about my NC State visit was that I left my gloves and scarf in the back of an assistant coach's car and desperately needed them for the harsh Ohio winter. On the Monday after returning from North Carolina, I called the university's office and spoke with Coach Holtz. He asked me how my visit went and whether I was still interested in joining the Wolfpack. I told him I was but wanted to visit a few more colleges and, in the meantime, I needed my gloves and scarf. He jokingly told me that if I committed to NC State, I would get my gloves and scarf back.

I saw Coach Holtz at a corporate event in 2012 and reminded him of the story. I told him it was a cold winter in late 1974 and would have been a little toastier if I had gotten my winter items back. He laughed and said I pretty much got, or didn't get, what I deserved.

A few weeks later, I went to Seattle and watched the University of Washington basketball team upset number two ranked UCLA, before UCLA went on to win the NCAA championship later that spring. At the campus party after the big upset by the Huskies, I was hopeful that someone had paid off the campus police, because the drugs and debauchery I witnessed were monumental! If the players had a game in the next forty-eight hours, they would have had to forfeit due to their inability to stand, let alone run up and down a court and utilize some level of hand/eye coordination.

I next visited Bloomington, Indiana, where I watched an Indiana team that beat in-state rival Purdue, as the Hoosiers were building a team that went 32-0 the following year and won the national championship. A notable incident that happened during my late January 1975 Indiana visit occurred when another recruit and I went to play a pickup basketball game in a university gym the day before the big game against Purdue. I later realized that after being encouraged to play recreational hoops during all my visits, which I enjoyed doing anyway, was the football coaching staffs' sly way of getting a look at various recruits' athleticism while not violating NCAA rules regarding athletic testing on recruiting visits. I picked up on this after seeing a football coach at Kansas hiding up in the rafters, behind a pole, watching another recruit and me playing a game of one-on-one. I assume he was scribbling down whether I had a good first step, some hops, and appropriate lateral quickness. On Indiana's campus, head football coach Lee Corso, who had visited me in Youngstown at least three times and even came and watched one of my basketball games, suggested that another recruit and I go kill some time and play some hoops on campus before dinnertime. After dressing in the football locker room, we headed to the student gym but decided to take a detour to the gym we were told on a campus tour was where the Indiana basketball team practiced. We entered through a side door to hopefully catch a glimpse of the Indiana team, and, much to our amazement, we saw soon-to-be famous Coach Bobby Knight conducting practice with his team. This team was undefeated at the time and went on to have a 29–0 regular season, only to lose in the elite eight to Kentucky, finishing with a 31–1 record. We stood there in awe, and when Coach Knight looked up, he blew the whistle to stop practice and came our way. He was bigger than life, and both of us nearly urinated on ourselves as he approached. Coach Knight asked us if he could help us. I said, "We are football recruits and just wanted to watch practice for a minute." Without skipping a beat, Coach Knight softly, but firmly, replied, "This ain't football! Get the hell out of here!" In a state of shock, we both turned around and nearly tripped over each other trying to quickly get out the same door we entered. Just outside the door we doubled over in laughter and then yelled to each other, "That's messed up!" When I told Coach Corso the story, he said, "Yeah, that's just Coach Knight. I should have told you guys to stay out of there!"

My most outrageous recruiting visit experience happened when I was stranded in Chicago at O'Hare Airport during a massive snow storm. From Youngstown Municipal Airport, there were no direct flights to anywhere of significance other than Chicago or Pittsburgh. If I was going anywhere east or south of Ohio, I had to fly to Pittsburgh and catch a connecting flight. If I was visiting a school west of Ohio, I generally had to fly to Chicago and make a connection from there. I usually left for my recruiting trips on a Thursday morning and returned Sunday afternoon, and I did this so frequently and regularly in the winter of 1974–1975, that I pretty consistently had the same flight crew, at least the same stewardesses, as they were called in the seventies. The stewardesses back then were generally pretty good looking. Today, that would be rightly deemed discriminatory. Nevertheless, the beauty requirement worked for me back then. Because of my nearly fifteen-week frequency of being on a plane headed due west to Chicago out of Youngstown, or southeast to Pittsburgh on Thursday mornings, the stewardesses in both directions got to know my face a bit. One even asked me if I was some kind of very young businessman. I told her I was a football recruit visiting colleges, which she thought was pretty cool. In any event, when I got to Chicago, on my way to the University of Kansas in Lawrence, all flights out of Chicago were shut down for the balance of the day due to a blizzard in Chicago that affected many states west of Illinois. I called my recruitment coach, Jeff Rutledge, at Kansas and told him of my plight, and he told me to head over to the Hilton at O'Hare Airport, where he would arrange for me to check into a room for the night, and he would get me on a plane to Kansas the next morning. When I got to the check-in desk at the Hilton, the stewardess crew from my Youngstown to Chicago flight were in the adjacent line. As they received their keys and filed by me, one of the brunettes in the crew said they needed a fourth card player and asked if I knew how to play. It just so happened that I was a prolific card player growing up at games like gin rummy, spades, tonk, and blackjack. I also played the board games Risk, Stratego, Life, and Monopoly rather than dodging bullets, sniffing glue, or defending myself on the mean streets of Youngstown. The stewardess asked me what room I was in and I told her. When I got up to my room, I flipped on the television and began watching a movie, basically casting aside the invitation, despite my card playing expertise, but about thirty minutes into the movie, my phone rang. It was the brunette, asking me to come over to her room and be her partner in a card game. I initially said no, but when she said they had ordered copious amounts of food, my stomach said *hell yes, I'll be right over!* When I got to her room and knocked on the door, she opened it, and all three of them were in the hotel bathrobes. I was clearly overdressed in my sweatshirt and bottoms. Soon after we started playing cards, the food arrived.

As we played and ate, the conversation turned to my recruitment opportunities. Brunette number one asked me about the recruiting process; the blonde asked what I thought of the various schools I had visited; and brunette number two asked me specific questions about football. I fielded their questions, but when they started drinking alcohol, I decided it was time for me to leave, as I was a non-drinker then, and remain one today, and started to feel a bit out of place. Besides, all the food was gone! I thanked them and told them I hoped to see them on my next Youngstown to Chicago flight, as they told me they generally flew this route on Thursdays as a crew, to set them up for weekend work excursions from Chicago.

No sooner had I gotten back to my room when there was a knock on the door. I opened it to find brunette number one standing there, asking if she could come in. As soon as she got in the room, she discarded her robe to reveal her birthday suit and teach me how to … *interact* with her! About an hour after she left, my mind still blown at what had just happened, the blonde stewardess paid me a visit and took her pound of flesh! I wasn't complaining, despite being in a state of absolute shock. About thirty minutes after she left, brunette number two showed up to show me what she looked like without her Hilton- robe. By late that evening, I was hyperventilating as I was blowing up the phone lines back to Youngstown, telling my male friends what had just happened. One of my buddies asked me if I was at the Playboy mansion or at the Hilton in Chicago! I assured him that this was better than anything that could have happened in Holmby Hills in Los Angeles.

Well, I made it to Kansas the next day and was understandably pretty spent from doing my Hugh Hefner imitation at the O'Hare Hilton. I told the coach that the weather layover took a lot out of me, as I dragged around campus. At lunch, I met NFL Hall of Fame running back Gale Sayers at the University of Kansas, where he was an assistant athletic director. One of the assistant coaches referred to Gale as the Kansas Comet, Sayers' nickname from his record-breaking college days at Kansas. The coach stated that perhaps I could be a two-time All-American like Gale if I matriculated and worked hard. In my mind that weekend, I was already a three-time All-American, albeit at the University of Hilton at O'Hare!

I couldn't wait for my next trip west, to visit Notre Dame. I was excited to visit Notre Dame, but more excited to perhaps see my new friends on the flight to Chicago and pray for extremely bad weather upon arrival. I got on the plane in Youngstown, and much to my pleasure, there were *Derek's Angels*, looking extra special, but my big smile and excitement quickly turned into bewilderment, as all three of the stewardesses totally ignored me and acted as if we hadn't shared something special just the week before. Brunette number one asked me what type of soda I wanted, with or without ice, gave me a bag of chips, and went on her way. The other two never even made eye contact or even acknowledged me. I felt totally used and rejected. I'm not sure if there was a lesson to be learned in all of this, but I learned this much: be happy for what I've got, steel my heart, and move on.

All of my remaining recruiting trips were for my heart, and male pride, in an eastern or southern direction relative to Ohio, so I flew from Youngstown to Pittsburgh, with the wheels of the plane seemingly just clearing the tree tops for the twenty-minute flight to make my connecting flight. My next recruiting trip was to Yale University in New Haven, Connecticut. Yale was coached by the legendary Carm Cozza, someone with whom my dad was familiar and liked very much; however, after visiting Yale in an Ohio-like snowstorm and going to a sure-'nuff square dance in the bowels of one of the residential colleges, I wasn't feeling too excited about the non-academic side of the Yale option. Furthermore, and more importantly, since the Ivy League didn't, and still doesn't, have athletic scholarships, and provides financial aid determined by a family's finances, I hesitated to commit to a college situation where my parents would have to dig into their shallow pockets for even a nickel. I remembered that only a few years prior, our family was getting government cheese after my dad was laid off from his job, and I was determined not to dip into the slim financial coffers of my parents when I could go elsewhere, and to damn good schools, essentially free. I also wanted to play Division 1 football, even though many preached to me about potentially being a superstar in the less competitive Ivy League. My dad was so intent on me going to Yale after I got my letter of acceptance that he tried numerous strategies to try and get me to commit to become a Yalie. First, he asked Coach Cozza to promise me my high school number 32 for my jersey number at Yale. Second, he had numerous people in town talk to me about the value of an Ivy League degree. Third, he talked to me about the numerous people of color that had historically gone to Ivy League institutions and done well because the Ivy League had accepted and promoted the tenet of people of color excelling and going on to success. Regarding the two thousand dollars we would have to pay annually, he told me that he would mortgage the house and come up with whatever money Yale determined we needed to contribute. After these many approaches failed to sway me, he went deep and tried to bribe me with a car. Just to temper him a bit, I told him that I wanted to make a few more visits but that Yale would definitely be in the final calculus, which it was.

I visited a few other schools, including the University of Maryland, West Virginia, Northwestern, Ohio State, and Michigan, after Yale, which were all fine institutions, but one school stood out after my campus visit: Duke University, in Durham, North Carolina. I immediately loved the stunning campus as assistant coach Lee Moon initially drove me up Chapel Drive, which framed the majestic chapel at the top of the drive. I salivated over the combination of a beautiful, first class, prestigious academic institution, and the opportunity to play Division 1 football against many traditional football powers. I also liked the people I met in the sports administration, as well as the players already enrolled. Given my interest in becoming a doctor, the school even arranged for me to sit in on an operation by the team's orthopedic doctor who was operating on someone's wrist at Duke Medical Center. I was sold and left campus knowing Duke was the place for me. Now I had to figure out how to convince my dad that this was the best choice for me versus his dream school, Yale. My mom simply wanted me to go where I would be happiest, and she didn't even want to be around when I discussed my final choice with my dad. She knew that discussion was going to be a difficult one because my dad, unbeknownst to me, had already told his buddy, Coach Cozza, that he would deliver me to New Haven.

The day I got home from Duke, my dad woke me up when he got home from work around midnight. He asked me how my visit went, and I told him I really liked the school. His first retort was, "Derek, I don't want you going down South. You don't need to be subjected to how black people are treated in the South." He walked out of my bedroom shaking his head as he turned off the light. I stayed up the rest of the night with a knot in my stomach, trying to figure out how I was going to convince my father that Duke was the right choice for me. Over the next few days, I even thought about dismissing both Duke and Yale and going to Stanford; however, that potential plan fell through when the Stanford assistant coach who was recruiting me called, very annoyed that I had taken all these recruiting trips and was pressing up against the March signing deadline. He sternly told me to "make a damn decision," and he had also heard that I was contemplating a recruiting trip to the University of Hawaii. He was partially right, but the Hawaii coach previously told me that they were not going to continue to recruit me because they felt the probability of me leaving the Big Ten Conference was slim, and they essentially couldn't afford to fly out recruits from the upper 48 unless a recruit was intently serious about matriculating. He said that a lot of recruits take visits just to see *paradise*. I was in that category. Given the Stanford coach's impatient and somewhat harsh demeanor, I thanked him and told him that he had helped me narrow my list to Duke and Yale. Now it was back to mental gymnastics with my dad, who was far better prepared for this household warfare than I was.

I had about two weeks before the national signing day, and nearly each day, my dad gave me something positive to read about Yale and the Ivies and something negative to read about the South. I'm sure he searched long and hard to dig up some dirt on Duke, but none was found, I guess, because none was presented. He did do some research on Duke President Terry Sanford, who was the governor of North Carolina from 1961-1965, before coming to Duke in 1970. I think that backfired, because he was hoping to find out that Sanford was the Grand Dragon of the KKK, when, in actuality, Sanford vehemently condemned the Klan and fought for racial desegregation and quality education for all. I conversely gave him something positive to read about Duke and something less positive about the Ivies in general. One day, I left Duke's four-year football schedule on his dresser, with opponents like Southern Cal, Michigan, Florida, Miami, Tennessee, and the Atlantic Coast Conference schools, versus Yale's schedule of Lehigh, Colgate, and the Ivy League members. When I went into his headquarters after he went to work, to see if he had read the personally prepared "opponent comparison report," I found the document in tiny pieces in his bedroom circular file. On to plan B.

The week leading up to national signing day, my dad reluctantly gave up the fight. An incident at my high school caused my dad to first blow his top and then to reticently embrace my choice of Duke. Many interested parties at my high school, ranging from the head coach, Mr. Pat Ungaro, to my fantastic linebacker coach, Chester Leone, to the school principal and various teachers, as well as my teammates, were interested in my college choice. One guidance counselor saw my obvious angst and confusion about what school to attend when a Penn State coach named Jerry Sandusky (yes, that Jerry Sandusky) visited my school, very late in the process. He said that anyone with the last name Penn, playing linebacker, should be at Linebacker U, Penn State. The guidance counselor, who overheard Sandusky's sales pitch, suggested I should make it easy on myself and go to local Youngstown State, where'd I'd be a big fish in a small pond and a local hero. He gave me a Youngstown State University (YSU) brochure, which I added to the pile of the other hundred-plus college brochures that were stacked in the corner of our dining room. I had no intention of enrolling at YSU, even though they had a pretty solid Division 2 football team. Little did I know that my dad came in from work every night and looked at what mail I had received from the various colleges. After seeing the YSU brochure (my dad's alma mater), he woke me up around midnight and asked me where I got it. While in a sleep stupor, I told him the guidance counselor gave it to me and suggested I go there. While I went back to sleep, I think my dad stayed awake thinking about how he was going to handle the situation.

One of my classmates told me that he witnessed my dad addressing the guidance counselor, mobster-style, telling him to stay in his lane or face extinction. The next day, my dad told me to go to Duke and knock the cover off the ball academically and athletically. That guidance counselor came in very handy, in a very fortuitous way.

3

DUKE UNIVERSITY

After signing my athletic letter-of-intent to become a Duke Blue Devil, the news became public via the local paper, the *Youngstown Vindicator*. I received congratulations from far and wide. The televised and prominent signing ceremonies in high school gyms of today hadn't hit the scene in 1975, but in a football-mad town like Youngstown, any gridiron news spread quickly. I thought my commitment fanfare, which had spread to my dad's workplace, General Motors, would have further warmed him up about me attending Duke, but he was still concerned that I had made a mistake in turning down admission to Yale.

My dad's concern was on full display as the whole family drove the 540 miles from Youngstown to Durham, North Carolina, to attend Duke's spring football game; all the recruits and their families were invited. During the roughly nine-hour drive, my dad was virtually silent as my older brother and I shared the wheel of our late model Cutlass Supreme. We made sure to put soothing music on the radio and drove as carefully as possible so as not to provoke my dad in any way.

My Mom had assured me that once my dad got to Duke and saw how beautiful it was (even though she'd only seen it in the brochure), he would embrace my decision. I know how impressed I was when I saw the stunning Duke Chapel during my recruiting visit a few months earlier, so I hoped my dad would feel the same, since I know how much he appreciated beautiful buildings, especially churches.

After checking into the local Holiday Inn, I gathered the family to take the drive to Duke and up Campus Drive to see the world-famous Duke Chapel. I nearly ran over the curb on the inclined road as I drove, trying to watch my dad's expression as we got closer and closer to the majestic chapel. In the early evening light, I caught a quick but distinct smile on my dad's face that melted months of my college selection anxiety, at least for a short time.

My dad's positive attitude lasted about twenty-four hours, until he attended a cocktail party at the Holiday Inn for the recruits' parents and the influential booster club known as the Iron Dukes. The parents of the recruits weren't the problem, as most of them were similarly middle-class people like my parents, and many of them from north of the Mason Dixon line; however, the old school southern boys, many of them ardent Iron Dukes, complete with the accompanying southern twang, made my dad recoil.

The next morning, my mother had that "good luck son" look on her face, a look I'd seen many times before when I had screwed up and no words from her could save me from my dad's wrath or, more often, lesson teaching.

When I caught up to my dad at breakfast, he said, "Are you kidding me? Your mom and I had cocktails with the Ku Klux Klan last night! All we needed was for the Grand Wizard to show up! No damn way you're going to school here!"

It was a long ride back home, as now I was thinking that I'd have to renege on my commitment to Duke, but since the Ivy League is not sanctioned by the same commitment rules and regulations of the NCAA, switching to Yale wouldn't be much of a problem, even though my heart was set on Duke. I had one more secret weapon to try and win over my dad—MOM!

My mom, like most moms, had keen insight into all the family tactics and when and how to use them. It was one thing for me to give my dad the cold shoulder, and vice versa; it was another for her. After my mom had a few private conversations with my dad, with the unsolicited help of many of my dad's friends whose intellect he respected, he *finally* relented with the following: "Go down there and work your butt off academically and athletically, and don't venture into any of those quiet towns in North Carolina or anywhere else in the South. It wasn't too long ago that they were stringing people up down there!"

■ ■ ■

Before I headed south in August for the beginning of preseason football practice at Duke, I had two other high school-level athletic events to address. I was selected to play in the Ohio North-South All-Star game in Columbus, Ohio, at Ohio State Stadium. This game supposedly pitted the top thirty Ohio high school players in the North, of which I was voted a member, against the top thirty players in southern Ohio. I was also selected as the top scholar-athlete on the North team and received the award from Ohio State football legend Archie Griffin at a ceremony during the two weeks of practice preceding the game. I ended up as the leading tackler on the North squad, as I started at outside linebacker, with three other linebackers that all ended up as All-Americans at their respective universities (i.e., Tom Cousineau, Ohio State, and the number one draft pick in the 1979 NFL draft; Bob Golic, Notre Dame; and Jimmy Browner, Notre Dame). Other than leading my team in tackles, my second biggest contribution to the August game was comical. The day was very hot, and the temperature on the artificial turf was clearly above a hundred degrees. I was wearing fancy white sneakers on the smoking hot turf, trying to look fly, and managed to land a picture-perfect tackle on an opposing running back coming around my end. I firmly planted, took the runner to the ground with my helmet in his chest, got a rise out of the crowd and my teammates, and ran back to the huddle for the next defensive call. As I ran back to the huddle, my feet seemed hotter than usual, and when I glanced down to check them out, I realized that I only had the tops of my sneakers; the heat had melted the glue that held the tops of my shoes to the bottom sole. The referee called a timeout as I gathered the soles of my shoes, which were stuck in the turf in the place of the tackle, on an upward angle, consistent with my foot plant after I hit the running back. Players on both teams laughed their asses off as I ran to the locker room, soles in hand, with my shoe tops flopping, to get another pair of radial tires! My North team won convincingly.

The second game I was selected to play that summer before heading to Durham came three weeks later, on the Big 33 Ohio team, which, theoretically, featured the best thirty-three senior football players in Ohio against the best thirty-three players in Pennsylvania, in a game in Hershey, Pennsylvania. The best thing I can say about that game is that Ohio won for the first time in many years, but it was costly for me, as I broke my left forearm blocking a field goal. I was successful in blocking the goal, but a Pennsylvania player, whose injurious act I would revenge in college, dropped his head and helmet on my outstretched arm and caused me to spend the second half of the game at Hershey Medical Center getting plaster wrapped around my broken arm.

My arm injury prompted the Duke athletics medical staff to send me to the Cleveland Clinic a couple days after the game to assess the extent of the break and do whatever was necessary to make sure I healed properly and quickly. Not that Hershey Medical Center hadn't treated my injury properly, but the Duke sports doctor had a colleague at the Cleveland Clinic that he knew and trusted to determine the best course of action to get me ready quickly for the upcoming Duke football season. My dad was impressed with the concern and responsiveness to get me the best health care possible. Not only was my broken arm put on a path to, hopefully, quick and efficient healing, but my dad's psyche was also undergoing positive therapy as it related to Duke and my matriculation.

■ ■ ■

My dad and I drove down to Durham in early August of 1975 to drop me off for preseason football practice. This ride was much better than the previous one, as my dad had finally come around and was cautiously excited about my becoming a Blue Devil. Along our journey, my dad offered all sorts of fatherly advice regarding work ethic as it related to academics, athletics, women, and life in general. I only realized a few days later, after he dropped me off, that the idea of the trip being just him and I was purposeful on his part. He was very cunning and smart in that way, amongst other ways, and I only realized this as I matured.

Preseason practice was brutally hot, especially inside a helmet. The learning curve to understand everything that could be done with eleven athletes on offense, defense, or special teams was steep. The three-a-day practices left me sore, exhausted, and depleted, but I persevered, all the while dragging my healing left arm around in a new fiberglass cast. I also got to know my teammates, especially my fellow freshmen. My indoctrination into the Southern culture, both on and off campus, was also noteworthy. My first request for a pop (a soda to Southerners) was met with puzzlement. When the team held a picnic sponsored by the Iron Dukes boosters, I was introduced to both North Carolina cuisine and the bewilderment of Southerners as it relates to Northerners, and vice versa.

I recall filling my plate with a ball of vinegar-soaked pork, which was very different than the barbeque I grew up with in Ohio, so I said, "Where's the bone in the barbeque?" When I reached the end of the line and was about to check out, the hostess said, "Hon, go back and get yourself some hushpuppies." When I couldn't find them under the food tables, she said, "Hon, what are you looking for down there?"

"I'm looking for the hushpuppies!" I said.

With a perplexed look on her face, she pointed to some little barrels of fried flour and cornmeal on the top of the table, in large aluminum bins. Shaking her head, she said to everyone within earshot, "I don't know if number thirty-two is going to make it here coach. He ain't too bright!"

Hell, for me, and most Northerners I knew, hushpuppies were something with soles, insoles, and laces!

Another early football chore was to test the physical fitness, speed, and strength of each of the football players as we came into preseason camp. This regimen helped the coaching staff figure out who had worked out over the summer and who kicked back on their local beach. I found it hilarious, but not surprising, that the white players dominated the long-distance run, a test that required the players to run two miles in under fifteen minutes. In the forty-yard dash, the black players dominated, with me leading the freshmen class, running the distance in 4.5 seconds, fiberglass cast and all. When some of the faster black players failed the distance run, one of the coaches chastised the group for not being able to accomplish the endurance feat. One of the black players said, "Coach, I haven't seen too many two-mile runs for touchdowns, but I'm damn sure I have seen some forty-yard ones. Which type do you want?" That wise guy ran many unwanted disciplinary laps around the track at Wallace Wade Stadium. I think the coach was trying to show him that long twitch muscles were just as important as short twitch ones.

After I conquered the cuisine issues and got through the onerous preseason preparation, it was time to dive into the books in the beautiful gothic buildings on campus. This started on a poor "oh shit" note as I got into my first class, Math 19, Duke's lowest level math class for freshmen. I knew I was in trouble when the professor asked how many people had taken calculus in high school and my football teammate and I were the only two people to *not* raise their hands. "Oh boy," I thought. "Here we go!"

The academics were way over my head in nearly every class. As I continued into my early pre-med curriculum, I was stumped at every turn. My frustration with not performing well boiled over when I studied every waking hour for an introductory chemistry class exam and received a score of eighty percent, which was an unacceptable grade to me. I wished that I had scored higher, but at least my score got me in the B range, if my high school grade chart held true to form. The professor then proceeded to put the range of scores on the blackboard, the letter grades associated with those ranges, and the number of people that scored in each range. After he put the chalk down, I realized, much to my disappointment, that I received a D, along with one other person. I walked out of the class, exam clenched in my fist, searching for answers as I dragged myself back to my dorm room.

After a sleepless night wondering if I had made the wrong college decision and determined to have the professor address what I thought was an unfair D grade, I paid him a visit and asked how in the world an eighty percent proficiency could render a D. He then explained how the curve grading system worked. As I grew more agitated, he said the curve grading system and subsequent letter grade was based on how each person did relative to the others. He then explained that, technically, he could have given me an F, since I was at the bottom of the class.

I was boiling mad at this point and told the professor that he should call an ambulance. With a look of compassion and absolute concern, he asked if I was feeling okay and whether I really needed medical attention, to which I responded, "No, *you're* going to need an ambulance after I put a 'curve' in your jaw if you don't change my damn grade!"

Thankfully, my disposition calmed a bit and I refrained from taking a swing at the professor before I stormed out of his office, saying, "I can't do any better!"

Later that day I got the expected phone call to come to Mike McGee's office, the head football coach, before practice. I knew I was in serious trouble. When I arrived, he spared no expletives. "WTF were you thinking?" His basic message was that I couldn't threaten my professors and that I'd just have to study harder and longer.

I spent the next week running the stadium steps at six in the morning as punishment.

■ ■ ■

My initial freshman advisor at Duke did nothing to ease my academic discomfort; in fact, he raised my paranoia and angst to another level until I was able to process his racist insult by talking with my father.

During one of our meetings, I consulted with him about potential classes I should take in my second semester. I suggested a few science classes, consistent with my pre-med thoughts at the time, and he looked perplexed. When I asked him why he had a quizzical look on his face, he said, "I don't think you people belong on Science Drive (Science Drive is the road at Duke University where most of the science-related buildings and classrooms reside). I ended our session and immediately called my dad when I got back to my dorm. I could tell he was ready to eat up some road and come to Durham with guns blazing, but he calmly said, "Get another advisor, and do it tomorrow. Don't let a racist determine your future."

Conversely, I found extreme kinship with the many black Duke workers on campus. The maintenance workers, groundskeepers, cafeteria workers, and waitresses in the campus restaurant, the Oak Room, were like mothers, aunts, and uncles to me. I think our connections served us equally well. For me, it was having people who understood me, my ways, my mannerisms, even my black thoughts. I can't tell you how many times I got an extra scoop of ice cream on top of the famed Oak Room banana split, or an extra piece of bacon on my BLT sandwich. They all respected me and treated me well, because for them, it was almost as if the black students' matriculation and success was also their success. I believe, and rightly so, they helped to pave the road for the black students to attend a school like Duke, which wasn't integrated until 1963 by five black undergraduates. This was evident when I returned to Duke after graduation, on a recruiting trip for my first Wall Street firm, Morgan Stanley. I went to the Blue and White Room, the main cafeteria, to see a few of the workers and grab a bite. Nearly ten black workers, both male and female, came out from behind the counters and the back kitchen and hugged me. I was nearly in tears at the outpouring of love, as they couldn't have been prouder of me and my success. One woman, who had worked at Duke for nearly thirty years at that point, whom I absolutely loved during my time on campus, said, "Sir, you look so good in that white man's suit! I'm so happy for you. Don't you take no shit from them white folks!" I said, "Yes, ma'am! I hear you."

■ ■ ■

My first year on the football field went much better than the academic side, even though the team ended the season a disappointing 4–5–2. My broken arm prevented me from playing in a game until the sixth game of the season, when we took on Clemson at home, in Wallace Wade Stadium. My first start was playing as a stand-up defensive end/outside linebacker. Across the line from me was Clemson All-American stud, tight-end Bennie Cunningham, who fortunately went out more on pass routes versus attempting to block me. I fully planned on using my quickness to make sure his 6'5" 270-pound frame didn't fully touch my 6'1" 220-pound frame.

We upset Clemson 25–21, and I was on the books as a player after recording a few tackles. The next week, I started at Florida in Gainesville at outside linebacker, albeit in a losing cause (24–16), as the Florida fans touted us loudly as "Gator Bait!" We finished the season with another loss, one win, and two ties. Team-wise, the season was a disappointment, but I had managed to establish myself as a bona fide starter for the Blue Devils at linebacker.

Another highlight of my freshman year was seeing Duke start a black quarterback, Mike Dunn, something that hadn't happened in the history of Duke football. Mike was an even more highly-touted incoming freshman than me, and the fact that this highly respected university was starting a black quarterback was noteworthy and newsworthy. I didn't make the opening season game to Southern Cal due to my broken arm, but the guys that made the trip told me that the black players at Southern Cal all stood when Mike came into the game. It was an historic moment for a school like Duke to have a black quarterback. Ironically, USC also had a black quarterback,

Vince Evans, who was an acclaimed starter, but a black quarterback at Duke was another story. Dunn was a top ten recruit coming out of high school and maybe the highest ranked high school football player to ever enroll at the prestigious institution in Durham, North Carolina.

■ ■ ■

I got wiser and smarter my first year at Duke, away from the classroom and the football field. I was amazed at the apparent wealth of my fellow classmates, certainly relative to my family's tax bracket. One student, who later became a friend, apparently didn't mind flaunting her family's wealth by driving a bright orange Mercedes sports car her freshman year that seemed to say, "stick it up your ass." Prior to my arrival at Duke, I had never seen or heard of a BMW automobile. My freshman roommate, Jeff Crunkleton (also from a steel mill town in New Castle, Pennsylvania and also a member of the football team) and I compared independent research notes on these BMWs and discovered that BMW stood for Bavarian Motor Works. Our next question was, where is Bavaria, and is it near the Ford or General Motors plants in Ohio, Michigan, or Pennsylvania? In the meantime, while I was figuring out how to get back to Ohio during school breaks and debating whether to take a bus or hitch a ride with some other financially challenged classmates who had a family jalopy at school, many of the other students were jetting off to the beach. While they enjoyed the sun, surf, and unsupervised alcohol consumption, my breaks involved coal, smokey haze, and hot beverages while traipsing through soot-laced snow in Ohio.

My dad sent me pizza money to Durham on a pretty regular basis, but I thought I could augment my income by volunteering for different experiments over at Duke University Medical Center. In the back of the student newspaper, the *Duke Chronicle*, many times there were ads to make $25 to $50 by being one of the hospital's research subjects. A few of my financially challenged teammates and I would subject ourselves to different research regimens because it always seemed that the research required healthy, young human specimens, and it was easy and needed money in our eyes. I once did an underwater test for $25; another time, I got in a massive dryer and rotated around wearing some sort of monitoring bands; and yet another time, I took a shot of something they told me was a mega-vitamin and they then wanted to monitor my response to the vitamins. I casually mentioned this to my dad once and he nearly came through the phone. He told me to stay the hell out of the hospital unless I had a "broken leg!" After I pushed back and told him it was easy money, he nearly had a cardiac moment on the phone. He went on to tell me about the so-called Tuskegee experiment, where black men with syphilis were not told they had the venereal disease and were left to suffer to be studied to see how the disease affected them long term. He said this unethical and racist government-sponsored experiment had only been recently revealed after many years of black men being guinea pigs. He also mentioned how black women had been unknowingly sterilized during medical checkups to keep the black population in check. He made me promise to never participate in another medical test at Duke or, as he said, "any other goddam hospital or medical facility." The only time after my father's directive that I went to Duke Medical Center during my undergraduate days was to get an x-ray on a separated shoulder.

On campus I encountered classmates that clearly hadn't spent much time around black people or people of color in general. For instance, at times I felt I was back in elementary school with the Solomons and Cohens, as more than a few of my white classmates wanted to touch my large, round afro. Afro hairstyles in the mid-seventies were quite prominent, but many of the white Duke students had only seen them on television. I brought them Lincoln "Linc" Hayes, from the popular television series *Mod Squad*, in living color. I also felt like the odd man out in the classroom, because whenever I spoke up or was called upon, the room went eerily quiet as my classmates waited to hear what I had to say and how I would respond. In one class, a real cute blonde Southern belle used to totally turn around in her seat if she was sitting in front of me to intently watch me whenever I spoke. I thought she was trying to visually connect to my smooth baritone voice. After I got to know her, she told me that in Alabama, she had never heard a black person speak with such eloquence and authority, unless the person was on television. I took it as a compliment but always wondered afterwards where in the hell in Alabama she grew up?

One of my all-time highlights at Duke came when the student government club invited comedian Richard Pryor to campus for a stand-up concert in the spring of 1976. Pryor was the number one comedian in the land at the time and had recently launched a hilarious and controversial weekly television show. His comedy on television was borderline R-rated for the time, and I think the student group that invited Pryor, certainly the administration, thought they would get an edgy R-rated, Pryor, not an X-rated Pryor. That thought was quickly extinguished when Pryor came out in Cameron Indoor Stadium and announced, "Damn, there are a lot of white MF's in here! Didn't they sell no tickets to black folks? Duke University! Institution of higher mf-ing learning!" His colorful language continued when he talked about the football team.

"Y'all football team went out to Southern Cal last season and got your mf-ing asses kicked! Them boys out there don't fuck around. If they lose, they get thrown in the fucking ocean! Y'all need to keep your asses here and not fuck with dem boys out there!"

My teammates and I rolled in the audience for ninety minutes. He was absolutely hilarious, but there were more than a few tight faces in the audience, and in the next issue of the student newspaper, the *Duke Chronicle*, much was made about the selection process for entertainment on campus going forward.

■ ■ ■

My sophomore year at Duke was a little smoother on all fronts, but I still was struggling academically, at least as it related to the curve grading nonsense. I was full bore into my chemistry major at this stage and somewhat expected that I would be a lifelong average student at best. I was behind the average student in math and science, primarily because most of them had already seen the material or were exposed to some aspect of the coursework in an earlier life. I thought the only courses in which I could excel, relative to my peers, were English courses, where I felt I had a strong foundation, going back as far as elementary and middle school. I declared an English major as well, given that I loved the courses and thought good grades in English could balance the poor ones I was bound to receive in chemistry, as I pursued a double major in chemistry and English.

One of the more hysterical memories of my sophomore year was when I enrolled in a German class, in an attempt to learn another language. After all, I had taken Latin for four years in high school and gotten straight As, and I was quite proficient in English composition. Besides the typical professor-led instructions at Duke, we also had a lab where you could independently listen to tapes, in whatever language, and then repeat what you'd heard while recording your effort on a reel-to-reel tape to increase your pronunciation proficiency. During my very first lab class, I must have threaded the tape in the recorder improperly, because when I looked up, my tape was like spaghetti and was crisscrossed and wound thirty ways around the spindle. I immediately pulled my tangled tape off the recorder, full of embarrassment, and hoped that no other student had witnessed this carnage. I then marched out of the lab with my mangled tape and went over to Perkins Library, where my sophomore roommate, Harold Morrison, was quietly pretending to study. When I showed him the tangled tape, we both burst out laughing. That was the end of my German experiment; however, I did learn one sentence for my troubles, which I'll never forget: *Der hund est in the kirche*, which translates to there is a dog in the church!

Another memory I have is learning how important it was to pay strict attention to the professor's instructions. My roommate during freshman pre-season practice, Larry Doby Jr. (son of Hall of Famer Larry Doby, the first black baseball player in the American League and second black after Jackie Robinson in the Major Leagues), was in a philosophy class with me. We got an assignment to write a two-page paper about some aspect of philosophy. I got a little giddy and wrote a five-page paper that I thought was superb. When Larry came over to my dorm room, I asked if he'd finished the philosophy assignment that was due the next day. He had totally forgotten about it, so I gave him my paper as an example. When the professor handed the papers back after grading them, Larry, whose two-page paper was largely a slimmed down version of mine, received a B, while I received a D, with the message scribbled next to the grade, *I stopped reading after two pages!* Lesson learned. (Larry still jokes about it to this day.)

■ ■ ■

Athletically, I started all eleven games at linebacker my sophomore year. Our record was 5–5–1, with an opening victory at Tennessee, where we silenced 100,000 fans dressed in bright orange. We won 21–18, and I had a game-saving tackle when I caught their All-American receiver and punt returner, Stanley Morgan, from behind, as he broke out on a punt return on his way to paydirt. My college nickname, Speedy, was solidified at that very moment. It also provided for some comedy in the weeks to come, as when I reached for Morgan, I tore away two different parts of his tear-away jersey before I was able to corral him and prevent him from scoring.

My next memorable game was when Tony Dorsett and his nationally top-ranked Pittsburgh team came to Durham. We held Dorsett to, reportedly, one of his lowest rushing totals (126 yards) of his career, but their quarterback, and my fellow Youngstown gridiron star at a crosstown rival high school, Matt Cavenaugh, was named *Sports Illustrated's* Player of the Week for crushing us, by throwing five touchdowns for over 300 yards in a 44–31 victory for Pitt.

The last memorable game for me that year was a loss to our arch-rival, North Carolina, which prevented us from having a winning season and ending up at 5-5-1 instead. North Carolina was down 38–31, with a little less than three minutes to play, and had to drive about eighty yards to tie the game. Their ACC player of the year, running back Mike Voight, vacuumed up yards on his way to a touchdown and a 38–37 deficit before the Tar Heels had the audacity to go for a two-point conversion to win the game. Needless to say, their audaciousness was rewarded as we walked away with a loss and a huge knot in our stomach, knowing we had blown a very winnable game that would have made for a satisfying season, especially having beaten our biggest rival.

■　■　■

During Christmas break in 1976, I was excited about returning home to Ohio to see my family and friends for a few weeks. I was prepared to fly home, but my teammate, Carl McGee, also a fellow Buckeye, talked me into riding home with him to his home in Cincinnati and then either taking a bus or renting a car for the balance of my journey home. Something told me to use my $150 airline ticket and fly home, but my teammate and fellow linebacker buddy appealed to me to keep him company on his ride home. I could also save some money, as $20 back then may as well have been $1000. He also told me he was giving a ride to a female law school student from nearby North Carolina Central who had the hots for him, but the attraction wasn't reciprocal, and he thought it would be easier for him to thwart her efforts if I was in the car.

Off we went, though, with her in the backseat and me riding shotgun. As we approached the mountains of eastern Tennessee, the weather got progressively worse, and a few miles into the mountainous region, the snow was coming down hard. More than a few cars and trucks had pulled off to the side of the road due to slippery conditions and low visibility, but we trudged on. As we rounded one curve, a state trooper on the side of the road was motioning for everyone to slow down. Still, we rolled along in Carl's rose-colored Ford LTD at about thirty-five miles per hour, listening to Roy Ayers' "Running Away" in the tape deck. I closed my eyes for a second, behind some rose-colored shades, muttering Roy's lyrics, "shooby doo, boom, boom, boom," when all of a sudden, BAM! We had slid across the road, hit the cement median, and were now sliding back toward the guardrail on the other side of the road in what seemed to be slow motion! As I braced for the guardrail hit on my door, it was as if the car just jumped and skipped over the guardrail and turned with the front of the car facing the rocky, downward slope. My next view was a steep incline of about fifty yards, with a frozen river at the bottom. I later learned that this river, in Maggie Valley, was a tributary of the Tennessee River. As we slid down the mountainside, the woman in the backseat was screaming, and Carl was clutching the steering wheel. I braced my hands on the dashboard, all the while the guts of the car were being ripped out from underneath by the rocky terrain. It's a miracle the car didn't explode or turn over. It went straight down like a sled. As we approached the frozen river, the woman in the back now singing superlative soprano, a wheel on the car went flying. We hit the frozen river and immediately broke through the ice. The strong current carried the car about twenty yards through the broken ice floes, fortunately lodging the front of the car onto a massive rock. As the front of the car was caught on the rock, the back of the car started to sink. Instinctively, I rolled down the passenger seat window (thankfully, the windows weren't electric), and as the car began to sink, I climbed out the window, got on top of the sinking car, jumped onto a portion of the rock and then from one rock to another, until I hit land and sprinted up the hill in a state of shock. When I got to the top of the hill, a trucker who had pulled over met me at the guardrail and asked me if I was okay. As I got my bearings about me, I remembered there were other people in the car, and so I started back down the hill. The trucker said, "Nobody else is coming from there. Don't go back down. You're the first person I've ever seen survive a crash over this guardrail!" Just as he said that, I saw Carl and the woman climbing out of the freezing river and onto one of the rocks near the shoreline. I was thankful to see that they weren't hurt, just wet and cold. Having jumped out of the car before it sank, I was still wearing my sunglasses, with nary a scratch on me, dry as a bone. When I approached Carl and our female companion at the guardrail Carl said, "I see why they call your ass Speedy now! How in the hell did you get up here so fast?"

A state trooper took us to a local motel to clean up and make some calls. Back in those days, there was no ESPN; otherwise, the NCAA ticker would have read something like Two Duke football players go over a cliff in a car in Maggie Valley, Tennessee, but survived. The three of us eventually made it safely to our respective homes in Ohio, but the story of our ride down the mountain circulated, and as my grandmother said at the time, "Boy, I have to pray for you 24-7! This is the second time you were at death's door!" (I fractured my skull as a five-year old and was in a coma for a week.)

■ ■ ■

By my junior year at Duke, I had started to feel more comfortable academically and athletically. I also had gotten a good feel for North Carolina and its social norms, at least until I was tripped up by one incident. Since I had spent the summer in Durham taking a few courses in summer school, I had access to the athletic training facilities on campus. Outside of weightlifting, I spent some time on the track at Wallace Wade Stadium working on my fitness, to ensure that I could pass the football two-mile run in August, when preseason practice started. The track around the football field was generally occupied by fifteen to twenty people exercising and jogging at any given time (the track has since been removed from the football stadium and relocated to a new outdoor facility). I noticed a beautiful blonde running a few times during my late afternoon training, and after about the fifth time, we spoke to each other. We became friends and occasional jogging partners that summer. I learned that she was a winner in a statewide beauty pageant, and when I inquired a bit about her family background, she was a bit uncomfortable. When I pressed her about her family, she told me that her father would be very disappointed that she had become friendly with a black man. Nevertheless, our platonic friendship extended into the fall semester, and on occasion we had lunch together or studied together in Perkins Library. Then one day, one of my football coaches, a black man, pulled me into his office and asked me to tone down my appearances with "the beautiful blonde." When I got defensive and said, "Coach, she's just a friend, and I'm not with her all that often. It's really walking from a class that both of us are in, or back in the summer on the track. I have a girlfriend (who later became my wife) here at school."

"People are watching, and you must remember that this is the South," he said. "People are talking a bit, and I don't want to see you get in a pickle."

I walked from the football office at Cameron Indoor Stadium in a stupor, thinking, *damn, my dad was right.*

My junior year on the football field was a very mixed one. We opened with a bad loss to East Carolina (17–16), and then headed up to number one ranked Michigan, to take on Bo Schembechler's Wolverines. We were about 28-point underdogs, as I recall, and given very little chance of even scoring on the Wolverines, let alone winning. When we arrived at Michigan Friday afternoon and went to the stadium, known as The Big House, for our usual Friday walk-through before a Saturday game, the Michigan players were in the stands waiting for us to exit when we were leaving the field, so they could do their walk-through. The Michigan players were ridiculing us as we departed, and one of my former Ohio all-star teammates who was on the Michigan team yelled to me that he was going to crush me tomorrow. When we got back to the hotel, our head coach, Mike McGee, was furious at the disrespect shown us and told us, in his uniquely fiery way, that we had "better let the Wolverines know tomorrow that no one disrespects a Duke football team." He got us all riled up, and when the local sportscaster in Ann Arbor basically stated that the game should be a laugher on the evening news, it led to an even more interesting pre-game breakfast. I called my father and told him to "bet the farm" on the game, as my dad was prone to bet every now and then, because there was no way the Wolverines would beat us by three or four touchdowns. Well, the final score was 21–9, and a play here or there, and there could have been a monumental upset in front of 104,000 Michigan fans and about

1,000 Duke fans, including my family, who had driven 225 miles to Ann Arbor from Youngstown. I had a solid game, with a number of tackles and a few nice face-offs against my fellow Ohio all-star offensive tackle, wearing the maize and blue. After the game, I felt good about our showing. All my friends and family in attendance had that surprised look about them, as they realized that we had a chance for a huge upset; however, my dad looked sad. When he hugged me, I asked him why he was so down, because we actually beat Michigan everywhere but the scoreboard. We out-toughed them, out-hit them, but made a few mistakes, like a blocked punt that killed us. He whispered in my ear, "I thought you were bullshitting me. I didn't bet the damn game!"

■ ■ ■

Contrary to my athletic success, the first semester of my junior year was a self-inflicted academic disaster, as I put myself in a technical situation that would nearly prove fatal the second semester. I started with the standard four classes, but made a poor decision to drop one of those four classes that I absolutely hated—physics—planning on taking it in summer school, when I could better stomach the material. This reduction in classes meant that I was required to receive a C or better grade in the remaining three classes. Ironically, I failed an African studies class taught by a black female professor that seemed to truly have an issue with a bunch of jocks in her class. Every one of the football players in her class received failing grades, and this failure technically put me out of school for the second semester. The athletic department was in an uproar because of the treatment of all the football players in this professor's class, but what was done was done, despite numerous unsuccessful appeals. I was understandably distraught, but then foolishly added to my pain by pulling perhaps the dumbest stunt of my entire life. My father had generously let me drive his brand spanking new Datsun 280-Z back to Duke at the beginning of my junior year of school. Even now I think about how generous and bighearted my dad was in giving me a car that he truly loved. Many times, I thought, and still do, to some degree, that it was very selfish of me to have driven this wonderful car to Duke, but my dad always tried to put his children in the best possible situations that he could afford and provide. As I waited for my academic appeal to play out, I spent nearly every afternoon in an old gym on campus known as Card Gym, playing basketball and letting off some steam and frustration. One afternoon, I came out of Card Gym, started up my dad's gold-colored 280 Z, and immediately noticed that the radio wasn't transmitting. I stepped out of the car, checked the antenna, and realized that the internal part of my antenna had been unscrewed, which rendered the radio useless. Furious, as this had to be vandalism, I made one of the worst decisions of my life: I considered pilfering someone else's 280-Z for their antenna piece. I rode over to the medical center parking lot and in quick order found another Z. I brazenly stopped my car in the lot, walked over to the other Z, and proceeded to screw out the internal antenna piece. Fortunately, my senses returned and I screwed the antenna piece back in before I totally removed it. I walked back to my car, without the antenna piece, and slammed my door, at which point two undercover policemen who had been watching me from the back of an unmarked vehicle stepped out and told me to halt. I peeled off in my car and went back to my apartment on Central Campus. After sitting in my car and realizing how stupid I was, I drove back to the parking lot where the police were radioing in my license plate. One of the policemen was an older white man who looked straight out of a KKK movie. The other policeman was a black man that I personally knew. When our eyes met, he had that look of, *what the hell are you doing man?* I told the white policeman that I really hadn't done anything, despite my original intentions. He wasn't hearing it. He said he hoped the owner would press charges for felonious tampering, or something to that effect. The officer located the owner of the car in the medical center, and the owner came to the parking lot about thirty minutes later, where the three of us waited. She was a white doctor at Duke Medical Center and, fortunately, an avid football fan. She recognized me as a Duke football player that she had watched on many Saturdays at Wallace Wade Stadium. I told her what I had stupidly done and why. She basically asked me if I had learned my lesson, and much to the chagrin of the white officer, she said, "No harm was done, and I don't want to get this young man in any trouble. I want to see him in class and on the football field next fall." The white policeman was furious. The black officer told me to take my ass home and think about what I was about to throw away, and to pray that I never do something this asinine again. I did exactly as the black officer told me, but I did hear from Coach McGee the next day. The white officer had called him and told him of my foolish act. Coach McGee said, "I think you need to go back to Ohio for a few weeks, since you're not in school anyway, think long and hard about your actions and your academics, and we'll talk in a few weeks."

The drive back to Ohio was the longest journey of my life up to that point. I couldn't imagine telling my dad all that had happened, nor could I reconcile potentially not returning to Duke to continue trying to get my academics straightened out, nor continuing my promising college football career as a Blue Devil.

When I finally arrived back in Youngstown and saw my father, I think he was in a state of shock. He said very little, but every now and then he just shook his head and wondered out loud how my situation had gone so sideways. My mother was the typical loving mother—very understanding and trying to make my life as pleasant as possible. I also think she was trying to balance out the inevitable explosion that was surely looming in my father, which, fortunately, and utterly surprisingly, never happened. He basically told me that I had a decision to make. Was I going to be a failure or a success, and was I willing to put in the work to prevent the former and make the latter happen? I think at that point he had also realized that his work on me was primarily done and hopefully all the lessons learned would somehow kick in, in a positive manner, soon, before I made mistakes from which I couldn't recover.

After being readmitted to Duke for the summer session and talking with Coach McGee, he told me to come back to Durham, get situated, get a summer job, and make up the four classes I missed that spring semester. I think I got three Bs and an A during the summer session. I also got a summer construction job, which was the hardest physical work I have ever done in my life. A fellow football player, Stanley Broadie, and I were tasked with knocking down a solid concrete wall at the medical center with a jack hammer and a sledgehammer. We had to hold the jackhammer parallel to the floor, with one of us supporting the ninety-pound tool and pulling the trigger, with the other one directing the chisel end to the wall. The area was enclosed on both sides, as this wall was being taken down to provide for an access point between the emergency room and the monorail system at the medical center. The combination of the hot and heavy protective clothing we had to wear, the throat clogging cement dust that stirred, and the North Carolina August heat and humidity was overwhelming. Our immediate supervisor, a Caucasian, called me Duke. He was a very nice man, fifty years old, and he said one of the most prophetic things anyone had said to me up to that point. "Duke, unless you want to be doing this kind of back-breaking work the rest of your life, you'll get that damn Duke degree!" To which I replied, "You are goddam right I'm going to get my degree. No freakin' way am I going to be doing this type of work the rest of my life!" I certainly had developed a profound respect for people that do this kind of torturous work, but I thought it wasn't for me, at least not long term.

■ ■ ■

By my senior fall semester in 1978, as a Blue Devil, I finally felt a sense of calm. I had proven to myself that I could do the academic work, and I was well on my way to completing a double major in chemistry and English. Athletically, I was firmly entrenched as a leader on the football team and calling the defensive signals for our team from my linebacking position. We started 2–0 after soundly beating Georgia Tech in our home opener and followed up with a victory over South Carolina and their eventual Heisman Trophy winning running back, George Rogers. For our third game, we were primed to go back to Ann Arbor and once again put the fear of God into the Wolverines a second year in a row. This was also our chance to be nationally ranked, with at least a solid performance against them. Michigan was ranked fourth in the nation, and we wouldn't be able to sneak up on them this year like we did the previous year. I recollect that we were ten-point underdogs, but I knew my team was not as good as my junior year team. I told my dad that he shouldn't bet this game, because Michigan would probably beat us by more than ten points. I also knew from conversations with Michigan players over the previous summer that their coach, Bo Schembechler, had worked the devil out of them after their narrow victory over us the previous year, as they dropped from number one in the nation to number eight because of our close game.

During the first play of the game, I hit their offensive tackle—my former Ohio all-star teammate—and separated my right shoulder.

I stayed in the game, running around blocks and trying to hit only on my left shoulder the rest of the game. When we watched the game film the next Sunday morning after the game, I looked very foolish on film while trying to protect my injured shoulder; however, I didn't get too much grief from the coaching staff because our entire team looked foolish and bad on film. We lost 52–0, and if we had played another quarter, it would have been 102–0! So much for scaring Michigan and getting nationally ranked. The only person who felt worse than I did after the game was my dad. After my mom hugged me and asked if I was going to be okay, my dad looked like he was in more agony than I was. He gave me a hug and said in my ear, "Dammit. I bet the game. Don't say anything to your mother, because things are going to be tight for a bit!"

As one of my Duke teammates said, "We took Allegheny Airlines up to Ann Arbor and took Red Cross Airlines back," as Michigan put a hurting on not only me, but the whole squad. We finished the season 4–7, ending with my last game at North Carolina and us losing in the final seconds, 16–15, as a running back named Famous Amos Lawrence weaved his way into the end zone, seemingly eluding all eleven Duke tacklers, including me. As we were undressing in the locker room and showering, the seniors knew that not only had we played our last game in a Blue Devil uniform, but our performance also probably (and did) seal the fate of our head coach. Most of us felt Coach McGee knew on the bus ride back to Durham that he would be fired in the next twenty-four to forty-eight hours, as he went to each and every player on the bus and shook our hands, something he didn't customarily do, even if it was the last game of the season, and the last game in a Blue Devil uniform for the seniors. The news of his termination came Sunday morning. It was the end of my Duke football career.

4

THE NFL AND CFL

I n the spring of 1979, a number of professional football teams' scouts streamed through Durham to chat with me and a few of my teammates and to get a look at us on the field at Wallace Wade Stadium and on the track surrounding the field. (The track was removed and relocated elsewhere on the athletic campus in 2015, during a major stadium renovation.)

The primary interest in me was due to my reported 4.5 and occasional 4.4 seconds, 40yard dash speed. Specifically, the New York Giants, Pittsburgh Steelers, San Francisco 49ers, and the Miami Dolphins visited campus and showed interest in me as a free-agent strong safety or, to a lesser degree, as a linebacker, my natural position, although I would be an undersized linebacker in the NFL at 6'1" 225 pounds. After a couple good sprints down the track and an exhibition of decent agility on the field, I made two team visits: the defending Super Bowl champion Pittsburgh Steelers and the Miami Dolphins. I accepted a visit to Pittsburgh because they were my favorite childhood team, having grown up 70 miles away and watching them notch a few Super Bowl victories (1975, 1976, 1979) during my Duke tenure. I was also a huge fan of the Steel Curtain, led by Mean Joe Greene, while also an admirer of running back Franco Harris, who wore my long-time jersey number 32. (I wore number 32 from little league through college because of my dad's and my admiration of Cleveland Browns' running back Jim Brown).

The highlight of my Pittsburgh visit was meeting members of the Rooney family, notably cigar-smoking Art Rooney Sr., the founding owner of the NFL franchise. Mr. Rooney, head coach Chuck Noll, and a few other position coaches watched while I guarded their fourth-round draft pick, wide receiver Calvin Sweeney, from Southern Cal, while he ran pass patterns with quarterback Terry Bradshaw. At the conclusion of the workout, I was offered a free-agent contract, with a $2,500 signing bonus. I told them I would get back to them after my visit to Miami.

When I returned to home base in Durham, Miami offered me a $7,500 signing bonus if I would commit to them immediately before coming to their mini-camp. I asked Pittsburgh for a counteroffer, but they stuck to their original $2,500 offer. The fact that the director of player personnel for the Dolphins, Bill Davis, was from my hometown, attended my high school, and was the one who reached out to me, sealed the deal for me to head south, rather than north, to the Steel City. I arrived in Miami a few days later for their mini-camp, where they tested all their draftees and free agents and gave us their weight and strength expectations upon returning for preseason training camp in July. I went back to Durham with my defensive play binder and thoughts of wearing a nautical aqua and orange uniform for the next chapter of my football career. I lifted weights in the Duke football weight room in the mornings and worked on my fitness running the stadium steps in the afternoons. At the top of the steps, at the conclusion of one afternoon session, I walked onto the concourse with my hands on my hips, sweating profusely and breathing heavily. A voice said to me, "Does your workout count for both of us." It was the famous comedian, Jackie Gleason, who was standing near his red Jaguar. I recognized him and walked over and introduced myself and asked him what he was doing in Durham and at the track. He said he was attending the famous Duke "Rice Diet" program to hopefully lose at least a hundred pounds, and he was going to walk a few miles around the track daily to get started. He then looked at me, drenched in sweat, and said, "I think I'll start tomorrow!" We both laughed as he jumped back in his Jaguar, drove off, and beeped his horn twice.

If I thought Durham's heat and humidity were bad, Miami's was worse, especially when I arrived for training camp at Biscayne Community College in mid-July. Camp started off great, as I peeled off a 4.5 40-yard dash on grass, recording a tie for the fastest time amongst the rookies. A third-round pick from Alabama, running back Tony Nathan, clocked the same time as me. The next drill, commonly known as the shuttle drill, allowed me to really display my quickness, as I recorded the best rookie time; however, I came up short in the weight room, where I was only able to bench press 225 pounds, for 8 reps. A couple rookie linemen surpassed 20 reps.

My first experience of the reported exalted life of a professional athlete came during fan appreciation day. I thought every fan would be lined up in front of stars Bob Griese, Larry Csonka, Nat Moore, or Bob Kuechenburg, or anybody but a lonely free agent like me. Hell, I wanted to get in line and get their autographs! Nevertheless, many women and children stood in my line. One kid told me he wanted to get my autograph before I became famous so he could say to his friends that he recognized my talent before everyone else if I made it big. I told him that I hoped his name was Nostradamus as I signed his notepad. The number of kids in my line was also because the other lines were much longer. As for the women, I presumed they were single because a few of them wrote down their telephone number when they passed their piece of paper to me to sign. One woman even came with a self-addressed sealed envelope, which I later opened to find a G-string, photo, and phone number. I don't know if her "gift" was specifically intended for me or just random. I thought the latter after talking to some teammates. When I mentioned her forward behavior later at the training table to one of the veteran players, he said, "What do you expect? This is the big time. You haven't seen anything yet! If you make the team, they'll be lined up at your door, but if you can't handle it, rook, pass it on to me. I'll take care of it!"

The hazing process started on day one, as all the rookies were expected to stand up on the dining table and belt out whatever song was requested by the veterans. I tried to take care of my forced commitment early on to get it out of the way by picking my own song, but they liked my rendition of Bill Withers' "Lean on Me" so much that I was unfortunately called upon at numerous lunches and dinners to belt out this classic. I thought about balking after my fourth encore, but after I saw the treatment a fellow rookie received after refusing to sing (he was dragged out of his bed and thrown into the center of the nearby pond that reportedly had a gator or a snapping turtle in it), I brushed up on the second stanza of "Lean on Me" really quick.

I figured my days in camp were numbered after they moved me from the strong safety position, where they were three deep, to an outside linebacker position, where I was fourth team and undersized. Nevertheless, I thought I'd quickly make my mark on a blitz, where I managed to slip through the offensive line clean, due to my quickness, and took out Hall-of-Fame quarterback Bob Griese, with a flush blindside hit, but I held him up and didn't put him on the ground; I just banged him pretty hard. Linebacker coach Bill Arnsparger went ape shit, while head Coach Don Shula looked very displeased. Arnsparger stormed over to me and asked me why I thought Griese was "wearing a red jersey" while everyone else on offense was in white. I guess I didn't provide a good enough answer, so he told me to start running laps until either he got tired of watching me pass him on each lap or I figured out a better reason why I shouldn't put the franchise quarterback on the ground. Suffice it to say, I lost a few precious pounds that day.

What happened a few weeks later during a scrimmage late in the preseason sealed my fate. We bused to Vero Beach to scrimmage the New Orleans Saints. Thus far, I had only gotten a chance to get my uniform dirty during occasional special teams play. In Vero Beach, it looked like more of the same early on. I camped out on the sideline next to Arnsparger, hoping that he would tire of seeing my expectant face and insert me into the game. More than a few times in the first half, he gave me that annoyed "would you get lost look," but still refused to insert me. Finally, late in the scrimmage, he said in a very reluctant voice, "Penn, get your ass in there at left outside linebacker." I couldn't have been more pumped, as it was third and three for the Saints. I sprinted into the game, got the defensive signal call, and lined up with inside foot up, outside foot back, in a semi-crouched stance, with head turned into the quarterback, ready to explode. Ideally, in this situation, one prefers that the first play not come directly to him, so that you get a chance to see a few live plays and get acclimated. Regardless, I think I could have taken out King Kong if he had on a Saints uniform, given my intense adrenaline at that point. Inevitably, at the snap of the ball, an end sweep around my side started to unfold, as a duo known as "thunder and lightning" started to bear down toward this undersized linebacker. Tony Galbreath, a 6'1" 230-pound fullback, charged at the Dolphins defensive end to my right, and they ended up in a stalemate heap in front of me. Now it was just me and the running back with the ball, Chuck Muncie, the 6'3" 230-pound running back, who was the third pick in the 1976 NFL draft. From my vantage point, Chuck looked like a bull poised to run over a bull fighter who had lost his cape. His nostrils were flaring as he saw me in between him and a lot of open space where he could showcase his Olympic-quality speed. His square black goggles rested above his nose, behind his triangular face mask, as he went from 0 mph to above the expected speed limit in two steps. As he bore down on me, it appeared that he had made a conscious decision to run me over and leave tread marks on my chest, rather than juke me and potentially make me look silly, grasping at air, as he sprinted down field. Well, he should have tried to finesse me, because I laid one of the best hits of my eighteen-year football career on him. I caught him in the numbers with my face mask in his chest and proceeded to dump him on the ground with no gain. The crowd roared! I jumped up from my picture-perfect, textbook hit and sprinted to the sideline as the punt return team came on the field. I don't think my feet hit the ground on the way to the sideline, as I felt I could have tackled the entire Saints team on that play. On the sideline, I gave the pound (today's equivalent of a high five) to anyone with arms and hands. As the punt team lined up, I put my hands on my knees to catch my breath. While my head was down, a coach came over and gave me a congratulatory pat on the back. I thought it a bit strange, as he was wearing black shorts and the Miami coaches wore aqua or orange shorts. As I rose up, the coach said, "Son, that was one hell of a hit, but you are on the wrong sideline!" Embarrassed, to say the least, I took the longest run imaginable across the field to the Miami sideline after the punt play. I tried to avoid Arnsparger's glare while many of my teammates were laughing hysterically. That was a very long 140-mile bus ride back to Miami. I think Arnsparger was even more offended when I got up amidst all the razzing on the bus and announced, "I did wax Chuck's ass, though, didn't I?" The bus went crazy!

The next morning, an aide knocked on my door, telling me that Coach Shula wanted to see me in his office with my playbook. I had my exit interview with Coach Shula, which was respectful and sensitive. He said I was talented and that the embarrassing gaffe in Vero Beach had no bearing on their decision. He said I handled the ribbing well, but it just came down to a numbers game as they tried to get down to the 45-player limit on this next-to-last preseason weekend. During our meeting, I asked Coach Shula about his coaching philosophy, something that I follow to this day. I asked him why he seemingly had different rules for different players, which included everything from some players being fined for being overweight while others weren't, to some players being allowed to smoke in the locker room while others were discouraged from doing so, to some players being able to enjoy a cold beer in the locker room after practice while others received disapproving stares from coaches. Coach Shula said he learned a long time ago that a coach needed to know what made different players tick. Some players and people shut down when disciplined. Some respond well to structure. Some excel when given some freedom. Some go off the rails with their freedom. He also said that one must have some general and broad parameters that no one can violate, but it was important to treat players as individuals within those parameters. He said, "If I tell perennial all-pro guard Larry Little to stop smoking in the locker room, he won't perform up to his capabilities. I'd rather let him smoke." In a nutshell, what I took from that conversation, other than an airline ticket back north, was to treat people who work with me as individuals. Get to know their personalities, understand their positive and negative triggers, and hopefully massage and maximize their strengths while giving them some individual room and freedom. Shula's adopted philosophy worked well for me during my many years of managing people on the trading floor.

■ ■ ■

My next football stop was the Canadian Football League, after I unsuccessfully tried to catch on with the Steelers or one of the other NFL teams that was originally interested in my services; however, by that time, teams were close to having their own rosters already set for the regular season, and there was little room for an unproven free agent at that point. Subsequently, I went to a tryout for the Saskatchewan Roughriders in Washington, DC. I busted a 4.4 40-yard dash, and they signed me on the spot.

I was suspect of the move to the thriving metropolis of Regina, Saskatchewan, before I even arrived. I took a flight from Washington, DC, with a change of planes at Chicago's O'Hare Airport. When I got to the departing gate in Chicago for the flight to Regina, I thought I was at the wrong gate. This many brothers couldn't be headed to Saskatchewan! As I looked around, a number of us looked at each other and one said, "I betcha I know where all of us are going!" About three hours later, a plane load full of black football players landed in a cornfield in Saskatchewan. The team had three vans ready to transport us to the Roughriders' training camp at the local university.

My stay in Regina was about as long as it takes to get a cup of coffee. The team's first-round draft pick, out of the Canadian university system, would have had a tough time getting off the bench on my Duke team. The talent was marginal. Practice was a drag. The town had nothing entertainment-wise to offer outside of a pub in town where people went to drink and listen to country music on a jukebox. Some of the veteran Canadian players told us there were two ladies down at the pub who would "take care of us" if we got horny! I passed on Emily and LuAnne. Most of the black players ended up playing the official card game of black folks, Spades, during our down time. I primarily hung out with a fellow ACC player from the University of Maryland, Brad Carr, who played one helluva piano, as I tasked him with playing whatever song I could think of while I belted out the associated Motown lyrics in the college dorm lobby. A few weeks after my arrival, my desire to play football had diminished significantly, and I basically determined my own termination fate with a waning degree of enthusiasm. Furthermore, in the CFL, there was a limit on the number of American-born players each team could have on their roster, and it was reported that a group of American players got traded all over the league every year to playoff contenders, and I fit that player profile. (That limit today for American players on a team is around 20. I believe in 1979 it was significantly less.). Also, I felt like it was time for me to move on with my non-football life, get out of this soon-to-be-realized violent game while I was still healthy, and find a conventional job, or go to graduate school. The year before I got to Saskatchewan, the team was 2–14, the same record the team had after I left. Clearly, *I* wasn't the answer.

5

REAL JOB HISTORY PRIOR TO BUSINESS SCHOOL

After my "cup of coffee" in professional football, I set out to join the so-called real world in Washington, DC. I managed to leverage my Duke chemistry degree and got an offer from a small chemical firm located on the northern outskirts of DC, in Silver Spring, Maryland. The job was with a firm that worked as a contractor for the National Cancer Institute, a part of the National Institutes of Health in nearby Bethesda. The contractor was tasked with taking in potential anti-tumor agents from every corner of the world, and even from some unknown places, and then visually representing on paper the stereochemistry (the three-dimensional arrangement of atoms and molecules) associated with that potential agent. The substances arrived in all sorts of packaging imaginable, and the paperwork and samples were forwarded to NIH for analysis. The firm also went out to various research settings, like universities, and took samples of potentially promising anti-tumor agents. Back on the home front, one of the firm's senior staffers would take an agent into the lab, in full hazmat suit, and study and analyze the substance for further stereochemical properties. After about six months of endlessly representing these compounds on paper with carbon and hydrogen bonds, I noticed a few oddities around the office. One woman was always hoarse; another woman had small patches of her hair consistently missing; and one guy always seemed to have some sort of skin rash. Around my one-year anniversary, I decided that the chemistry lab, at least this one, which seemed to have an impact on one's personal health, wasn't for me.

While still at my chemistry job, I also took on a night job working as a security guard (really an employee anti-theft guard) at Lord & Taylor department store in Chevy Chase, Maryland, a close suburb of DC. This job allowed me to sit at a desk in the bowels of the store and occasionally glance up at a security camera, in between checking to make sure employees didn't leave with fuller purses, pockets, and more bags than when they came to work. My two-year tenure at Lord & Taylor ended when two female thieves rolled out a rack of expensive lingerie while I happened to be out walking on the sales floor. As I stepped out of the store to politely ask the women to return the expensive La Perla lingerie, one of them said that her friends Smith & Wesson were accompanying her and really wanted her to have this lingerie, which caused me to quickly decide it was too cold to be outside the store in the winter without a coat!

During my brief stints at the National Cancer Institute and Lord & Taylor, I began freelance writing, utilizing some of the writing skills I had developed during my school years. I managed to catch on as a stringer for a science periodical called *Clinical Chemistry*

News in DC. I wrote over twenty articles about various happenings at NIH, science associations, hiring in the scientific world, and, on occasion, a new scientific finding or drug. Seeing my byline in this monthly periodical, published by the American Association of Clinical Chemistry, was quite gratifying, as I was able to leverage my chemistry and English degrees in one effort. I also branched out a bit on the freelance front and submitted a first-person piece to *Sports Illustrated* about my transition from eighteen years of playing football to my then current standing. Despite the piece never being published, I got paid for it, which allowed me to come to New York to have lunch with the managing editor of the magazine, Peter Carrey. His advice was for me to continue writing to perfect my craft and to go to journalism school, preferably Columbia, right in the city, if I could get admitted.

I also wrote an article that I hoped to sell to the *Washingtonian* about the illicit use of pharmaceutical drugs in DC. I had managed to interview a number of drug addicts that were at a nearby rehab center and got firsthand insight about the significant problem in the district with legal pharmaceutical drugs. I presented the article to the *Washingtonian* and they sat on it for a few weeks. In the interim, a new city magazine, the *Washington Times,* called to inquire about my work, as they had heard through their sources about my visits to the rehab centers. I sold the article to the upstart, and obviously struggling magazine, and got a cover story; however, I think the magazine went under in less than two years, despite my Pulitzer Prize-worthy story!

My writing and knowledge of some of the inner workings of the federal government landed me a job as a lobbyist for the American Academy of Child Psychiatry (AACP). My tenure in the lobbying world was characterized by one event. There was a press hearing on Capitol Hill about various aspects of child psychiatric health. I was asked by my boss to go and cover the event for the organization.

When I got to the Hill, there was a chair for an AACP representative at a table along with a few more chairs for other lobbying representatives. I was asked to represent my organization and take a seat. My initial response was, "What?" My second, internal, thought was, *oh shit!* This was at a time before cell phones, so I couldn't call the head of the organization and ask her to get to the Hill in time, and I certainly didn't want the only unoccupied seat at the table to have been for the American Academy of Child Psychiatry. I think I may have invented the phrase "fake it till you make it" that morning! When I got back to the office and told the horrified woman in charge what had gone down, she screamed, "What the hell did you say?" I told her that I had little to say, made only a few basic comments (i.e., "the mental health of children is paramount" was my profound statement), and that I didn't embarrass the organization. She then called everyone she knew in the metropolitan area who could have possibly attended the event to confirm what I reportedly said. Despite confirmation of my limited words, and my unabashed and dull performance at the press conference, the trust was lost. Both of us realized that this position was not the career path for me.

■ ■ ■

On January 13, 1982, it all came together. Before then, I realized that none of my jobs or education had prepared me for a potential career in any type of business. When I was with the Miami Dolphins, the woman who did payroll asked how many withholding allowances I wanted taken out of my paycheck. I said, "Ma'am, I want as much money as possible in my pocket!" She just looked at me, shook her head, and put down ten while wishing me good luck. I didn't know the payback period for the commercial application of a potential anti-tumor agent, nor did I know the difference between a penny stock and a blue-chip stock. But what happened that day in DC helped me to realize it was time to get serious and try and build something a bit more lasting and substantial in my young life.

■ ■ ■

The DC Metrorail suffered its first fatal accident when a train derailed after trying to back up when the conductor realized he was on the wrong track. The front car was crushed against a concrete tunnel support, killing three people and injuring twenty-five others.

I rode the Metro every single day, and was on the system that day, albeit on another line; however, the much bigger tragedy that day, ahead of an impending major snow storm, was the crash of an Air Florida plane into the Potomac River. The plane crashed about thirty minutes before the Metro derailment, and I heard about both tragedies as I walked to my apartment across from Meridian Hill Park, in Northwest, DC. After watching the news that night and over the next few days, listening to those tragedies played over and over, I reassessed my young life and realized that tomorrow isn't promised by any stretch of the imagination and one should maximize and optimize his time above ground. That Saturday, I walked down to edge of the Potomac with a Duke friend and fellow football teammate, Marvin Brown, and watched the authorities pull a large wing of the plane from the river. That tragic image left an indelible mark on me until that horrific image was replaced on September 11, 2001.

Realizing my profound business ignorance, after never taking a single business course at Duke during my undergraduate tenure, I decided to correct this educational void. At Duke, I had spent my entire academic career on Science Drive, where all the science buildings were, or in the Allen Building, which housed most of the English department. Marketing to me was going to the local A & P grocery store, so I applied to three business schools. Even though

I was accepted at all three, the Fuqua School of Business made this a very easy decision for me by offering me a full fellowship. I was honestly shocked at the financial award and called the school to ask on what basis they thought I deserved such a gratuitous award. The financial award representative and assistant director of admissions, Jane Novick, said, "We know what you went through, we know you played football, we know you had one of the harder curriculums at the University, and we are sure you will thrive and be successful here. Do you want the award, or not, because we can quickly find someone else to give it to?" I apologized for doubting my candidacy and the school's selection criteria and told her she'd see me in August. (Sadly, Ms. Novick passed away from cancer not long after my graduation, but I am forever grateful that she overlooked my ignorance. I also want to thank the director of admissions, David Miller, who obviously played a major role in my matriculation to Fuqua).

6

DUKE UNIVERSITY'S FUQUA SCHOOL OF BUSINESS

n August 1982, I entered the Fuqua School to begin the next chapter in my education toward a business degree. I enrolled with the largest class of black students to attend what was then known as the Duke Graduate School of Business. Out of a class of approximately one hundred sixty-five students, the second-year class had three black students, and my first-year class had a record seven black students out of an approximate one hundred eighty students. One of the second-year students, and one of my best friends to this day, Owen May, remarked, "Now we can have a basketball team"; we could combine the three black males from his class and the four from my class and rock the intramural team.

Three of the students in my first- year class were from historically black colleges and experienced culture shock right from the outset.

One of those students, who lived in the same off-campus apartment complex as I did, told me that he had thought he had made a mistake in coming to Duke, given the scarcity of people of color. He was intellectually intimidated and thought he was in way over his head, despite having graduated with honors and having a business degree from his undergraduate institution. I shared with him my undergraduate trials and tribulations and assured him that the school hadn't made a mistake by admitting him. If he was willing to put in a one hundred percent effort and reached out for help early, when he felt he was behind or sinking a bit, he would be successful. Unfortunately, he didn't last beyond the first year, and, to this day, I think it was due to a preconceived notion that he was out of his league. His failure left an indelible mark on me, as I was determined to have a much better academic performance in graduate school than I did as an undergrad, and I strived to live up to Ms. Novick's declaration and expectations.

As I got my head around debits and credits and tried to stay current with my classmates who had already seen much of this material while pursuing their business degrees in undergrad, I found myself having to work twice as hard. Thankfully, my math background from my undergraduate science curriculum was something on which I could lean, which allowed me to focus more on nearly everything else. The first semester was tough, but I started to get my sea legs by the end of the second semester, at the end of the first year, and finished the year in good standing. By that time, I also began to focus on the all-important summer internship. I had intended to go to work for a health care consulting company in Rockville, Maryland, one of the close suburbs to DC. The president of this small consulting firm had seen some of my science writing while I was living and working in DC and thought I would be a good fit, not only for the summer but, perhaps, longer, after I received my MBA. I had an interest in health care and thought it might be a good fit, given my scientific writing and familiarity with various health-related organizations around the Beltway and in DC;

however, a few second-year friends in business school told me they thought I had the rough and tumble personality of a Wall Street trader and that I might be a good fit in that industry. My first thought was, *what is a trader?* After a few conversations with classmates and some research on my part, I started looking at Wall Street as a viable possibility, given my personality and interests. An industry as close to a meritocracy as possible, dynamic, fast-paced, the potential to do well financially, in the Big Apple, and where I could curse and scream just like on the football field, sounded quite appealing.

I managed to get in contact with the uncle of a fellow Duke football player, Robert Vowels, who was a significant figure working on Wall Street at Salomon Brothers. The uncle, Milt Irvin, was willing to have me come to New York to spend some time with him and others on the trading floor, which, at the time, was the largest trading floor in the world, where securities ranging from mundane treasury bills to exotic derivatives were traded. When I stepped on the Salomon trading floor, I was immediately smitten. The cacophony of sounds was spine tingling and reminded me of the football field. Constant yells and screams, with a few four-letter words mixed in, had me salivating. I had no idea that an environment like this existed outside of the Roman Coliseum or some similar sporting venue. And one can get paid handsomely for this if they bought low and sold high. Count me in, I thought; however, after talking with Mr. Irvin for about an hour and watching all the blinking and confusing screens, data inputs, and listening to the strange trading floor language, I told him I had second thoughts regarding my ability to do this seemingly intimidating and confusing multitasking job. He said, "Wait a minute! You played football for eighteen years at a pretty high level. You went to Duke and got two degrees. Nobody on this floor is any smarter than you. I'll let you sit with some of these folks for a while. You'll see; trust me. They aren't any smarter than you, and probably half of them aren't as smart as you."

I managed to get a formal invite a few weeks later for an official summer internship interview with Salomon. One of my interviews was with one of the mortgage traders, and he asked me what kind of memory I had, given that a good trader needs to remember historic trading levels, what specific clients care about, and at what levels. I told him that I thought I had a pretty good memory, so he challenged me and asked for my wallet. I hesitated, but he assured me that he'd give it back. He opened it and asked me which credit card I used the most between the three cards I had. I told him my American Express card. He then asked for the account number. I was dumbfounded and said, "Excuse me?" He proceeded to tell me that he could remember his nine-digit New York driver's license number and the account numbers of all of his credit cards. He said that I should be able to remember similar numbers if my memory was as good as I thought it was. I thought about this for a second, as I saw my Wall Street career careening off a cliff, even though I thought this was a grossly unfair and bewildering interview question. When I realized that I did know my fifteen-digit Amex number, only because my bill payment was generally late and I had received multiple notices reminding me, I spouted my number. He looked at me and said, "Your pre-interview intel must have tipped you off. I guess I have to come up with a different shtick!" Despite this seemingly successful interview, as well as what I thought was a solid performance in the other interviews that day, I didn't receive an offer for summer work with Salomon.

Before I packed up and left Fuqua in May 1983 for my summer internship with what I thought was the secure job with the health care consulting firm in Rockville, Maryland, an opportunity to make a few bucks presented itself at Duke. Frank Sinatra was coming to town for a concert in Duke's Cameron Indoor Stadium, I believe to assist in the fundraising efforts for Duke Hospital's Children's Classic event. Tom D'Armi, the head of athletic facilities at Duke, asked me and a few athletes if we wanted to make a few dollars guarding Sinatra's dressing room during his concert. After realizing he only needed one athlete to assist with Sinatra's own security detail, he said whomever knew a Sinatra song would get the job. Well, none of us knew more than a few lyrics to any Sinatra song, so Tom told us to go learn a song and come back tomorrow and sing it for him, and the one with the best rendition of Sinatra would get the job. The other athletes, all black, said, "Screw that! I ain't learning any Sinatra song!" But I went to Perkins Library and looked up and wrote down the lyrics to one of Sinatra's famous songs, "Summer Wind," for which I knew the basic melody but not the lyrics. Guess who got the job despite Mr. D'Armi saying "You sure ain't fuckin' Italian" after hearing my soulful, Motown-like rendition of "Summer Wind"?

The next night, I reported for duty at Cameron Indoor Stadium and met Mr. Sinatra and his entourage. He was much shorter, smaller, and older than I anticipated, but that didn't stop him from having a few extremely good looking, young women at his beck and call. While I did my best to check out all the women who were hanging with Frank, it was his righthand man, Jilly, with whom I got closest. Jilly and I watched the door to Mr. Sinatra's dressing room in the corner of the stadium during the entire concert, but, unfortunately, it was out of the line of sight of the performance area. I only got one or two peeks at Frank as he crooned, forgetting a few lyrics, but the crowd was quite enthusiastic and elated with Ol' Blue Eyes' presence and performance.

Jilly was a character. He had a rather large nose, perfectly white teeth, a gravelly voice, and wore a thick gold chain around his neck. He called me Duke. We shot the shit in the hallway outside the dressing room for two hours, and in that time, I told him a little bit about myself, including that I was from Youngstown, Ohio, an area he seemed to know quite well. He said, "Duke, you ever come to Philly, you tell 'em Jilly sent for you, and no fuckin' body will ever fuck with you! You got that?" Who was I to disagree! He grabbed me by my head and neck, rubbed my medium fro with his knuckles, and said, "Fuckin' guy! I like you!" He repeated, "You come to Philly and see me, you fuckin' hear?" I respectfully said, "Yes sir, Mr. Jilly."

After my memorable evening with Jilly, I refocused on trying to get a Wall Street internship, even at this late date, but was once again unsuccessful. I shifted back to the health care consulting firm in Rockville, which was always my ace-in-the-hole, or so I thought.

Once settled in a Georgetown townhouse with a few other students, I reported to the consulting firm bright and early one Monday morning. The owner of the firm welcomed me and invited me to breakfast. I thought this was a good start. At breakfast, the owner told me that my job was contingent on a government contract that hadn't yet come through. When I asked what that meant, he said he expected the contract to come through in a matter of days or weeks and to just enjoy the summer in the meantime. I wasn't happy about this and relayed to him that, despite my willingness to work for free to get some experience, I felt mislead and my trust had been broken, as I had made some financial decisions based on the expectation that I would be earning a few dollars over the summer, but now I would have to scramble.

I returned to my Georgetown room and contemplated what to do next. I needed to earn an income, and at this point I wasn't concerned about resume building. I simply needed a job to afford my one-room empire and not have to eat ramen noodles all summer, but what job could I get for eight to ten weeks? I then remembered a temporary work agency in downtown DC and immediately went there and filled out the required paperwork. Within forty-eight hours, they had me up and running.

My jobs for the temp agency included working for a tree surgeon, doing accounting work for Fannie Mae, and working for a moving company. I remember telling the temp agency that I wanted diversity if I couldn't land a job at one firm for the entire summer, but this degree of diversity seemed a bit ridiculous.

After about two weeks of this nonsense, I decided to get serious and started pounding the pavement for a real job. I put on my best suit and tie, grabbed my portfolio with the Wall Street Journal peeking out of the top, along with some freshly printed resumes, and marched over to the Washington, DC, K and L streets corridors looking for names like Prudential Bache, Dean Witter, and Merrill Lynch.

At Prudential Bache, near Dupont Circle, I was told there were no summer jobs available by the greeter at the front desk. I left a resume but saw the receptionist drop it in the waste can through the reflection in the window as soon as I turned toward the exit door. I then crossed the street to Dean Witter, where I got a little further into the office, but was eventually told that I was too late in seeking summer work, as the summer was already in full bloom. Despite this second rejection, I felt my confidence growing as I continued to get my "sell story" refined. Nevertheless, I knew I needed to try and get in to see a decisionmaker at one of these firms in order to truly present and sell myself.

After eating lunch downstairs at a restaurant nearby a Merrill Lynch office, I walked into the elevator lobby of the Merrill building and saw a sign listing the different executives. I committed the top name to memory and proceeded up to the appropriate floor. As I exited the elevator, I confidently told the receptionist who I was there to see. When she learned that I didn't have an appointment and was just "a friend, in the neighborhood, she buzzed the office and said, "His name is Derek Penn, who says he's a friend ..." Surprisingly, she gave me directions to his office.

Awaiting me on the other side of the door was a white man in what looked to be his late fifties, graying, and wearing glasses. He looked confused, as this strange twenty-six-year-old black man with a mid-height afro, who claimed to be a good friend, entered his office. He immediately asked, "Who are you?" I handed him my resume and proceeded to tell him my story and why I was there. As he studied me and listened in dismay, I fully expected him to either hit a button under his desk and a trap door under my feet swallowing me whole or him calling security. But after my ten-minute soliloquy, he sat back in his large leather chair, behind his large cherry desk, and said, "If anyone can be that creative and have big enough gonads to wiggle their way into my office, I guess there should be a place for you here somewhere. I can't pay you much, but when can you start?"

■ ■ ■

My summer at Merrill Lynch, basically for lunch money, couldn't have been more eye opening. I believe I was told the gentleman for whom I worked was the son-in-law of then U.S. Secretary of the Treasury, Don Regan. He initially placed me in the back office, operations area, where I did what was expected of me in that department. After spending about two weeks in operations, I was asked to come out on the sales floor and be a sales assistant to one of their top brokers, whose sales assistant had unexpectedly quit. This particular broker was championship boxer Sugar Ray Leonard's broker. Looking at Sugar Ray's significant account balances gave me some understanding of municipal bonds and their tax advantage particulars. Even though I believe I was supposed to be registered and have at least an industry Series 7 license, I was answering phones, taking orders, and sending in trades after having them approved by the broker. I loved the transactional nature of the business. I developed friendships with a few people in the office, in particular, with one middle-aged brother who gave me some very good advice about two weeks into my internship. He said, "Keep your head low and just work and learn. Don't even let them know you're working on an MBA, because they might treat you differently, and all you want to do is learn and become familiar with the vocabulary of Wall Street. Secondly, leave the women in this office alone, especially the white women. That can only be problematic for you." I never forgot that latter advice and have repeated it to every black man I've mentored in my thirty-four years on Wall Street.

■ ■ ■

When my interesting and creative summer was over, I returned to Fuqua, fully loaded and intent on securing a Wall Street job. I had gotten a taste of it during my visit to the Salomon trading floor and gotten familiar with a lot of the terminology of Wall Street during my few weeks at Merrill Lynch. I was also nearly caught up academically with my business major classmates at Fuqua, so the academics were less stressful as well. I was also now taking elective courses that truly interested me versus the core courses that were less desirable; however, if I never see a managerial accounting or statistics textbook again, I'd be thrilled.

The second year, as most B-school enrollees are aware, is basically spent securing a permanent job. The time during fall and Thanksgiving breaks were well-suited to interviewing and pounding the pavement in search of permanent employment. My most eventful job search occurred when three of my classmates and I went to New York after having set up some informational interviews. We stayed in a fellow classmate's parents' pied-à-terre on the upper westside of Manhattan, and for four days, we scurried all over the city to our respective interviews.

My first day of interviewing had me on my heels quickly, as I pulled the most arrogant and ignorant move imaginable. I had an interview at Morgan Stanley at nine a.m., with the head of the Fixed Income division, John Mack. Despite my "immense" knowledge of Wall Street gained from my six-week Merrill Lynch experience, reading the *Wall Street Journal* daily, and watching Louis Rukeyser's *Wall Street* television shows, I didn't know what I didn't know. On the morning of my interview, I went down to Wall Street (the actual street) and walked up and down the eight-block stretch a few times, but didn't see Morgan Stanley. I saw Brown Brothers and a few other firms, but no Morgan Stanley. I went to a pay phone (before cell phones) and called the head of the division and arrogantly said, "Sir, are you sure that you're a Wall Street firm? I'm down here, and I've walked up and down this entire street at least three times to no avail." Mr. Mack replied, "Where the hell are you?" He proceeded to tell me that Morgan Stanley is in Midtown and that if every Wall Street firm were on Wall Street, the street would stretch to Canada! He gave me the directions and instructed me to get there pronto … before I heard a click.

If I had had a change of underwear, I think I would have changed them right there in the phone booth. I almost decided not to go to the interview, but I figured, at this point, I had nothing to lose, except, perhaps, the job.

When I arrived for my interview, some 45 minutes late, I checked in at the lobby desk and proceeded to the 32nd floor. I was met by a receptionist, who was looking at me and subtly shaking her head. I nearly turned around, but decided to take it like a man. A few minutes later, she walked me over to a glass-cubed office on the Fixed Income trading floor. John Mack, the head of the Fixed Income division, came out of his office and announced to anyone within earshot, "This is the guy who thought we were down on Wall Street!" After a chorus of boos and some "Send him back to Duke" remarks, the gentleman shook my hand and took me into his office to talk. He could have further tortured me, but he didn't. He got down to business pretty quickly, and I ended up spending some time with him and a number of other employees in the department.

I went on a few more interviews that week before returning to Duke to continue bolstering my knowledge and creating a game plan to gain employment in New York. I had decided that I wanted to be a trader. I didn't care if I traded stocks, bonds, commodities, or refrigerators. I loved the action, the quick thinking and energy required, the stamina needed, the pulling of the trigger, and the nearly instantaneous feedback that one got from a good or bad trade. The trading floor also reminded me of two of the environments I had enjoyed and succeeded in most up to this point—the locker room and the football field, respectively.

The balance of my second year at Fuqua went very well academically. I also had significant success in securing a job on Wall Street. I was invited back to New York to interview with four firms, and I eventually received an offer from Kidder Peabody, Goldman Sachs, and, yes, Morgan Stanley. That spring, the Fuqua School also had a host of business titans visit the school and make presentations about their business, their leadership principles, or something else germane to business school students. One of the more interesting visits was from the CEO of General Electric, Jack Welch. I was on some sort of student welcoming committee and, as a result, was close to Jack for a good portion of his visit. As students and a few professors stood around listening to Jack at the post-presentation cocktail reception, Jack, for whatever reason said, "I really like students from Columbia (business school). In New York, you have to have an edge, have grit, you ride the subway, you have to be on your toes at all times. I like those types of kids." Without saying a word, the look on all the Fuqua students' faces, as well as that of the professor who was standing there with us, read, *Well, excuse the hell out of me! Why the hell are you here in Durham then?* The professor later told me that comments like that were Jack's way of riling people up and seeing what kind of intestinal fortitude one has. Hmmm.

■　■　■

A few weeks before Christmas break in 1983, I came back to Morgan Stanley for my official interview. The first person I interviewed with was the nicest, most humble, and, perhaps, smartest man I think I have ever met on Wall Street, Richard (Dick) Fisher. Unbeknownst to me, Dick had just been named the president of Morgan Stanley a few days prior to my interview. I knew he was quite powerful at Morgan Stanley, just given the size and placement of his office on the floor, but I didn't realize that he was *the man*. He asked me a few basic questions; like what books had I read, how did they impact me, and why I wanted to be a trader? But perhaps the most important question he asked was what did integrity look like to me? After a few more interviews, I was brought back into Mr. Fisher's office, where Mr. Fisher and Mack made me an offer of employment. It was the greatest Christmas gift I could have received.

7

NEW YORK AND MY JUNIOR DAYS AT MORGAN STANLEY

After securing the early and unexpected offer from the lips of Dick Fisher, John Mack, and Morgan Stanley, I returned to the Fuqua School in January for my last semester, feeling very fortunate and about eight feet tall. I didn't accept the offer immediately from Morgan Stanley because I thought it was prudent to look at other Wall Street firms that had shown some early interest in me, and I also thought that learning a bit more about the other firms would help me better understand Wall Street and my eventual competitors if I indeed did join Morgan Stanley. The firm was great about my desired competitive education, and John Mack merely asked me to inform them if my head started to turn toward another firm. After on-campus interviews, I was invited back to New York with three other venerable Wall

Street firms. I interviewed with Lehman Brothers and met the tenacious cigar-toting trader and then CEO, Lewis Glucksman. I visited with individuals at Kidder Peabody and also sat down with Max Chapman, their CEO, and endured some ribbing from him due to the fact that he was a former football player at the University of North Carolina, a huge rival of my alma mater. I also spent time with Goldman Sachs in their New York and Philadelphia offices and was impressed by everyone there who just seemed to ooze money. At the end of this recruitment, I made the call to Morgan Stanley and asked them to reserve a seat for me. I thought the culture, the people, and the opportunity at Morgan Stanley was best suited for me.

My first extended period of time in New York was compliments of my new employer. The firm had assembled twelve MBAs in their first formal MBA training program for sales and trading. I felt quite fortunate to be one of those individuals, as we all had enrolled from prominent business schools such as Duke, Stanford, Penn, Chicago, Columbia, Dartmouth, Harvard, and UCLA. Our first assignment was to find housing before we started the training program a few weeks later, and Morgan was gracious enough to provide a prepaid real estate broker to help us uninitiated individuals. I was paired up with a lovely young lady named Eve, and my first thought was to ask Eve if she needed or desired a roommate. After thinking that a beautiful woman like Eve probably already had a companion, I was nevertheless feeling that if she was representative of the women in the Big Apple, my existence here was going to be superb, at least on the dating front. As Eve and I sat at breakfast chatting on our first day of working together, she asked me what my budget was for an apartment. Given my topnotch advance research and my Morgan Stanley signing bonus of $10,000 burning a hole in my pocket, I figured that I could handle a $500/month, one-bedroom apartment, preferably on the Upper East Side of Manhattan. After all, I had a

$210/month two-bedroom apartment in Durham, North Carolina, and that came with access to a tennis court, basketball court, and a swimming pool. No reason why I couldn't step up and hit New York *right* on the apartment front. Well, Eve nearly coated my face with coffee as she expelled her liquid due to my naivete. She said something like, "This isn't North Carolina; if everyone that wanted to live on the Upper East Side lived there, the island would tip over, and you'll be lucky to find an efficiency for $500/month." After I picked my chin up out of my eggs and bacon, she offered to show me what $500/month would yield in terms of an apartment, and we could go from there. The first apartment she showed me was an efficiency, in a five-story walk-up, with a one-burner stove and a refrigerator that could accommodate one casserole dish. Nope. The second apartment was so disgusting at the downstairs entrance door to the building that I told Eve there was no point in going inside. The subsequent Upper East Side apartments left me thinking that I was going to be Morgan's first homeless employee, or a roving resident in the bowels of Grand Central Terminal. I asked if the apartments would be better if I shifted neighborhoods, but Eve assured me that unless I planned on spending more, I should lower my expectations substantially. As we exited the last disaster on the second day of my search, Eve's beeper went off (remember, still no cell phones yet); it was a message from the office. She had been communicating with the office throughout the day, reporting on our progress, or lack of it, and checking to see if any other apartments had become available. After getting one of the messages, Eve stopped in her tracks and said, "Derek, we need to head to the Yorkville section of Manhattan right now." She pushed me into a cab and told the cab driver to hurry to East 90th Street, between First and Second Avenues. I asked her why were we leaving the prime Upper East Side area, which I was told was between 57th Street and 86th Street, and she turned motherly, saying in a stern voice, "Do you want an apartment or not?"

When we arrived at 320 East 90th Street, we walked up to the fourth floor. Eve told me that this apartment had just become available because the person who had supposedly secured it that morning had failed the credit check. The apartment had just undergone a complete renovation, and despite it being only 450 square feet, it was more than adequate, certainly relative to the hovels and closets I had already seen. The bedroom could *just* accommodate a queen-size bed, but one would have to go sideways into the room to get past it. The bathroom behind the bedroom would allow one to sit on the toilet, put his feet in the tub, brush one's teeth in the sink, and play with the light switch all at the same time! I envisioned a small dining table, one dining chair, and half a couch in the living room, which was positioned off the five-foot-wide kitchen. The apartment had two slender closets as well, but I would have to shrink my wardrobe down to two pairs of slacks, two shirts, and a short summer coat. The puffy winter coat would have no home. Nevertheless, despite this accommodation for a Lilliputian, based upon my eye-opening apartment hunting experience, this apartment had to have an $800–$900 monthly price tag. When Eve said it was $650/month, I felt like I was back on the football field and nearly tackled her on a blindside blitz! I immediately screamed, "I'll take it! Call whomever! I'll take it! Hurry!"

Now that I had secured what I later learned was the least expensive apartment in my entire training class, I had four more days on Morgan Stanley's dime to experience the city from my base, the famed Essex House Hotel on Central Park South. The day after my apartment coup, I hooked up with a fellow Fuqua school friend, Owen May, who lived in Mt. Vernon, a suburb in nearby Westchester County. Owen and one of his native pals, crazy Phil, must have written the first book on how to enjoy, eat, and navigate

New York City on a dollar a day! They knew where all the free happy hour food was, even though we were supposed to be drinking and paying for our libations, both of which we weren't. They knew how to get into the movies free of charge due to a projectionist hook-up. They even knew how to go see Sarah Vaughn at Carnegie Hall for free, but that adventure did require some unexpected, at least on my part, extemporaneous sprinting up back steps, a sharp right turn at the top of the steps, and a quick disappearance into the crowd of paying patrons, ala 007. I decided that there wouldn't be a repeat of that experience, feeling that Morgan Stanley probably had little desire to employ a two-bit con. A few days later, as I legally strolled by myself up and down the avenues of Manhattan, ducking in and out of the many small boutiques, convenience shops, and food establishments, I saw a sign advertising gefilte fish and wondered why I had never heard of this species. I further learned that *pop* didn't exist in New York; here it was called soda, and I only learned that after a rather frustrating five-minute discussion with a small store owner. When I told him I wanted a pop, he looked at me as if I was from another planet, or Ohio. I pointed to a can of Coca Cola and he said, "Yeah, that's a soda." We argued back and forth a bit over our differences of opinion on the matter until, in disgust, I paid for a ginger ale and scurried out the door shaking my head and wondering how in the world's greatest and most vibrant city they didn't know the difference between a pop and a damn soda!

A few weeks later, Morgan Stanley paid a mover to pack up all my belongings in Durham and transport them to my humble abode in the German-influenced neighborhood of Yorkville, on the extended Upper East Side. Once I got settled," it was time to party a little bit before immersing myself in the Morgan Stanley training program. I started at the top, attending a party in which the reigning Miss America, Vanessa Williams, was in attendance. The next weekend I managed to get through the selective admission line of the famed Studio 54. Another weekend I visited a nightclub called Area, which had different themes on various nights, highlighted by naked women, dancing in the themed windowed boxes. The absolute wildest and most bizarre nightclub I ventured into one weekend evening, after midnight, was called Paradise Garage, in lower Manhattan. It had different floors devoted to different types of music and people. Whatever vibe you preferred, ranging from house music to salsa to disco, there was a spot for you. I also recall that more people than not were in their own worlds, dancing with themselves, totally oblivious to everyone else on the dance floor. I tried to break in on one young lady who was grooving hard, and she waved me away, saying, "I'm a solo dancer! Keep it movin'!" Welcome to New York!

■ ■ ■

On June 25, 1984, my official Wall Street career began. After a few orientation meetings, my twelve-person training class began our three-month rotation around the firm's different product areas in the Equity and Fixed Income Sales and Trading divisions. Each product area visit (i.e., mortgages, treasuries, FX, equities, research, operations, etc.) was prefaced by a teaching session given by one of the area professionals. In the rotation, each MBA trainee would essentially sit next to an established professional on the sales and trading floor and listen to their conversations with clients and co-workers, take notes, and ask questions while trying not to disturb the professional's train of thought and flow. We also got to know the personality of the individual and could loosely extrapolate that to the personality of the product and the group. For instance, the mortgage traders tended to be a bit more mechanical and mathematically inclined while the FX salespeople tended to be more transaction focused and quickly moved on to the next sale or trade without much post-trade thought. The corporate bond traders seemed to be a bit bored, even though their desk was one of the two premier trading desks at the firm; the other being the equity desk that traded blocks (then defined as roughly 10,000 shares or more) of stock for institutions like money managers, asset managers, hedge funds, insurance companies, and municipalities. Relative to the fixed income traders, who seemingly tied up outrageous sums of slow-moving capital, the equity traders always appeared to be hopping, as their product traded more often and with much more volatility and velocity.

After spending a week on Morgan's equity block desk, and feeling much more attached to the product and the personalities working on this desk, I surmised that this was the place for me, if they would have me. Thankfully, the firm made every effort to try and match up the candidate's primary desire and the firm's needs, and this happened for me. The head of the firm's training program, and a senior human resource executive who became one of my all-time best friends, Mike Giorgio, told me that I was going to be "our Jackie Robinson" in equity sales and trading, as only two people of color, Trish Payne (on the retail trading desk) and Greg Place (a clerk on the block desk who was hired a few months before my arrival) were on the thirty-third floor of the Exxon Building, at 1251 Avenue of the Americas, in 1984. I was selected to be the first person from the firm's nascent MBA sales and trading training program to join the firm's prestigious equity block trading desk. (I should add that Morgan Stanley had hired MBAs for years prior to me and my contemporaries' arrival, but I was told that my 1984 class was the first formal MBA sales and trading class in the history of the firm). When I talked to my father after getting my placement at Morgan Stanley, I told him I was placed on the block desk. He said, "What the hell is that? You're on the *black* desk? What kind of nonsense is that?" We both had a good laugh after I "educated" him on the matter.

After gratefully being selected for the block desk, I spent time with the order clerks on the desk handling small retail orders to get a foundation in the mechanics of trading and to begin building an astute vocabulary for the world of equity trading. The first big lesson I learned was the huge and critical difference between the words *for* and *at*; you bid (buy) for and you offer (sell) at. In other words, if you are a trader relaying a market to an equity coworker, it would sound something like, XYZ, 28 bid for 12,000, 30,000 at 28¼. Someone is willing to pay $28 for 12,000 shares of XYZ, and someone is willing to sell 30,000 shares of XYZ at $28¼. Conversely, if you said 12,000 at 28, the experienced person would think that someone is selling 12,000 at $28 rather than trying to buy 12,000 for $28. Most likely this error would get caught by a seasoned professional, but no point in chancing this, given the velocity of trading and the dollars involved. (Note: This market quote is from the days when stocks traded in eighths, not decimals, as they do today, but more on this monumental change later.)

One of my biggest and most helpful learning experiences was spending two weeks on the floor of the New York Stock Exchange. I spent two weeks in the various Morgan Stanley booths on the NYSE floor answering phones and taking orders from the upstairs block traders while a senior clerk listened in to make sure I recorded the instructions properly. Here I learned how one word out of the proper sequence could cause serious financial problems and broken eardrums due to the trader screaming, after an erroneous execution, "What the f*** happened? I told you my limit was 28, not 28¼!" I realized why complete accuracy was paramount. Perhaps the biggest lesson I learned was to always repeat exactly what you had heard from the instruction provider, so both the order giver and the order taker spoke and heard the same instructions and could cross-check each other. With the average block trade valuation being in the multimillions, dollar-wise, getting the right directions and subsequent execution was paramount. Rarely was a buy order mistaken for a sell order, and vice versa, but the bid or offer price and how the trade was to be executed—aggressively, slowly work, participate, etc.—were standard areas of possible angst.

I rotated through the various Morgan Stanley booths in the various rooms (i.e., the garage, the main room, and the blue room) on the floor of the NYSE to get to know the different phone clerks and execution brokers who would be handling and executing the stock orders that I relayed down to the floor. One of the biggest impressions I got from my time on the floor was how physically and mentally exhausting working on the floor could be. I was in great physical shape at the time but, nevertheless, every evening I came home, my feet and legs were screaming. The working conditions on the NYSE were such that an order clerk was basically confined to an area as far as the phone cord would stretch, and he stood on his feet from 10:00 a.m. till 4:00 p.m. (The NYSE began opening at 9:30 a.m. in 1985). I also needed to mentally de-stress, given that the execution instructions taxed the mind, certainly for a neophyte trying to make a good first impression. The Morgan Stanley floor personnel, led by the legendary and now deceased Tony Landi, was arguably, in my view, the best NYSE staff ever assembled by an NYSE-member brokerage firm. I became close to various floor personnel, including brokers Dennis Valentino, Ronnie Frost, Mark Feeley, Donnie Whelan, and Jimmy McDermott, to then clerks Jimmy Riley, Eddie Landi, John Wall, Bobby Delfino, Stevie Brandon, Dudley Devine, and Mario Truglio. Mario was the first clerk I really befriended, and he was also the first person who schooled me on the racial epithets I hadn't heard before. One day after work on the NYSE, I was out having a beverage with Mario and bumped into someone who called me a moolie under his breath, which Mario heard. He asked me if I heard what the guy said, which I hadn't. When he repeated the word and I asked what it meant, he said it was a derogatory term for a black person and was derived from the name for eggplant, moulinyan, which is black in color. I said, "Clever! Better than the N-word, I guess!" Mario shared a few other despicable terms that aren't worth repeating, but I obviously missed this "education" in my previous life.

Once my two weeks of trying to perform what was, in my view, the toughest job on Wall Street was complete, I returned upstairs and began to build on what I had learned on the NYSE floor. Thankfully, I learned much more than a derogatory name for every ethnic group known to mankind from Mario. As a baseline, I gained a ton of respect for the floor personnel and vowed that I would never unreasonably raise my voice at them or remotely disrespect them for an execution mistake. I had already witnessed spewed vitriol more than a few times from some of our upstairs position traders.

Around this time, our MBA training class was also tasked with studying, and hopefully passing, the various industry competence NASD (National Association of Securities Dealers) exams. (The NASD is the predecessor of the regulatory association now known as FINRA). Our training program was told that no MBA in the history of Morgan Stanley had ever failed the primary licensing exam, known as the Series 7, and that no one in our class should be the first. The salespeople and traders around the firm were making bets on who in our class would be the first person to break this passing streak. A couple of the white salesmen and traders took out bets that the two black guys in the training class, Ivan Smith (out of Harvard Business School) and I would be the two that would fail the exam. Ivan and I both made a pact that we would study our asses off and not thoroughly embarrass ourselves or the entire black race. Looking back on that, and even to this day, I still wonder why, as a black person, that my individual failure, in almost anything

I do, will make the entire black race look bad. I realize this is just mental baggage and *my* issue, but it is an issue that I share with many other people of color, as each one of us represents the entire race. Regardless, I studied every night for two weeks, intent on not letting down the entire black race by becoming the first MBA in Morgan's history to fail the Series 7 exam; I later found out this wasn't true and that others had failed before. I took the exam on a Saturday morning at Murray Bergtraum High School, in Midtown Manhattan. After the written exam (the exam became computerized years later), the proctor told us that our respective firm's compliance department would get a phone call from the NASD in a few days, informing the firm whether we passed.

Back at Morgan Stanley, the entire twelve-member training class felt confident that we had passed the exam, especially given that a seventy percent score was a low hurdle to get over. Ivan and I felt confident as well, but I recall him saying that he wouldn't doubt if those white mf's sabotaged our scores to embarrass us and also to collect their bet money. One member of our training class felt particularly overconfident, believing that he may have scored a hundred percent on the exam, so one of the senior managers decided to prank him. He led the boaster to believe that he could call the NASD and get his score beforehand. Little did the trainee know that he'd be told he didn't pass the exam! The senior manager had arranged it so that everyone could listen in on the fake call. I listened in too, as did nearly everyone on the trading floor. The trainee nearly fainted when the dispatcher said, "I'm sorry, you didn't pass!" Despite his cries of "There must be a mistake! There is no way I failed that exam," the dispatcher repeated that he could take the exam again next month. While his battle cry continued, those listening in were nearly underneath their desks exploding with laughter. I personally felt bad for my fellow trainee, but I wasn't about to step in and thwart their devious efforts, especially since

I'd be working with them. In the end, the *boaster* ran out of the building and later called my human resources friend, Mike Giorgio, and told him he resigned!

About thirty minutes after the incident, I got a call from Mike, who said, "Okay, tell me what the hell happened up there!" When I explained what happened, Mike instructed me to go to the guy's apartment and tell him it was a cruel joke. I could tell by his tone and the expletives he used that he wasn't too happy, and he didn't accept my argument that I was working on the desk. He reiterated, in no uncertain terms, that I was to bring him back now, or I might be joining him crying in my apartment.

Aside from sidestepping the embarrassing and numerous conspiratorial comical bombs of a trading floor, and passing all the necessary industry competence exams (everyone in my training class passed the Series 7, including the boaster and I), there was the chore of getting technically acclimated to the profession of securities sales and trading. I was also adjusting to my new colleagues and the rough and tumble world of sales and trading. Even though Morgan Stanley was known as a conservative, ultra-prestigious Wall Street firm, primarily because of its corporate finance and mergers and acquisition personnel, sales and trading was a different story. Many of the senior personnel in sales and trading did not possess the elite academic credentials that the under-thirty crowd possessed. Nearly every single person under thirty years of age possessed a degree or more from a so-called prestigious school. Even the young sales assistants possessed degrees from elite schools. So, two cultures were being mixed in this dynamic environment: one jagged and a little edgy, and the other polished, highly educated, and a bit snooty. I had experience with both cultures. For instance, there were *Playboy* pin-up centerfolds on the walls behind the equity block desk. Today, if a magazine like *Playboy* was even in sight with the cover closed, it would be grounds for dismissal. The disrespect for women in general was also very palpable. Some members of the trading floor had cards numbered one through ten that they would flash as grades as woman passed by. There was even a member of the trading staff who routinely asked at least one woman as she approached the trading desk to "show me your tits!" Not that my then wife had any interest to be in this business, but I would have strongly discouraged her from joining the ranks of Wall Street, at least in sales and trading. I envisioned waiting outside the firm's doors with a baseball bat for the individual who disrespected my wife and sent her home in tears. Having said that, I had tremendous respect for the women who were in the business who took it and maintained their femininity; even better, sometimes they gave it right back to the offender. The woman who was routinely asked to show her tits once shot back, "Show me your little dick and I'll show you my big tits!" One female salesperson, who had become "one of the men" in her daily approach to the business and the associated gutter verbiage, let loose unfairly on one of the mature, grandmotherly types who worked in human resources. She was trying to collect everyone's answer to an HR survey that asked about moving the firm to Stamford, Connecticut. She politely asked the saleswoman to either return her survey, as this was the last day for responses, or to fill it out while she waited. The irritated saleswoman asked for a blank survey, which the HR rep was carrying, and wrote three words on it in all caps: SUCK MY P***Y! I only found out the details of the story after my friend in HR, Mike Giorgio, called and relayed what happened. This particular saleswoman's notorious tongue was feared by many of the men on the trading floor, and she could go toe-to-toe with any man on the floor when it came to salacious language or penetrating responses to improper comments.

■ ■ ■

As a young guy from Ohio, I had to familiarize myself with the New York City lingo my first year on the block desk. All ten traders on the desk were born and raised in the tri-state area, and they knew that I didn't immediately understand the language, so to speak. One of the New York born and bred traders yelled out, "ok guys, we're ordering pies! What kind do you want?" I thought, damn, this is a strange request for lunch time, but ok. "I'll take a lemon meringue if they have it (lemon meringue is my favorite pie). Everyone on the desk heard me, and immediately turned my way. One of the traders said, "Donnie, (the head trader), where in the hell did you get this guy?" I responded, adding to the comedic drama, "do they only have apple or something?" One of the more sensitive guys said, "Derek, a pie here is a pizza!" That produced a chorus of laughs I said, "shit, where I come from, a pizza is a goddamn pizza, and a pie is a goddamn pie! Screw you guys!"

Lingo barriers aside, there was never a dull moment on the equity floor. A few weeks after learning what a New York pie was, I was introduced to Chessie, at the invitation of the head trader. Chessie was a stripper from Jersey City and had some size G knockers. She came up to the floor wearing a rain coat, which she quickly removed, stripping down to a G-string and bra in front of the trading desk, embarrassing an elder statesman whose birthday surprise this was! She dragged her size Gs all over his balding head, as she gyrated in fishnet stockings and eight-inch heels. I committed to never reveal my birthday to anyone on the trading floor.

As I continued to adjust socially to the Wall Street equivalent of a football locker room, and had become reasonably technically solid as a clerk for one of the senior traders, the real-world social issues began to sprout. Even though most of the other ten traders on the block desk, all male, grew up in perhaps the most diverse and cosmopolitan tri-state area in the world, some were still quite naive about certain aspects of the life of a black man in this diverse city.

Case in point, I came to work one morning fairly irritated, and pretty antisocial, after being refused a yellow taxi cab ride for the second time that week. The guys on the desk were incredulous after I explained that I routinely had issues with not being picked up by an empty yellow cab that went right down the block and picked up a white person after passing me. It was even more perplexing given that I am very light-skinned and the taxi drivers would have a hard time deciphering my race, given my paleness from where I flagged them down. Regardless, I went to the Taxi and Limousine Commission and filed complaints about blatant non-service on average three times a year in my early New York days. (As of the writing of this book, I am 15–0 at the TLC, even though I haven't been there in about ten years.)

My fellow traders were unconvinced of my plight until we were all headed to a desk dinner one evening. I tried hailing a taxi for us, but taxi after taxi passed us by, so one of them stepped in and, finally, was successfully able to hail us a ride.

Another one of my more eye-opening social interactions with the desk came on a Monday morning, when one of the traders asked me how *Soul Train*, a dance show by, for, and about black people, was that weekend, knowing that I watched it every Saturday. When another trader overheard me comment about who was on the show, he derisively said, "Why in the world would you watch a black dance show?"

"Did you ever watch *American Bandstand*?" I replied.

"Yes, occasionally," he said.

"Well, I'm a regular with my show, but mine has a different flavor and better dancing!" I said. "You watch *All in the Family* and I watch *The Jeffersons*.

After that, I didn't hear anything more from him about my television habits.

One of the earliest and most personally debilitating racial events that I had at Morgan Stanley was one that still reverberates to this day. An NYSE specialist firm wanted to have a dinner with the block desk and some of Morgan's floor brokers. I was nearly six months out of the training program and was trying to learn as much as I could while establishing as many relationships as possible within the firm and broadly across the Wall Street community. I welcomed the opportunity to get to know another faction of the trading world, the NYSE specialist. My manager informed the desk to keep our calendars clear for a future dinner at the famed 21 Club in midtown Manhattan. A few weeks later, on the morning of the dinner, someone from the NYSE told me to forget about the dinner, so I was under the impression the dinner was canceled. The next morning, a few of the traders, and especially the floor brokers, asked me why I didn't come to the dinner. With my mouth agape, I asked my black coworker, Greg Place, if he attended the dinner, and he thought it had been canceled too. Through a subtle interrogation process, I determined that the 21 Club frowned on people of color being in one of their private rooms. It took me thirty-one years before I ever stepped foot in that place, and I've only been there twice since, at the request of clients. (The 21 Club announced in December 2020 that, due to the pandemic, it was closing down permanently).

A few other racially motivated occurrences inside and outside of the confines of Morgan Stanley's campus characterized my early years on Wall Street. The most horrific and embarrassing incident outside of work, but still connected to the firm, happened at a New York Jets football game in the winter of 1984. One of the managing directors in the Equity Division knew of my football background and graciously offered me two tickets to sit in the firm's luxury box at Giant Stadium. It was the dead of winter, with the temperature near single digits, but since I was going to be in the luxury box, the temperature wasn't really a concern. I invited my friend from business school, Owen May, who was from New York and would be a good partner at the game. We took a bus over to the stadium and excitedly proceeded up to the box, as neither one of us had ever been in a private suite at a professional sports stadium. When we arrived, I realized that everyone else in the box was from the corporate finance side of the firm, as they all had on the banker's winter uniform: horn-rimmed glasses, scarfs around their necks over merino wool sweaters with insignias, and shearling lined L.L. Bean boots. Owen and I knew we would have to keep each other company, and we were content with that arrangement. We had food, beverages, heat, a bathroom in the suite, and a great view of the field and game. We grabbed some munchies and beverages and plopped down in two corner seats in the front row, out of everyone's way, but by the middle of the first quarter, some drunken idiot started banging on the side window directly to our right. We were startled by the first bang and tried to ignore the subsequent bangs, hoping he would just go away; however, after about the fifth bang, I gave the guy a WTF look and raised my hands in an upwardly questioning fashion. This seemed to further inflame him, as he then moved from the side window of the suite to the window right in front of us. He had an enraged, red-glazed face, with frozen strands of beer hanging from his mustache like icicles. He then proceeded to expel big phlegm spitballs onto the front windows, with the loogies piling up and freezing on the windows almost instantaneously. At this point, Owen and I started laughing and realized we were dealing with a seriously drunken and crazed individual and tried to ignore him as best we could, but that was short-lived. When the man continued his antics, Owen suggested we go out and take care of him. I was worried how that might look and didn't want to ruin my chances of being offered tickets in the future, so Owen agreed we'd just wait it out. Thankfully, the idiot disappeared soon after, and we were able to enjoy the game until about halftime. It was then that the suite door opened and Owen and I heard, "I want the niggers! Send out the niggers!" We both leaped over the seats to deal with this drunken, racist fool, but by the time we had gotten to the door, the Morgan bankers had slammed the door on him and called security. To say we were enraged would be an understatement, but we got back to watching the second half of the game through the spit-stained windows.

No sooner had we settled in for the second half when, all of a sudden, at the back of the suite we heard the sound of flesh being hit! Apparently, the drunk had entered the suite again and punched one of the bankers in the face. Owen and I leaped up again, but by the time we got to the drunk, security had arrived and were standing in between us and this despicable character, while two others were holding the man down. The drunk looked up and once again started yelling, "I want the niggers! I want the niggers!" Owen and I both asked the security personnel to let him go, but they dragged him away with him continuing to yell "I want the niggers! I want the niggers!"

I was never so humiliated, as the bankers and their comrade, who bleeding from his nose, looked at us sheepishly. I don't think they knew how to address the situation, so they just kept quiet, but it left me wondering how the situation would be handled at Morgan Stanley on Monday morning.

On the bus ride back to the bus station, to add insult to injury, a drunken fan sitting directly behind us threw up all over the back of our seats, and his vomit drained under our feet! The smell on the bus was intense, and it caused a few other people on the hot bus to throw up. We couldn't get through the Lincoln Tunnel soon enough.

Once we arrived at the bus station and were walking to the subway, a homeless man threw a piece of food at me and cursed because I didn't respond to his request for some money. What a day!

On Monday morning, the managing director who gave me the game tickets approached me and asked me to join him in his office. My first thought was, *here we go with the corporate finance spin!* Fortunately, he said he had heard what happened and was very sorry that we had to endure such harassment, but he was glad that we handled it with class. Little did he know that if security hadn't intervened, the drunk would have endured a "classy" ass whoopin'!

For weeks, Owen and I both talked about our missed opportunity to put this racist in his place. In fact, the story has come up periodically over the thirty-plus years since it happened, and, inevitably, we both shake our heads in disgusted humor when retelling it.

■ ■ ■

Much of what's happened in 2020 and early 2021 has made it painfully easier to recall the earlier racial injustices I encountered all too often.

In 1985, on a morning research call that was piped into Morgan Stanley's various branch offices' sales floors (i.e., New York, Chicago, San Francisco, and London), an analyst in the UK was discussing a company that was reportedly misunderstood by investors and whose stock had been punished, if not just forgotten. The analyst very nonchalantly compared the out of favor stock to a nigger in a wood pile. When the racist comment went out over the transcontinental intercom system, Greg and I looked at each other in utter amazement, mixed with unbelievable disgust. We also felt that every set of eyes on the trading floor were focused on us as we recoiled. I sunk back in my chair and put my forehead on the desk;

Greg got off the desk and walked to the bathroom in a stupor. As news of the comment quickly spread throughout the firm, many of the few black people in the other departments called Greg and me to confirm the comment. A few of the more senior black personnel said they would take the protest reins and for Greg and me to hang in there and keep our heads up. Greg and I, and the woman of color on the retail desk, conferred and patiently waited to see how this would play out over the next several minutes and hours, as we knew that the wheels of disgust were churning at many points around the firm. About an hour later, we were told that the analyst was going to be suspended for a considerable time period, if not terminated. That set well with the three of us until the head of the entire worldwide equity sales operation approached my manager and asked, very disingenuously, and within obvious earshot of me, "How are the three blacks? They'll get over it!"

A few weeks later, when Greg was clerking for his designated senior trader, a typically hungover Irishman said, "What kind of nigger are you? You went to college, you play golf, you have no jail record, and you know both your parents?" When Greg, better known as Too Tall (a name given to him by the white traders due to his diminutive 5'4" height, which I never called him, as an act of defiance to what I considered a belittling name), told me about the Irishman's comments, I was ready to stuff this alcoholic's ass head first into a wine bottle, but Greg asked me to stand down, because he believed this asshole would one day get his. Ironically, the Irishman came in drunk one day too many and was terminated about a year later. I was given his trading pad and his list of technology stocks and was promoted to a senior trader, with direct profit and loss (P &L) responsibility.

A few months before I received my senior trading status, thanks, in part, to the Irishman's termination, I suffered a more personal racial hit. It was at a time when I had maybe one last step before I could graduate to getting my own trading pad and start really earning more money while utilizing the firm's capital and executing for its institutional clients. There was no timetable, as my promotion would only happen when another senior trader left or was terminated. Nevertheless, this was a final test, and I felt that there were a few senior salespeople who clearly didn't want me to take the next step, or at least they were going to make the transition as difficult as possible. One major thorn in my side was a white sales trader (a salesperson who is the intermediary between the client/buy-side trader and Morgan's trading desk) who rarely showed me any type of respect. On this particular day, he approached the trading desk and asked for a bid on a nice chunk of a very volatile stock that was involved in a takeover and was one of the so-called risk arbitrage stocks. In the absence of the head trader, who was downstairs getting in a quick workout, I checked the NYSE floor market, quickly got my thoughts together, and showed the salesman a bid that he clearly didn't like. As he turned away in apparent disgust, he quietly, but audibly, muttered, "This nigger shouldn't be on the desk!" If I could have jumped straight over the elevated trading desk and snatched him from behind, I would have snapped his racist neck. Instead, I walked around the desk and loudly told him to meet me in the elevator bank. I was ready to dismember him. Despite the offender's seeming bravado, though, he never met me at the elevator.

When I walked back onto the trading floor, I was fit to be tied. Loudly, I said, "If I hear that shit from you again, I promise you'll end up in a fucking ambulance!"

For the rest of the day, everyone on the floor steered clear of me unless absolutely necessary, including my best friend on the desk, Greg.

I was later told by Mike Giorgio, in human resources, that it wasn't worth losing my job over a scumbag.

■ ■ ■

In the fall of 1985, nature played its games with New York City and helped emphasize, understandably, where I stood on the totem pole at Morgan Stanley. In late September of that year, Hurricane Gloria was making its way up the East Coast and was due to hit the New York City area on the morning of the 27th. I arrived at work just in time for the managing director of the area to greet me and tell me to man the desk for as long as possible, as he didn't believe there would be much business, given the impending storm. I was still only a junior trader and wasn't sure I could handle the entire trading situation without the other senior traders, and I didn't think I was indestructible enough to give Hurricane Gloria the finger! But, thankfully, we all got to go home when the New York Stock Exchange shut down around 11:30, just as the eye of the hurricane was reportedly thirty minutes away!

Several weeks later, on a Saturday morning, Mother Nature struck again, as I was abruptly awakened around six a.m. by what I thought was a rumbling garbage truck picking up trash, but then, all of a sudden, the whole building shook for about ten seconds, with a grinding sound to the shake. I immediately thought that this old ass four-story walkup was coming unglued! No wonder my rent was only $650 a month! I turned on the television to the breaking news that New York City had just experienced an earthquake, about a 3.8 on the Richter scale, with the center of the quake north of the city. I couldn't then, and can't now, imagine what a 7 or 8 magnitude earthquake must feel like, and would prefer to keep it that way.

When I got to work on Monday, the first thing I heard was, "Derek, the brothers up in Harlem must have all been break dancing Saturday morning!"

"No, the epicenter was up in Westchester County, where you live (a largely white area, north of Harlem)!" I said. "The white folks up there must have all been banging drums at the Klan meeting in your backyard!"

■ ■ ■

Despite my occasional racial issues at work, I was thoroughly enjoying life in the big city. I loved the restaurants, the shopping, the entertainment, and everything else that New York had to offer.

In late 1985, I wanted to share some of my happiness and decided to do some Christmas shopping before I headed home to Youngstown to see my family. After work on December 16, I walked over to The Sports Authority, a sporting goods store on Third Avenue and 51st Street, to purchase some athletic gear for my younger brother. When I came out of the store, the neighborhood was crawling with cops and patrol cars, and the sirens were deafening. I knew something major had happened, but I didn't find out until I got home and watched the evening news that mob boss and leader of the Gambino crime family, Paul Castellano, had been gunned down in front of Spark's Steakhouse a few blocks away from the sporting goods store on 46th Street.

The hit on Castellano was the talk of the trading floor the next day. The same individual I had previously called to the elevator bank made a comment that the mob needed to start "taking out the darkies before they take over." I almost took the bait, but I remembered what my friend in human resources had said months before.

Despite all these racial incidents, I still believed I was at the best firm on the street and that, thankfully, there were more positive times than negative ones.

■ ■ ■

The year 1986 was an eye opener for me on a number of financial fronts at work. Every morning, during our sales and trading call, each position trader went through their list of company stock names they wanted to buy and sell and provided some reasons and brief analysis of their so-called axe for the day. At the end of this call, at least once per week, the head sales trader would announce the value of the points in the pool. "Folks, the points are worth $2,650 as of today!" He'd say, "Let's keep pushing!"

The points were given a value at the beginning of the year based upon the expectations of the revenue of the equity department. This value fluctuated throughout the year based upon the actual revenue booked up to that point. I never knew the starting value or exactly how it was determined, but I was told that there were a finite number of points in the pool, and you had to be voted into the pool. If you got into the pool, you only got points if they were taken away from someone else already in the pool. Needless to say, no one *in* the pool was happy if they had to give up points to a new entrant into the pool. I fantasized about one day being in the pool as I witnessed the pool participants pull out their calculators after each announcement to figure out approximately what their year-end bonus would be. I was also told that the individual's calculated bonus could only be affected negatively by 10 percent; in other words, if a person had 50 points and each point was worth $4,000, his year-end bonus would be no less than $180,000 (50 x $4,000—10 percent).

Toward the end of the year, individuals could essentially go without generating revenue, ride the coattails of others contributing to the pool, and still max out at 90 percent of their pool value. Mike Giorgio later told me this plan was the biggest revenue disincentive ever created by a firm for compensation purposes. A pool partici-pant was essentially *stopped out* in a range, less maybe 10 percent, and given the usual values of the pool, the person was handsomely rewarded for maybe 10½ months of work. The calls to the sales and trading floor from real estate brokers, car dealers, and boat salesmen usually picked up substantially toward the end of the year and was indicative of the defined structure of this pool, even though bonus time on Wall Street, in general, tends to unearth the same types of phone calls.

Another big eye opener for me was the initial public offering of Morgan Stanley that occurred on March 21, 1986, when the firm offered the public a 20 percent stake and raised nearly $283 million for its capital base. Approximately 5 million shares were offered at $56.50, and the first trade on the Big Board on March 22 was at $70, which brought about a big roar on the Morgan trading floor, especially from the partners (114) and principals (148) of the firm. The stock closed that day at $71.25, a 26 percent rise from the IPO price, with volume of 1.93 million shares. After Morgan IPO'd, there were only two prominent Wall Street firms that hadn't gone public yet: Goldman Sachs and Drexel, Burnham, Lambert. (Goldman went public in 1999; Drexel filed for bankruptcy amid a junk bond and related insider trading scandal in February 1990). I didn't participate in the offering at the employee insider price of $56.50 and was clearly pissed at myself when I saw the stock open at a 26 percent premium to the offering price, but I was very happy for the firm and its principals.

Shortly after the IPO, I went to the Downtown Athletic Club to play some hoops with some of the very happy and suddenly wealthier Morgan Stanley guys who had owned a few shares pre-public offering or bought at an employee discount immediately prior to the offering. While playing with my missing-an-ACL right knee that I tore in business school, I went up for a dunk, hit the front of the rim, fell back, and heard another pop in my right knee when I came down awkwardly on it. I immediately knew I had torn more cartilage and that an ACL reconstruction was definitely now in order to stabilize the knee. I called Dr. Norman Scott, the New York Knicks' basketball team orthopedist, and got on his calendar for an April ACL reconstruction operation.

A few days before the operation, one of the salesmen who knew that my surgeon was Dr. Scott said, "Derek, I hope your doctor operates on the right appendage when you go in next week. I just read here that some celebrity (Peggy Cass) sued your doctor for operating on the wrong knee. I hope he doesn't snip your third leg! Without a fourteen-inch Johnson, you guys are useless in society!"

"If he does mess up and takes a foot off, I'll still have one inch more than you!" I joked back.

Knowing a long and arduous rehab for my ACL reconstruction was in front of me, I took the last week of March off and flew to L.A. to head off the depression I was sure was going to quickly set in. When I initially hurt my knee in business school, I fell into the biggest depression I had ever felt up to that point, thinking that my very athletically active life was over. Not being able to play a pick-up basketball game was life altering in my view at the time. I went to L.A., rented a Porsche 911, stayed at the renowned Beverly Hills Hotel, and ate at the finest restaurants I could get into on short notice. One of my L.A. friends said that I was behaving as if I was going to the electric chair! In my mind, not being able to play a pick-up basketball game was indeed like going to the chair.

The first restaurant I called to make a reservation was Spago, a very popular restaurant in West Hollywood, on Sunset Boulevard. As was typical, I made the reservation using my American Express, under the name Jean Penn. A few days later, I pulled into the parking lot on the hill behind Spago and valeted my lemon-colored Porsche. Upon entering the restaurant, I was greeted by the maître d' and I said, "Good evening, reservation for one, for Jean Penn at 7:30," and I was pronouncing my first name as my parents intended with the

French pronunciation of Jean. The maître d' looked up for a quick second and told me to let him know the minute Mr. Penn arrived. Puzzled, I said, "Sir, Mr. Penn is here." Again, seemingly confused, the maître d' stepped from behind his stand and looked behind me and questioned whether he was in the parking lot. At this point, I thought I was on *Candid Camera*. I said, "Sir, I'm Mr. Penn!"

I was getting frustrated because the maître d' started laughing a bit too much for my taste, so I said, "Sir, I don't understand the humor in this situation."

Stepping from behind the podium again, he said, "Sir, can I see the credit card you used to make your reservation?"

He laughed even more as he looked at my card and said, "Sir, we thought Sean Penn was coming, not Jean Penn! I'm terribly sorry. I thought maybe you were his bodyguard or something."

I thought they were about to rescind my reservation when he said, "Sir, right this way."

I sat at a table for two, not too far from the kitchen, which was partially visible from my seat. After the waiter came over and took my beverage order, a guy in a chef's hat came out and sat in the empty seat at my table. He let me know how sorry he was about the confusion and said the meal was on them. That man was the owner himself, Wolfgang Puck.

It got better from there, as right after I finished eating my outstanding chicken dinner, Chef Puck introduced me to another patron at a nearby table. He said, "Robin, this is Derek from New York." Robin said hi back and told me he spent a lot of time in New York and was headed there next week to do a story. When I asked him what he did for a living, he said he did a television show called *Lifestyles of the Rich and Famous*. I looked at him a little closer and said, "Are you Robin Leach?" To which he replied, "In the flesh."

I told him I routinely watched his show, and then he asked for my name and address so that he could put me on the show's mailing list for its various "best of" publications. I received those lists for ten years and always looked forward to getting them. It made me feel a little bit like an insider.

A week later, on April 3, 1986, I had my knee reconstruction surgery, and Dr. Scott did indeed operate on the right leg. A week later, I went back to work at Morgan Stanley, albeit on crutches and in pain from my daily six a.m. physical therapy sessions before work.

The firm offered me something for which I will forever be grateful, and it showed their extreme class and generosity. One of the senior managing directors on the floor asked me how I was doing and how was I getting back and forth from my apartment. I told him I was taking taxis to and from home and to physical therapy until I could handle the subway or a bus. He said, "We'll get you a car service to pick you up from physical therapy every morning, bring you to work, and take you back home in the evening from here. You just get to physical therapy every morning. Does that work?" I was speechless and forever grateful for their kindness, which lasted three months.

■ ■ ■

The year 1986 was a big year for the firm, with its very successful IPO behind it. This helped set me up for a promotion to senior position trader, about a year sooner than I and most other people expected. After the unexpected and sudden firing of the technology sector trader, I asked the head trader, Donnie Crooks, for the opportunity, almost expecting him to say I wasn't ready. Surprisingly, though, after a couple days of thought over a long weekend, he shocked me on a Monday in early 1987 and told me the promotion was mine. He said, "Let's see how it goes. If you falter early, we'll quickly scale it back. You're trading a very high-profile group, the tech sector, and you'll be tested daily and all day. You'll start your pad a week from today."

In one of those *be careful what you wish for moments*, I went home that evening nearly unable to swallow, but very thankful, and I quickly came to the conclusion that this was what I had worked so hard for, and just like many other challenges in my life up to that point, I would figure it out, measure up, and succeed.

The first several months of being a senior trader went reasonably well, despite my occasional going home with a knot in my stomach. I made sure I worked out at the gym a few days a week to unwind and relieve some stress. I had promised myself that I wouldn't take the job home with me and wouldn't let the job change my disposition or who I was, but on occasion, I did take the job to the gym. There were days I felt sorry for the gym equipment.

8

MORGAN STANLEY SENIOR DAYS

My promotion to a senior trader in January1987, after roughly two years of on the desk training and now trading the premier volatile technology sector, was met with significant dismay by a few of the sales traders. For one, I took the place of one of their Irish drinking pals, and second, I had a "tan," a very slight one, but I had very black blood running through my veins and persona, and this was a new phenomenon for all of them, regardless of their support or non-support of the promotion. Any racial humor that was acceptable on the trading floor during those days might have to be reeled in a bit if there was any sensitivity to race in the room; however, I quickly found out there wasn't. Nevertheless, to this day, I applaud the head trader, Donald Crooks, not only for showing faith in me with the promotion, but just as importantly, for assigning me a prominent sector to trade. It was up to me to shine or implode. I also had the media and defense sectors under my trading wing, so I was definitely going to be hopping on a daily basis.

The first educational thing I did was order weekly technical chart books from a firm called O'Neill Charts. This firm produced a weekly book that showed the daily price changes in every publicly traded stock. The books were delivered every Sunday morning, and every Sunday afternoon or evening, I reviewed the chart of each of the hundred or so stocks that I traded. I had studied technical analysis at the N.Y. Institute of Finance, and at the very least, with the help of the chart book, I recorded the support, resistance, trend, and risk/reward for each of the stocks for which I was responsible. I went to work every Monday with a buy or sell bias toward each stock and adjusted accordingly as the trading day and week proceeded.

Not only did the sales traders have to adjust with a newbie trading the tech sector, but the NYSE personnel also had to adjust to the nuances of my trading style. Given the idea that the better you personally know a coworker, the better the working relationship, I began having breakfast with the NYSE clerks and floor brokers. One particular breakfast almost ended my career as a senior trader at Morgan Stanley before my tenure even began.

Dennis Valentino, one of the senior floor brokers who could have played one of the Corleone's in *The Godfather*, and someone with whom I became close friends, and I used the bathrooms on the executive dining floor. This floor also housed the opulent offices of the firm's top executives. I always "made donuts" before the trading day began, as it was rare that a trader could get off the desk for a bathroom break during the six hours of hectic trading. In fact, it was rare to get off the desk to run and get lunch in the cafeteria, but, every now and then, you could get an adjacent trader to watch your pad and positions for you while you got your food. Inevitably, that lunch costs you some dough. We used to call it the $10,000 sandwich, because that was the minimal damage that being off the desk usually tallied on your long or short positions.

Anyway, on this particular morning, Dennis and I decided to use the executive floor bathrooms before he jumped on the subway to go back to the NYSE and before I went back to the 33rd floor trading floor. We weren't aware of any restrictions regarding non-executives from using the bathrooms on the executive floor, so we said, "What's the big deal?" When we both entered the bathroom, we immediately realized how much nicer these bathrooms were than the standard bathrooms. They had marble floors, pedestal sinks with brass handles, cloth towels, good smelling soap, and four-ply toilet issue! We were like, "Damn, what the hell! Let's enjoy this!"

As Dennis and I took up residence on the fancy toilets, we began to enjoy some rather raunchy and racist banter between the two of us, but we soon heard someone else entering the bathroom, and then the door to the stall between us opened. I then noticed a cane and thought, *oh shit!*

I knew that Dick Fisher, the CEO, used a cane due to childhood polio. The next thing I heard was Dennis flushing the toilet. I don't think he even wiped, as he obviously saw the cane too and was intent on getting the hell out of the bathroom as quickly as possible. While I was trying my best to get out of there quickly too, I heard Dennis opening the door and, like a true son-of-a-bitch, saying, "I'll talk to you later, Derek Penn!"

I was flabbergasted and not quick enough to rat him out as well, so I just got out of there as quickly as I could and hoped it was someone else in the middle stall and *not* Mr. Fisher!

When I got to the trading desk, I asked no one in particular if we were allowed to use the bathrooms on the executive level. The consensus was that everyone thought they were for the execs and their visitors only. My heart sank. I called the NYSE and told the clerk in Dennis's room, the garage, to have that SOB call me when he gets back to the floor!

After about thirty minutes of anxiously waiting for a phone call from Mr. Fisher, one of the NYSE floor lines from the garage lit up. I knew who it was. I picked up the phone, and I said, "Do you realize who was in that stall?"

"Yeah, that's why I got the hell out of there!" Dennis said, laughing hysterically.

As I continued to reem him out, all he said was, "Nice working with you," and hung up, still laughing!

I tried calling him back but got his clerk again. I left a message to relay: "If I go down, I'm taking his ass with me!"

As the trading day proceeded, I grew more and more confident that it wasn't Dick in that stall. Certainly, if it was, he would have summoned me or had HR come and get me, but it didn't help that Dennis called every thirty minutes to sarcastically inquire whether I still worked here, as everyone else on the floor razzed me about the now floor-wide publicized incident!

A few days went by without me getting the dreaded phone call, but two weeks later, I was standing at the elevator on the lobby level waiting to go to the 33rd floor, when Dick Fisher walked over to catch the elevator to go to the executive floor. I tried to avoid making eye contact, because when I saw his cane, I knew that it had indeed been him in the middle stall! Sidling up next to me, he said, "Hi, Derek, how are you?"

I could barely get the words out, but I said, "I'm good, Mr. Fisher. How are you?"

"Oh, I'm well. Let's go get 'em!"

As we rode the elevator to our respective floors, my heart was in my throat. Just before Dick got off on his floor he said, "You and Mr. Valentino are quite amusing. Just keep in mind that clients might not be so amused. Have a good day."

I didn't know if I was going to throw up or shit my pants, or both! I was in such a daze that I rode the elevator all the way to the top floor of 1251 Avenue of the Americas. I called Dennis and told him what had transpired, but all he said was "Holy shit," and hung up the phone.

I had major respect for Mr. Fisher before this incident, but it now went to a whole new level, and not just because he didn't discipline or fire me. He seemed to make light of the incident but still got his point across without reprimanding me. Dick Fisher still remains the classiest, most eloquent, elegant, smooth, and intelligent executive-level individual I have met during my thirty-four years on Wall Street.

The major lesson I learned through this ordeal is that whatever you do, someone, somewhere, might be watching or listening, so be mindful of your actions. As my head football coach at Duke, Mike McGee, routinely said, "You determine your fate. Don't let anyone else determine it for you."

■ ■ ■

The year grinded on as I honed my craft, and the equity market churned higher as it climbed the proverbial wall of worry. By August 1987, the Dow Jones Industrial Average (DJIA) was up 44 percent, and for the first time in my career, I heard the characterization *bubble*; however, as this bubble was building, I was being further indoctrinated in the ways and norms of Wall Street, at least from a Morgan Stanley sales and trading perspective. Aside from learning the technical aspects of how to trade stocks and service clients, I was also learning the social do's and dont's of the trading floor.

One of the senior salesmen asked me if I knew how to have longevity in this business. "Sure," I said, "if you continue to learn and be good at what you do." But his response was quite different.

He said, "Nope; don't mess with any white women here! You never know whose white man's sugar you may be dipping your stick in!" And I never forgot that. During my entire Wall Street career, I made sure I steered clear of any remotely sexual relationship with *any* woman at the firm, whether white, black, or brown.

I've tried to impart that lesson to other men, of all races, in subsequent years on the job, as there are enough women outside the firm to date; there's no need to complicate your life and career by dating a coworker.

■ ■ ■

In my first year as a bona fide trader for Morgan Stanley, I was sent back to Duke's Fuqua School to recruit second year MBAs, and I also went to UCLA and Harvard in early 1987 to seek out talent.

In early 1987, Morgan Stanley had made an offer to a young man named Joe Jett, of Harvard Business School, to become a member of their fall training program. Jett is largely credited (or discredited) with bringing down Kidder Peabody in 1993/1994 with a fictitious trading strategy that seemed quite foolish to outside minds, including mine. Jett's entrée to Wall Street was with Morgan Stanley, and I was sent with another black colleague and member of my training program, Ivan Smith, to go to Boston and convince Jett, also black, to commit to Morgan Stanley. Ivan and I took Jett out to what seemed like the only restaurant in Boston at the time, Legal Seafood, and we were told not to come back to New York until Jett assured us that he was coming to Morgan after graduation from HBS. I called Mike Giorgio, my human resources friend, who was running recruiting, and told him that I thought Jett was on board. Mike wanted to know if he was definitely coming, and I told him I was pretty sure. But that wasn't good enough for

Mike, so he insisted that Ivan and I stay in Boston until he signed the necessary paperwork.

We met with Joe the next day and basically threatened him, as we both wanted to get back to New York. Jett ended up spending two unremarkable years at Morgan Stanley as a junior mortgage-backed securities trader before he left and went to First Boston for a very short run. He ended up at Kidder Peabody as a government bond trader in 1991 and quickly rose to run the desk before his trading strategy came undone in early 1994. During his Kidder tenure, the various securities' regulators reportedly claimed that Jett recorded false profits of over $350 million, while in actuality he was responsible for approximately $75 million in losses. When the news broke in 1994, I was working at Merrill Lynch and was visiting the firm's London office. My HR friend at Morgan Stanley, Mike, called and asked if there were more questionable characters at Morgan Stanley that I recruited. I told him *he* was the one who told me not to come back to New York without his signed offer and to not put that shit on me.

We ended up laughing about the recruiting scenario in 1987, and although I didn't know Jett well, I felt bad for him. I didn't know all the details of his supposed transgression, but I believed many at Kidder had dropped the ball if he was able to do this on his own, which was highly unlikely, in my professional opinion. I was more concerned about the optics of a black man reportedly taking down a firm. I also carried the associated guilt that if one black man screws up, it's like we all screwed up; at the very least, I felt that the majority painted us all with the negative brush of one perpetrator.

■ ■ ■

In mid-1987, I witnessed a major awakening regarding the global nature of Wall Street research and how news in the U.S. can have major financial implications overnight in another country. This scenario played out with two companies in the U.S., but the financial damage was done in another country before it reverberated back to America.

One evening, the Hospital Corporation of America (HCA) had an earnings press conference in New York, attended by a number of Wall Street research analysts. HCA stated it was going to report a quarterly loss the next morning for the first time in a long time, if not the first time ever. Up until this point, very few analysts realized or thought about overnight equity trading of U.S securities in other countries. Some, even at major firms, didn't even realize they had trading desks in other countries that trafficked in U.S. securities during non-U.S. hours. Well, some enterprising trader in the UK called Morgan Stanley's trading desk in London and asked for a two-way market not only in HCA, but in another health maintenance company as well, American Medical Institute (AMI). Morgan Stanley's equity trader in London, who was not informed about the news of HCA because he didn't receive a call from the New York-based research analyst, and due to the lack of the twenty-four-hour news cycle of today, laid out a two-way market to this savvy Brit competitor. Morgan's bid was hit in both securities in major size. When we arrived at work in New York the next morning and looked at the positions of the desk that London had accumulated overnight, there were a lot of red faces after we had read and heard the HCA *lack of earnings* news. The research analyst was harshly called on the carpet for not relaying the earnings info to anyone the night before. He said he didn't realize that we traded U.S. securities overnight and had planned to give everyone an update during the usual morning meeting. Too late. A couple million dollars later, and an analyst's career truncated, proved to be a painful day on the desk as we unwound our long positions in both companies. We also suspected that the informed London trader had loaded up other bulge bracket firms—Goldman Sachs and Salomon Brothers specifically—with shares of these two primary health concerns as well, which caused the two stocks to be even further depressed, with the aggressive unwinding by everyone.

We learned the painful lesson that all significant company news needed to be quickly communicated firm-wide, regardless of geography. To soothe some of the pain, Morgan Stanley hired the savvy trader from the small brokerage firm in London who sold us the HCA and AMI.

As the fall of 1987 approached, a number of clouds began to hover over the Street, despite the three major stock indices (i.e., S & P 500, Dow Jones, and Nasdaq Composite) hitting record highs in late August. The internationalization of the Street was gaining traction as foreign investors, looking to participate in the strong U.S. market, were throwing major cash at U.S. securities, further exacerbating the bubble. Interest rates were ticking up. The trade deficit was heading higher, and the strong dollar was putting pressure on exports. A flawed product called portfolio insurance was created to hedge significant stock gains by shorting stock index futures. Clearing and settlement of stocks was three days, while settlement of futures and options was one day, which created somewhat of a mismatch of available values.

We didn't have market circuit breakers or trading curbs like we have today, to allow for a regrouping, reassessment, and a slowdown in times of major market dislocation. Hostile takeovers were consistently being announced and financed with risky high-yield debt in a rising interest rate environment. And Congress was considering instituting a takeover-related tax bill that would undo some of the significant merger and acquisition tax breaks, which made the risk arbitrage community very nervous.

It didn't help that the Street was still reeling from the major Ivan Boesky insider trading scandal that unfolded in late 1986. In fact,

I was interviewed by the SEC and another federal entity before the crash, regarding my selling of CBS stock for Ivan Boesky's trading firm, named Seemala, after his wife. Apparently, the arbitrageur had acquired a substantial stake in the CBS network in late 1985 and early 1986. At the direction of the feds, and before his plea-bargain was made public, Boesky was ordered to clandestinely liquidate all his holdings. It was the ultimate insider trading, and in this case, by the federal, and maybe New York state, government.

I'm not sure what the feds' angle was in interviewing me and asking how I got the sell orders (from the salesman covering the account), how I was told to execute the daily orders (carefully), and how much I sold (millions of shares).

■ ■ ■

The week preceding historic Black Monday, as October 19 ,1987, was called, was eventful and a foreshadowing of what was to come. The equity market drained 3.8 percent on the Wednesday before Black Monday and lost another 2.4 percent on Thursday. On Friday, October 16, the DJIA dropped another 108 points, closing down about 9 percent for the week. That 4.6 percent implosion on Friday presaged in miniature what would occur on Monday.

I personally missed the Friday sell-off, as I was at Duke University, at the Fuqua School of Business, participating on an investment banking panel with my boss, Donnie Crooks. Both of us were a little concerned about being away from the desk during these uncertain times, but neither of us imagined that Monday was going to be the monumental day it became. We figured that a bounce-back was in order on Monday, given that the market was down 9 percent for the week already. Another small, but hopefully positive, consideration was that the UK securities' markets were closed on October 15 and 16, as The Great Storm, a deadly cyclone, roared through that geography, exacting a devastating toll. Closed markets provide no liquidity and rattle investors, so we were hopeful that on Monday, the U.K. would help provide some stability, despite maybe having some catching up to do on the downside.

On Monday, October 19, the carnage started in Far East markets like Hong Kong, then quickly drifted to Europe, with the UK adding fuel to the fire rather than dousing it (FTSE was down 11 percent), setting up a rude awakening in New York. We all arrived on the Morgan Stanley trading desk earlier than usual that Monday, knowing that overseas markets had gotten clobbered. When we left the desk the previous Friday, there was hope that the market would rebound from the 9 percent deficit of the week. It was obvious, after looking at the volume, velocity, and carnage of Asia and Europe, that we would need our hardhats for the day, if not the week.

The worry around the 33rd floor was palpable. The NYSE didn't open for ninety minutes beyond its usual opening time, as specialists tried to digest the influx of sell orders, with many of the orders part of so-called large sell programs that indiscriminately whacked bids with reckless abandon. When stocks did open, it was absolute carnage. The average stock was instantly down over 20 percent, with many of the issues in *offer only* situations (no buyers at any levels). I had obviously never witnessed such financial destruction, and my heart was in my throat most of the day. I received a number of *bid-wanted* requests, and I priced everything down nearly 3–5 percent from the last sale. I was hit on 90 percent of my bids, despite the severely discounted pricing. At the end of the longest day of my career, up to that point, the DJIA had shed 508 points, or 22.6 percent. I went home long over $20 million worth of stock on my trading pad, and I believe the entire desk was long over $100 million collectively. Thankfully, we came in the day relatively flat; otherwise, we would have been carried out early and couldn't have carried the additional $100 million into Tuesday. I recall the absolute capital number after the day's close being kept very close to the vest, due to the severely unusual tie-up of balance sheet. I wanted to go to the gym that evening, but I was mentally, physically, and emotionally spent. I went home, ate for the first time that day, checked on the imploding Japanese market before bed, and slept for four hours before waking up and checking on the very weak European markets. I figured Tuesday would be crazier than Monday, given what I had witnessed that day.

All the traders arrived around six a.m. on Tuesday to check on our breaks (i.e., buy and sell, quantity and price, mismatches), as a break on just a few thousand shares could amount to significant losses (or gains), given the high volatility of individual stocks and the overall market; furthermore, every trader expects that the majority of the time a break goes against him, rather than presents an economic gift. Based upon how the U.S. market closed on Monday, near its lows of the day, and no visible rebound in Asia and Europe overnight, I expected more bloodletting on Tuesday.

Before the Tuesday opening, some corporations announced significant buybacks to not only scoop up some cheap stock, but also to hopefully prop up their weak shares and prevent them from imploding further. Banks also announced stepped up lending, which was echoed and backed by the Federal Reserve. Shortly after the opening, bids in the market started to reappear, and it was off to the races on the upside. That Tuesday and Wednesday saw the DJIA recover 288 points, or 57 percent of the Black Monday loss. The Morgan equity desk had its biggest revenue day and week in history up to that point, as we sold our $100 million portfolio into a rising market. Our biggest positive ticket came from a massive trade we had with financier George Soros, where we made close to $10 million, unwinding a position he had sold us the day before. Conversely, if the market had gone further south, my career, and that of many others, could have been short-circuited, in quick fashion.

The fallout of the 1987 crash, despite the quick comeback, caused significant job loss in certain areas. The municipal securities market was reeling before the October crash due to the Tax Reform Act and rising rates, and as a result, job loss was significant. Firms like the venerable Salomon Brothers totally exited the business, even though they held the number one market share. This downturn in the municipal securities business on both the trading and underwriting sides led to many people of color losing their jobs. The Street had ramped up hiring of minorities during the eighties, after black mayors in major U.S. cities overtly and covertly demanded people of color as their Street counterparts. Unfortunately, during the downturn in municipals in the late eighties and early nineties, a good percentage of the minority population on the Street was decimated. I don't have accurate figures of how many people of color lost their jobs behind the muni implosion, but anecdotally I would offer that the minority representation hasn't returned to those levels since and is dramatically down from whatever those numbers were. Perhaps the coldest dismissal I witnessed after the crash of 1987 was the head of research sales at Morgan Stanley meanly, and insensitively, calling an equity research salesman on his honeymoon in Hawaii and telling him not to spend too much money because he was terminated and a box with his belongings would be waiting for him when he returned home. Absolutely coldblooded, and many people, including me, experienced *schadenfreude* when this senior asshole experienced misfortune later in life.

In early 1988, as things settled down, I felt like I had gained years of experience just in the fourth quarter of 1987. I was much more comfortable and assured, as I felt that if I survived last October, nothing could dent my armor at this point. I dealt with the usual racial stuff, like my white trading assistant talking directly to me about the "niggers in the bad neighborhoods." When I said, "Excuse me, what the fuck did you say?" he replied, "I don't mean you, Derek. I'm talking about the uneducated and trouble-makers that we read about all the time. You're not that type."

I told him to never use the N word in my presence again or our relationship would implode more than it already had at that instant. I got off the desk and headed to the bathroom, shaking my incredulous head the whole way. Fortunately, some racially amusing things also happened that year.

One of the most outwardly racist sales traders went out at lunchtime and foolishly bought a VCR from one of the street hustlers on Sixth Avenue. (I was told he hated everyone, but I know for certain that he wasn't a fan of black people.) Over the weekend, the sales trader gave the VCR to his son for his birthday. When his son opened the box at his birthday party, he was greeted with a box of bricks!

One of the adults at the party relayed the story to my manager on the trading desk, and the manager couldn't wait to tell me the story, knowing I would howl. One for the brothers. This same sales trader was also deceived a few years later, after we both had gained a tiny bit of mutual respect for each other. Once again, he was swindled, when someone posing as my blood brother met him outside the building and told him that his car had broken down and that he needed $200 for a tow. He told the sales trader that I would give him back the $200 tomorrow. The next morning, the gullible salesman approached me and told me the story and asked for his $200. I took great pride in telling him that the brothers got him again. I think it had to be an inside job, and I think the brothers in the mail room, whom he showed little respect, set him up. What little relationship we had disappeared, as he probably, to this day, assumes I was part of the scheme.

■ ■ ■

In mid-1988, I married my college girlfriend. Prior to the official justice of the peace union, we stepped into New York's Diamond District, on 47th Street, between 5th and 6th Avenues, to buy a ring that my soon-to-be-wife wanted to design herself, given her artistic and creative bent. The jeweler was recommended by a senior person at Morgan Stanley, so I felt that I could trust the dealer. My wife and I took about an hour to carefully pick five diagonally shaped diamonds, out of hundreds of diamonds, for the ring she had previously sketched out. The dealer augmented our elementary education regarding cut, color, and clarity, and helped us with the selection of the five diamonds. After the selection process, the dealer said the ring would be ready in a few days. We returned a few days later and picked up the ring and the certification paperwork. Upon examining the ring, my wife immediately said, "These aren't the diamonds we selected." I concurred, because one was blurry, one was yellower than the others, and one was shorter than the others. The dealer swore that these were the same diamonds previously selected. I was willing to insist on a changing of the diamonds while we watched their placement in the ring casing, but my wife said, "Screw it. I want the ring. They are going to rip us off anyway." A few weeks later, we got the ring appraised and confirmed our suspicions. Lesson learned. The Diamond District is a scam. I never went back again.

Shortly after the ring fiasco, we stepped up our purchases and bought a condo on the Upper West Side. The condo was in a beautiful, new townhouse development and was one of the first of its kind in Manhattan. The building was six stories, with about twenty apartments in total. Each condo had two floors, with the ground level apartment having an enclosed patio and backyard. The condo in the middle two floors had a balcony in the back on one of the two floors. The top floor apartment had a balcony in the back and a roof deck. Each apartment had its own private entrance. I thought we were very lucky to have found these unique apartments, and the price was right because the stock market crash of 1987 had deflated the original pricing by about 20 percent; however, nothing in Manhattan so great comes without some "fleas."

Directly across the street, in an elementary school playground, was a basic drive-up drug dispensary for the tri-state area. Nearly every night in the evening, especially on the weekends, a car with a New Jersey, Connecticut, or New York license plate pulled up and got its order. Every now and then a car from Pennsylvania got its order fulfilled. We were unaware of this drug activity before purchasing this beautiful property, as were all the other buyers in the complex, as we discussed the situation at our first condo board meeting. A few weeks later, I was walking home from work and encountered a stare down from the drug lord of the street, right on our block. He mentioned that he saw me one day looking out the window of my apartment at the playground. He said, "Mind your own business." Rather than wisely just keep on walking, I told him that business on the block where I live IS my business. Thankfully, he didn't respond as I kept walking to my apartment. When I told my wife what had happened, she nearly soiled her pants. She was afraid she'd no longer be able to walk down the street, but I told her to just go the other way, as we found out where he lived on the block.

A few weeks later, I encountered him again, but this time he was with his young son, who was about eight or nine years old.

"Dad, that's the man that got my ball from over the fence the other day," the young boy said.

I had retrieved the kid's ball from inside a community garden next to our complex. At his son's remark, the drug dealer nodded, and from that day on, we shared a mutual respect, as much as one can respect a drug dealer.

At our second condo meeting, someone suggested that we all call the police, as well as our local councilperson, and complain about the drug activity.

One evening, approximately two months later, there was a lot of commotion outside, with flashing lights and sirens blaring outside our apartment window. We looked out and saw the police rounding up numerous drug dealers at the playground, handcuffing them, and escorting them into the back of a paddy wagon. I never saw my drug dealer "friend" again, but my wife did about a year later, when she was asked to serve on jury duty and my "drug dealer buddy" was on trial. She begged off the jury when asked, "Is there any reason why you can't serve?"

■   ■   ■

Toward the end of 1988, Morgan Stanley had our year-end bonus discussions, which set me back on my heels a bit, as I was hoping to refill the coffers after buying my condo. As I sat with two of the senior managers, I was told they had some good news and some bad news. The good news was that I was unanimously voted into the year-end compensation, bonus "points" pool. The bad news was that the pool had been eliminated for everyone because one of the pool participants had complained about losing some of his pool points and made a huge stink about it. Human resources had to step in and decided that this compensation model was fraught with issues, and the best thing to do was to go strictly to a discretionary year-end compensation model. I didn't feel any better when I was disappointed at my number, given the solid year I had, and was told, "Do you realize that you are making more money than anyone in your high school graduating class?" I'm sure my face spelled out *WTF* in capital letters. That high school comment made me feel like white folks had a visceral disconnect when it came to black folks making serious *white folk* money.

Not getting white folk money aside, by 1989, I was hitting my stride. I had a bevy of great research analysts that constantly kept me in the know in terms of individual company details like earnings expectations, corporate actions, trends, and industry minefields. My market share numbers for percentage of stock traded in a particular name were in the top one to three rankings on the Street in the majority of the stock names for which I was responsible. I was even consulted every now and then by the financial press for comments about the industry or a particular stock. I stopped this practice after a reporter consulted me and asked for a comment about the earnings report of a company called Digital Equipment (DEC). Within minutes of my "anonymous" comment about DEC having a poor quarter, it was up on the tape, with somewhat of a misquote that the "Morgan Stanley trader said DEC was a dead stock!" That same asshole, head of research sales, approached me and said, "What the fuck did you say to that fucking reporter?" I told him that I didn't say what was reported. As he turned around, he said, "Keep your fucking mouth shut and just trade the fucking stock!" If I could have thrown the heavy ass metal timeclock on my desk at him and taken that asshole out, I would have; however, I did heed his unwanted and harshly delivered advice going forward. Speaking to the press going forward would most likely not serve me well, and I never spoke to the press again for the remainder of my trading career, but I did try and continue to raise my voice inside the walls of Morgan Stanley.

When I became one of the top tech sector traders on the Street, I tried to make sure I was generally unassailable. I studied my stocks, nourished professional relationships that could assist my trading prowess, and respectfully put my foot down when anyone stepped out of line.

During one of our morning position trader/sales trader meetings, as I was going through my buy and sell list, some wise ass suggested that since it was Black History Month, maybe I had a special stock I wanted to push. I quickly responded, "Keep talking that black shit, and you'll be history!" That brought about a roar from the group, given that I had nicely silenced one of the bigger mouths on the floor.

I recall another humorous occasion, but not of my doing, when a few of the position traders went to dinner with some of the NYSE floor clerks at the Old Homestead Steakhouse in Manhattan. These dinners, especially when the senior executives were not in attendance, tended to get a little loud and crazy as the night wore on. After a few hours of food and drink (by others, as I don't drink alcohol) and lots of laughs, the waiter brought the check. I'm uncertain if we asked for the check, but shortly after the waiter dropped it off, the guys ordered another round of beers. A few minutes later, the waiter brought a new check, which included the last round of beers. My friend and eternal NYSE broker pal, Jimmy Riley, took the check from the waiter and put it in his mouth, chewed it, and swallowed it! The waiter looked as if he was going to shit his pants, as we all paused for a second and then fell out of our chairs laughing. With bits of paper on his lips, Jimmy yelled, "You fucking bring us a new check for five beers after we spent a thousand dollars in this MF? Are you nuts?"

After that outbreak, the manager politely asked us to leave ... after we paid the *original* bill. We were still laughing as we spilled out onto the sidewalk.

■　■　■

Internal dinners were commonplace with the position traders and Morgan's NYSE personnel to maintain relationships and get to know one another better. It is harder to sound off on a person or have a non-productive yelling match when you have a personal relationship. One notable dinner with some of the Morgan NYSE floor brokers was at a restaurant in Little Italy called Taormina. We were in the appetizer stage of our dinner when the door opened and in walked infamous mobster John Gotti and a few of his henchmen. Our mouths dropped when they sat down at a table about five feet from us. I suggested that we pay the bill and scat, as I had no desire to be part of a *New York Post* front page headline about six innocent bystanders getting taken out in a mob hit. It seemed like every month, some mobster in New York or New Jersey was erased, as the mob wars of the mid-to-late eighties were keeping gun, car bomb, and casket manufacturers busy. The rest of my dinner pals offered that if we just minded our business and kept an eye on the door and big picture window, we should be fine. Well, before I could even digest my appetizer or the suggestion to remain at dinner, one of the now slightly inebriated Morgan traders, Michael, got up to go to the bathroom and walked directly past the Gotti table. We all looked at Michael as he not only walked close to the table, but actually went up to Gotti and stuck out his hand for a handshake. Every one of Gotti's men had their hand in their breast pocket as Mike approached, and I don't think they were looking for their cigarettes or billfolds. Gotti reluctantly shook Mike's hand with a smirk on his face. Mike then proceeded to go to the bathroom, and two of Gotti's guys followed him. At this point, I was swallowing my last morsel of food before I thought I would calmly walk out onto Mulberry Street and hightail it out of the neighborhood before Mike was dismembered in the bathroom. When Mike miraculously returned to the table, I quietly asked him, out of the corner of my mouth, "Are you nuts, man? He ain't the Pope?" To my dismay, Mike said he didn't think Gotti was a bad guy, but I reminded him that he kills people!

I stuck around and ate my entree, but I skipped dessert and quickly got out of the neighborhood. A few years later, it was revealed that Gotti's primary meeting place was across the street from the restaurant, at the Ravenite Social Club, and that Taormina was Gotti's favorite local restaurant. The press even suggested that Gotti owned the restaurant

When I saw Mike the next morning, I told him that was the last time I would ever go out with his reckless, crazy ass. (I went out with him again three weeks later.)

■ ■ ■

The summer of 1989 brought joy and pain as it relates to life at Morgan. Some of the joy revolved around my human resource pal, Mike Giorgio, when Mike and I went to see Spike Lee's *Do the Right Thing*. Mike, being a socially conscious individual, wanted desperately to see the film, which was the talk of the summer, but he didn't want to go by himself. As a white guy, Mike was concerned for his well-being, as the critics hinted the movie would incite racist and violent responses and, perhaps, even cause actual race riots. I joked with Mike that if he championed bringing back the compensation pool with points, I would protect him in the theater!

Mike and I thoroughly enjoyed the movie and discussed it at length over a late dinner. Mike believed everyone should see it, despite one's race, so they could see and understand the perspectives of the alternate race. I was grateful that Mike and I shared such a special relationship, as we were able to see our race through each other's eyes.

Mike had an interesting perspective on life growing up in Jersey City, as he was bullied by blacks because of his race and by whites because of his diminutive size. A few times after seeing the movie, when Mike would walk on the trading floor and wave at me, he would shout one of the lines from the movie, like "How come ain't no brothers on the wall?"

I loved Mike and his stories, and I miss him dearly, as he passed away in 2014 at the age of 74, after battling pancreatic cancer. In my last conversation with him, as he was in the throes of his health battle, we both did complimentary Richard Pryor routines, which was the usual for us.

I called him at home while he was getting treated and said, "Anybody around here seen Jessie? We're looking for Jessie." This was from a Pryor routine about two cops breaking up a craps game in the back room of a black club, looking for a guy named Jessie.

Mike shot back, "Not me. No lie. I ain't seen nobody since 1922! Thought I was blind until I seen you walk in the door!"

"Cool Breeze, you seen Jessie?" I said.

"Nah, I ain't seen no goddam Jessie!" Mike continued. "What I look like, radar? They got some white Jessies! Why don't you go looking for those mf's. And, if you see the mf, send him to me. Mf owes me $25, and I need my money badder than a hog needs slop!"

Mike was the best and helped to smooth over many of the rough patches for me at Morgan Stanley.

The pain of 1989 was more closely associated with the usual events that happened in the financial world: investments. On a flight out to Morgan's San Francisco office to spend time with the sales traders, I was reading the in-flight magazine and stumbled on an article discussing the valuation of the various U.S. airlines. The article suggested that United Airlines was severely undervalued and ripe for appreciation. I was so convinced of this investment opportunity that when I got to the S.F. office, I made a point to call the firm's designated employee trading broker back in New York. I told the broker that I wanted to buy some United *out of the money* calls (calls are options to buy the underlying security at a set price within a certain time frame). The broker informed me that I hadn't funded an option account yet, and that I needed to have cash in the account to purchase the calls. After thinking about the different, but still problematic, ways I could get the cash into the account from San Francisco, I decided I would wait until I returned to New York and would fund the account the first Monday I was in the Midtown office. Well, after returning to New York, I picked up the *Wall Street Journal* left in the vestibule of my condo the next Monday morning and nearly fainted when I saw the headline touting the premium takeover bid for United Airlines! I sat on the wall outside of my condo to let my heart rate slow and the cold sweat dry up.

When I got to work, I slumped in my chair. I told the head trader that I just blew at least a $100,000 investment gain and all he said was, "Oh, they would have taken that gain from you anyway. It was your first options trade, and Morgan is the banker. No way you would have been allowed to keep that trade. It smells of insider trading." I told him I would have fought it all the way to the Supreme Court!

■ ■ ■

The nineties decade started sluggishly, as the effects of rising interest rates, decreased consumer confidence, rising unemployment, and the hangover effects of the 1987 stock market crash caused a dark cloud to form over financial markets. By July of 1990, the economic slowdown was officially called a recession. Wall Street firms were retrenching as stock performance slumped and volume decreased. At Morgan Stanley, management looked around to see where they could re-position people, and my face popped up. I was asked to move to Morgan's relatively new and lean Nasdaq trading desk. They had four seasoned traders and an equal number of sales traders they had recruited from other firms over the previous few years. I was asked to be the fifth senior trader, and given that I traded technology on the block desk, the transition wouldn't be too difficult from a stock understanding standpoint. When the opportunity was presented to me, I was totally against the move. I had a strong franchise on the block desk, had great research analysts and relationships, and had a following on the Street. My initial response was no, as I had no desire to move. Frankly, I don't know if I ever had the option to stay on the block desk, but after talking to a number of people, including the president of the firm, I reluctantly agreed to the move. One of the best pieces of advice I received was to learn something else. Learn a new product. Learn how to trade on a different platform. The days of being one-dimensional are over. Make yourself indispensable.

One of the casualties of the manpower repositioning was my best friend at the firm, and fellow block trader, Greg Place. Greg had arrived at Morgan about six months before I did, but he came in at a lower level than I did due to my coming in through the firm's official MBA-training program and Greg coming in as a direct hire as an assistant. The MBAs were expected to move to a senior position within a few years; that wasn't the case with hires like Greg. Theoretically, Greg could have stayed an assistant his entire Morgan Stanley tenure. He had moved to work with me in 1989 as my assistant, but I treated him like a senior trader by giving him half of my stock list and letting him roll. Our first year together, we knocked the ball out of the park, tallying the second most commissions on the desk, while tallying the lowest so-called loss ratio amongst our desk peers. (Loss ratio is a calculation that exhibits what percentage of losses you tallied for every dollar of commissions earned.) Since we were in the negative selection business, meaning that we bought when the majority of investors wanted to sell, and vice versa, it was expected that we would lose sometimes. Greg and I managed a 9 percent loss ratio, which meant for every dollar we earned, we only gave back .09 cents.

The head trader told me in a one-on-one meeting that Greg was going to be let go in two weeks, due to a floor-wide reduction in head count. I was absolutely apoplectic! I told the manager that Greg and I were kicking ass, and I needed him to continue putting up the numbers we had amassed in 1989. I also told him that I didn't think Greg deserved to be fired. The manager told me that I would have to go on my own, as no one was going to have an assistant going forward. At the end of the day, it was a numbers game. I asked if Greg could go to a previously scheduled industry convention in Chicago with me as his last hurrah. The manager thankfully approved the trip and told me to show him a good time. That was all I needed to hear to send Greg out on a high note and make me feel a tad better about his dismissal. I also told Greg about this impending dismissal under the old pal's act! The showing of a good time started at Chicago's O'Hare Airport. When Greg and I stepped outside to catch a cab to our hotel in downtown Chicago, we both spotted a long white limousine and immediately hailed the luxury liner. We sat in the back of what had to be a fifteen-person limousine, and Greg even invaded the driver's vodka stash. When we arrived at the hotel, we both requested room upgrades. Shortly after settling in, we went out to a steakhouse and ate all that would fit in our stomachs. We walked some of it off on our way back to the hotel, but when we got back to our rooms, I called Greg and told him to order every dessert on the room service menu, as I was doing the same. This type of outrageous and foolish spending went on for almost three days, and all the charges were on my corporate credit card. When I got back to Morgan Stanley on Monday, I submitted my expenses to one of the managing directors who had expense sign-off authority. He yelled out to one of the other sales traders who had also attended the Chicago convention and said, "Hey Matt, how is it that you spent four times the amount Derek spent in Chicago? Were you buying ass or something?" Greg and I looked at each other and said, "Damn, we can't outspend the white boys even when we try!"

Some of the items that ended up on the expense accounts at Morgan Stanley wouldn't get to first base today. Not only would the expense submissions be turned down, but in 95 percent of the cases, the individual would be immediately fired, if not prosecuted. I should add that this behavior existed across the entire industry; Morgan Stanley didn't have a patent on this behavior by any means. In fact, when I was at Morgan Stanley, the entire human resources department may have been twenty to twenty-five people, including entry level people to the head of the department. Today that number is understandably in the hundreds, I would guess. Not only is that because overall firm head count has multiplied, but also because more HR support is needed in these times of intense regulation, litigation, and general HR needs.

Speaking of humans and resources, one slow day on the trading desk, I answered the phone and the guy at the other end immediately started yelling at me. Before I could even get a word in beyond hello, he said, "You asshole, you owe me $100 to clean up all your sperm and shit in the back of my limo!"

I said, "Sir, who do you think you are talking to, and what are you talking about?"

"Is this Richie?" he asked.

"No, this is Derek. Let me get you Richie."

Before I could transfer him, he started yelling again. "Richie was in my stretch limo last night and he had sex with a girl in the back. He left sperm and alcohol all over my seats and carpet. I didn't know what he had done until I got in the car this morning and it was smelling!"

On another occasion, another employee's poor decisions were relayed across the entire floor. His managing director stood up and yelled out, "Let me get this right. You got four massages in two days and you didn't even get laid? You're paying for this just because you didn't even get laid!"

Infidelity, drug and alcohol abuse, and other related issues were commonplace all over the brokerage industry in the eighties and early nineties. I recall hearing a story about a married Wall Streeter who, supposedly, was seeing another woman every Thursday night, but telling his wife that he was bowling every Thursday as part of a bowling team and league. Reportedly, his wife bought him a bowling ball and a personalized bowling bag for his birthday. He thanked his wife for the bowling ball and put the ball into his personalized bag and the bag into the trunk of his commuter car. A few weeks later, the wife asked how the ball was working out, and he said it was perfect; he was "killing it" at the bowling alley due to his new ball. About six months later, the wife suspected something wasn't right when he reportedly went bowling in a foot of snow, when most things were shut down. She went into the trunk of the car over the weekend and pulled out the bowling ball from its bag. The ball was in pristine shape and virtually unusable because the husband hadn't even gotten the finger holes drilled into the ball! Game over! Gutter ball!

I moved to the Nasdaq desk in the second quarter of 1990, and just as I was getting slightly comfortable with the more automated world of Nasdaq trading, Iraq invaded Kuwait on August 2, and volatility in the financial markets kicked up considerably. The common assumption was that Iraq invaded Kuwait to take control of its oil reserves, even though Iraq claimed it was simply reclaiming land that was previously theirs, albeit land with vast oil reserves. President George H.W. Bush deployed U.S. Navy ships to the Persian Gulf, which put financial markets on edge on a daily basis. I learned how to trade Nasdaq stocks very quickly while under constant fire, due to the tense situation in the Gulf and its hourly headlines, which affected every asset class, from oil to gold, to stocks and bonds.

The next year started off with a literal bang as Operation Desert Storm was launched on the evening of January 17, 1991. President Bush announced that evening that air attacks had been launched on Iraq and Kuwait. We all arrived early Friday morning knowing that it would be a wild trading day, as markets around the world were down multiple percentages. As the Nasdaq traders on the desk began to mark down our price quotes, especially our bids to reflect the market weakness, the hum on the floor grew and grew. Right around the opening of the stock market, the phone lines on our turrets were all lit up. We were only answering the broker dealer lights, as more phone lines were lit than we had personnel; however, someone answered one of the outside lines and the call was for me. I told the desk person to hang up on the person, as I was too busy to pick up. About thirty seconds later, the caller tried again, and I once again told the same person to hang up. Another minute or so later I got the relay again. "Derek, please pick up the damn phone!" In a very irritated way, figuring that anyone who remotely knew me, knew what I did for a living and had to know the day was crazy, I picked up the phone and said, "Who the hell is this? Men are dying here! What could possibly be so goddamned urgent?" A startled, but soft voice on the other end said, "Oh my! It's your mother. Call me back when you get yourself together and wash your mouth out!" I heard my dad in the background say, "I told you not to call him. It must be crazy in there. He doesn't have time to talk to you!" As my mom was hanging up, and I was in an *oh shit* disposition, I heard her say, "I just wanted to see if he was okay. He may have to come back home. I've never heard him talk like that before!"

■ ■ ■

The financial markets settled down a bit as the world got used to the Gulf War and learned the difference between a Patriot missile (U.S. made) and a SCUD missile (Russian made and used by Iraq). As a sense of normalcy came back to the trading world, a number of interesting and personal social situations unfolded. My now seven-year successful tenure at the firm had led me to become somewhat of a beacon and big brother for the black support staff in the mailroom. I became closest to a young man named Raynard. Ray would deliver the mail and stop and chat with me a couple times a week when I wasn't busy. I would ask Ray how his love life was going or how his weekend turned out, and I also gave him my personal tickets to an occasional Knicks game. On one particular day, Ray got into a somewhat comical argument with one of the white traders, and they both started talking about what kind of weapon they would bring to a potential fight. The white trader said he would bring his nine iron in the office tomorrow and whack Ray with it. Ray responded with a look of puzzlement on his face, and said, "Well, you better be accurate, because I'm good with *my* 9!"

I had to explain to Ray that the trader was referring to a nine iron golf club, and I explained to the white trader that Ray was talking about a 9 millimeter gun!

In a rather cocky tone, Ray said, "Okay, bring your shit and I'll bring mine! We'll see who walks out this joint tomorrow!"

I howled at the exchange, but made sure Ray understood that he couldn't, and shouldn't, bring a gun into the office under any circumstances.

The mail room guys provided all sorts of comedy and reminded me of my home boys back in Youngstown. A few weeks later, I went to the bathroom and was hit by a wretched smell, the kind that makes you hold your nose and not breathe. As I was at the urinal, trying to pee as quickly as possible, while holding my breath, in walked two other brothers from the mailroom. I didn't know them as well as I knew Raynard, but I had spoken to them many times. One of them immediately said, "Damn man! Put some water on that shit!" The other one said, "That's ridiculous G! Nobody should be smelling up shit like that! I don't know what that dude was eating, but that's ridiculous! Don't you agree, D?"

I nearly pissed all over myself laughing at these two brothers, as I waved, showing my displeasure as I finished my business and quickly washed my hands, all the while trying to not take in too much bad oxygen!

■ ■ ■

One of the more socially sobering experiences happened one evening that took me from a natural high to the lowest of lows in a span of three hours. The head Nasdaq trader and I went to dinner with the head trader and his second in command of a competitor firm based on the West Coast. The relationship had soured due to some execution issues, and the competitor needed Morgan more than we needed them. The other firm asked if it could try and repair the relationship over dinner on them. The head trader at Morgan asked me to find the most expensive restaurant so that we could make them "feel it," as they were taking us out to dinner. I didn't feel comfortable extorting the competitor and told my manager it wasn't my style, but he insisted: "Find the most expensive restaurant, with some good food, and make a reservation for four. If we spend $10,000, it will be a drop in the bucket for them if we resume trading with them!"

I pulled out the Zagat's restaurant guide and selected a very well-regarded Upper East Side restaurant called Aureole (it has since moved to the base of the Bank of America building in Midtown).

The restaurant was located in a beautiful townhouse between Fifth and Madison Avenues and reportedly had a $10,000 decorative flower bill per week.

Dinner went well, as we discussed our differences and resolved them. As a celebration, and to further stick it up their ass as a future reminder, my manager ordered a $10,000 bottle of Lafite Rothschild. Being a non-drinker, and not knowing anything about any kind of wine or alcohol, I was incredulous at the price. In fact, I decided that if I was ever going to start drinking wine, I should start with a $10,000 bottle of wine! I had the sommelier pour me about $50 worth, as the other three discussed the bouquet, its legs, its dryness, etc. After taking a sip, I said, "This may as well be grape Kool-Aid, fellas. I don't get it." They said that wine drinking is an acquired taste and that I should keep trying, but I questioned why anyone would keep trying something if they didn't like it.

So much for my foray into wine consumption! To this day, I don't drink. Give me a ginger ale and I'm good.

The ride home in the cab deflated whatever high I had gotten from the successful and delicious dinner we'd had. I was wearing a beautiful Hickey Freeman suit, was carrying a nice briefcase, and had the Wall Street Journal sticking out of the side pocket. It was early evening and the sun hadn't gone down completely yet, so visibility was still pretty fair. I jumped in the cab and told the cab driver my Upper West Side destination. As we proceeded up Madison Avenue, the white driver started a conversation, asking what business I was in. Despite my general reluctance to engage in small talk with cab drivers, I told him I was in banking. He then asked what I thought about the recession we were in. Again, I answered him. He then told me that he had lost his job due to the recession and was driving a cab to earn a living. I told him that I was sorry and hoped the economy would pick up soon, so that he could find a job in his chosen profession. He said he didn't realize that driving a cab was so dangerous, and I asked him what he meant by that. He said, "You're aware of all the cab drivers getting shot up in Harlem, right?" I told him I was. (It was mostly gypsy cab drivers being assaulted and killed, but horrible either way.) The driver, who had a Polish name on his ID plate, said, "Yeah, one way to avoid that is to not pick up the niggers who want to go to Harlem! I don't go up there to pick them up and I won't pick up a nigger because they might want to go up there! That's one way to stay safe, huh? Plus, the niggers don't tip!"

I was startled by his remark, and before I could think of how to respond, he continued, "See, you're a nice guy and an intelligent guy. I could talk to you. I couldn't even talk to a nigger about the stuff we just talked about."

At this point, I was fuming, and I realized that due to my light-skinned complexion, he didn't know I was black. My first thought was to wish I had a gun that I could put to his temple and eliminate one more racist from the universe; however, once I settled down, I thought that maybe I could teach him a lesson. I remained silent, as did he, for the most part, for the remainder of the trip. I asked him to stop a block or two away from my building because I didn't want him to know where I lived. When he stopped the cab, he thanked me and said it was a pleasure talking to me. I told him I had to get out of the car to get my wallet out of my pocket to pay him. I went to the front passenger seat window and leaned in with the money, which included a hefty tip. I said, "You should really watch who you say these racist things to. I am a black man and I'm very offended by your comments. I wished for a second that I had a gun to blow your brains out like the others in Harlem. But, hopefully, you'll remember all the bad things you said and you'll start looking at people as people. Some people are good, some are bad. Both come in all races." With that, I tossed the $20 bill on the front seat and went and sat on a bench on Central Park West. The cab driver sat there for about ten minutes as I sat on the bench and watched him. I thought he was either going to get out of his car and perhaps try and harm me or, hopefully, he was reflecting on what I said to him about being racist and realized that his words could have prompted a real ugly situation. He eventually pulled away and turned his availability light on the top of his cab off. I agreed that he needed to call it a day.

■ ■ ■

The balance of 1991 yielded more racially distinctive comments on the trading floor, as Magic Johnson revealed that he had contracted the HIV virus. The news was obviously discussed in every corner of the world after he made the announcement on November 7, and it nearly brought me to tears as I watched his announcement on the television at the firm. My heart was steeled when a white colleague insensitively said that the Boston Celtics wouldn't have to worry about losing to the Los Angeles Lakers anymore, as "One of your brothers just bit the dust!" The same individual later made racial comments about New York Knicks' star Patrick Ewing inking the largest contract in professional team sports, when management awarded him a $33 million contract over six seasons. The sports racist told me that the "non-talking Ewing is the luckiest black man on the planet! Good thing for him that he had a white agent!" I responded, "Oh, if he was white and the star of the Knicks, would he be lucky to get paid?" The jerk responded, "No, it would have been appropriate."

■ ■ ■

Friday's on the trading floor tended to be filled with numerous no-table moments, most of them humorous, especially in the warm months. I think some of it had to do with the release of the pressure

155

that had built up from slinging stocks throughout the week. If it wasn't a visit from Chessie, or a purchase of an entire mobile ice cream stand from the Rockefeller Center area being brought up on the elevator to the trading floor, umbrella and all, and ice cream and popsicles handed out, it was the sex show across the street at two p.m. every Friday. On the 50th Street side of the Exxon Building was the Time-Life Building. Nearly directly across from our 33rd floor trading room was an office in the Time-Life building where a man got "serviced" every Friday, for months, by a well-endowed woman who performed oral sex on him while he sat in his desk chair. One time, he even had her stretched out against the shade-less window as he serviced her from behind.

The Morgan Stanley personnel who had desks near the window looking out on 50th Street noticed what was taking place one Friday, and word quickly spread throughout the trading floor. Soon, there was a small telescope set up near the window, and a few people even had brought in binoculars. Someone even counted the floors up from the bottom and the number of windows over from the front of the building and went to the Time-Life building to try and determine exactly what firm occupied that floor and perhaps identify who the recipient of the sexual pleasure was. I heard that it was someone who worked for *Sports Illustrated*, but I don't know how accurate that was. Nevertheless, this weekly occurrence garnered the interest of any "sport," and it certainly was "illustrated."

During one of our slower Fridays, in the midst of doing our midday recap call, the traders go on the intercom system (the "hoot and holler") and tell the sales traders what customer orders still remain, and what we want to buy and sell. This gave the sales traders another reason to call their buy-side counterparts to see if they could find the other side of the trade and reenergize the trading activity in the slow afternoon. For instance, I might say, "I leave 250,000 IBM to buy for a customer. I've already bought 400,000 on the day." The sales trader would then call his buy-side accounts and say something like, "We're a big buyer of IBM," in an effort to find the other side of the trade and get both sides of the commission (the buy and the sale) rather than have me buy it from the Street and not get the second sell side commission for the firm.

On this particular Friday, one of the senior managing directors announced on the hoot, "I have a Catholic fish Friday special for everyone. I can use 500,000 John Deere. Make some calls. There is a big seller out there. Get the seller in here."

When my turn in the afternoon recap came, I said, "I have a gefilte fish special. I have 300,000 Hewlett Packard to buy!"

Before I could finish my list of desired buys and sells, I heard some commotion nearby, and by the time I got off the phone, the Jewish managing director was standing in front of me calling me a racist and calling for my firing! I stood up and said, "What's the problem? Didn't someone just say something similar? I didn't see you go off on them! I meant no offense. I was just being a bit comical like everyone else in here!"

That inflamed him even more, and he told my boss, Donnie, to throw me out, spewing that I couldn't say shit like that.

While this exchange was going on, I looked to Donnie, and he just motioned for me to sit down and be cool. The Jewish guy stormed off, muttering all sorts of expletives, as the room tried to process what had just happened, even though comments like his were spoken on the trading floor nearly daily, and many of them from this individual.

The severity of his response to my comments were different though. Fortunately for me, nothing further happened, but I never spoke to the Jewish guy again unless I absolutely had to for a transaction. And despite us having a convivial relationship up to that point, it was all business for me when I interacted with him from that point on, as I realized we were on different playing fields. His field had no referees and mine had one on each side and one in each end zone.

At the other end of the sad versus happiness spectrum, the fall of 1991 brought me as much joy as anything, short of bringing home my two beautiful and healthy children from the maternity ward.

One day, I stopped in Youngstown to see my parents on my way back to New York from Chicago on a business trip. The house in which I grew up had degraded, and the neighborhood around it had imploded even further. One of my parents' neighbors had sold their house while I was gone and had since moved away. I asked my dad if he knew how much they got, and he said the house sold for $10,000. I was shocked and told him you can't buy a parking space in New York for $10,000! But he told me the neighborhood had changed dramatically and that he and my mom would be lucky to get $10,000 for their house, as the neighbors' house was brick and theirs was made out of wood.

That afternoon, I drove around the neighborhood and saw what my dad meant about the neighborhood going south. I had never seen abandoned houses in our neighborhood before, but I saw at least a handful now. About six blocks away, I saw a lovely house across the street from a beautiful neighborhood park with a for sale sign in the yard. I called the realtor listed on the sign and asked what the purchase price was for this brick home. He said it was $50,000. I told him I'd like to see the home before I left for New York, so I did a walk-through the next day and thought it was a steal at $50,000. This same home in Westchester County or Long Island in New York would easily sell for $250,000 to $300,000.

Over the next two weeks, I worked to purchase this house and delivered the keys to my mom and dad in September. It was one of the happiest days of my life, and my parents were ecstatic. I was elated that I could move them into a better house, in a better neighborhood, even if it was only six blocks away.

■ ■ ■

Year-end bonuses in 1991 made me realize that if I was ever going to make what the brothers affectionately called white boy money, I would probably have to leave Morgan Stanley and step up into a higher-level role. I had never seriously envisioned leaving the firm, as I had been treated relatively well until the early nineties. I was promoted to vice president in 1987, and for the first few years was paid fairly in my view; however, when I got to the senior level, I believed I was underpaid compared to my peers, especially when I was on the Nasdaq desk. I confirmed this underpayment when someone seemingly, purposely, left the year-end compensation sheet for all the traders in the men's bathroom on the floor in stall three. A parade of us went into the third stall to view the sheet, and I was clearly near the bottom of the compensation scale, despite a top quadrant P & L.

In the last eighteen months, I had been approached by a few recruiters and began to listen to potential offers. Nothing was appealing until I got a call from Merrill Lynch. Ann Mills, a former Morgan Stanley colleague and someone who was in the MBA training program the year after me, was running the European equity trading desk at Merrill Lynch in London and was searching for a counterpart to run the UK and European desk in New York. I had never managed a desk and, perhaps more importantly, I knew nothing about international equities. On an occasion or two, I had traded a Canadian equity, but that was about the closest I had gotten to trading a foreign stock. Nevertheless, Merrill's management felt I was absolutely the right person to manage the New York desk and that learning the nuances of foreign equity trading would come quickly. After discussing the matter with some confidantes, I once again was confronted with the thought that it was better to know how to do more than less. I had listed equity trading experience from my six years on the block desk; I had spent two years learning how to trade Nasdaq stocks; and now I was presented the opportunity to learn how to trade international stocks, albeit at another firm. The potential move also came with a substantial uptick in compensation, and the role was obviously a management role where I would be both a player and a coach. My decision to leave Morgan Stanley was further solidified when I was standing at the elevator to go home one night, the day bonuses were announced, and a senior salesman asked me how I did with my bonus. I always told people I was good with the number even if I wasn't. When I asked him how he did, he said, "Derek, you couldn't pay my taxes with your bonus!" Enough said.

Around this time, the thought of racial and gender diversity began to hotly percolate on the Street. Corporate America had developed so-called *diversity and inclusion* programs a few years before, some with teeth, most without, but at least the thought of a D & I program was commonplace in mainline corporate America in the late eighties and early nineties. A flame on Wall Street was also relit after the municipal hiring and firing of the eighties, and Morgan Stanley's senior management decided to try and address their inadequacies around women and racial diversity. A small black consulting firm out of Chicago, James R. Lowry & Associates, with the primary principal, Jim Lowry, was hired to look at Morgan's current status and make some recommendations about how to make the firm more racially diverse. An associate of the firm, Marilyn Cherry (after marriage, her last name became Booker), was also on the Lowry team. From where I stood, Lowry's firm resonated with Morgan's top management, but their recommendations died one or two management levels down.

Before I left the firm, I told my friend Mike Giorgio that unless diversity hiring was going to be strongly tied to compensation, this would be an exercise in futility, and he agreed, but he also thought the effort couldn't be force fed. I doubted it would work, as so-called natural diversity won't just happen, and certainly not in an industry where the mighty dollar is the first, middle, and last thought on most everyone's mind. Diversity isn't a priority.

To Morgan Stanley's credit, they hired the consultant associate, Marilyn Booker, as a full-time employee. Over the years, she rose to managing director in human resources and became Morgan's first global head of diversity. (At this writing, in June 2020, Ms. Booker is suing Morgan Stanley for racial discrimination.)

■ ■ ■

As I contemplated my professional move to another firm in late April 1992, the Rodney King trial was coming to a conclusion in Los Angeles. King was a construction worker in L.A. who panicked while driving when he saw a police officer trailing him and made the ill-fated decision to try and outrun the police. King had been drinking and was on parole, as a result of a robbery conviction the previous year, and figured his drinking was going to be looked upon unfavorably. When he finally pulled over in front of a large apartment complex on March 3, 1991, he was beaten by four LAPD officers with batons. King suffered 11 fractures and other injuries due to the 56 baton swings and kicks that, fortunately, for King, were caught on videotape by someone filming from a balcony at a nearby apartment building. On April 29, 1992, after a heavily scrutinized seven-week trial, the four white LAPD officers were acquitted of beating King, and blacks in America were outraged at the decision, and a major riot immediately ensued in Los Angeles. Other major cities saw nothing like the six days of riots in L.A., but every major city was on edge as L.A. instituted dusk to dawn curfews. In New York City, police reported making 121 arrests, over a 4-day span, after the verdict. The news also reported that 41 people were injured, including 33 police officers, in direct response to the King verdict, but none of those injuries were serious. As the violence out West grew, and reports of anger and isolated violence in New York hit the airwaves, some of my fellow coworkers at Morgan Stanley became concerned about walking to and from the job, especially the trip to the Midtown subways and train stations to go home. The black and Latino guys in the mailroom jokingly asked me to let my white counterparts know that they were available to escort the white people along the streets of the city for a fee! Little did they know that two of the Caucasian ladies on the floor actually did ask me to escort them to the subway, which I did. I did this quietly, but I did bust a few chops amongst my white male coworkers telling them that my posse was waiting for them outside. Despite my jocular attitude on the trading floor, I was outraged internally regarding the injustice of the not guilty verdict.

My announcement to leave in June 1992 was understandably not met with overtly positive comments by management, as I believe they thought I would be a Morgan Stanley lifer and was making a mistake to leave. My peers were very happy for me, as they had realized that things on the equity floor had recently changed for the worse. The firm had hired some talent from the outside, and one senior person in particular had seemingly singlehandedly changed the culture on the 33rd floor into a backstabbing, toxic environment. This senior individual was more concerned about how my leaving would play out in the executive suite, given that I had a relationship with one of the five or six most powerful people at the firm, than he was about me walking out the door to a competitor. But on June 12, 1992, I ended my eight-year career at Morgan Stanley. I thought I had left with the blessings of the senior people at Morgan Stanley that I liked and respected, but through various interactions with one or two of them I got a negative vibe about my departure from Morgan. Nevertheless, I didn't regret the move to Merrill Lynch one bit, as it finally allowed me to command white boy money, climb into the management ranks, and learn another aspect of equity trading: international equities. I will say that by the time I was two or three firms removed from Morgan Stanley, I realized that pound for pound, Morgan Stanley had been the best all-around firm on the Street, with the smartest and sharpest people, from top to bottom; however, according to insiders at the firm, and from those I left behind, the firm changed dramatically after the mid-1997 Dean Witter merger. Many people of the legacy Morgan Stanley told me that the culture and intelligence meter had changed dramatically, for the worse, and it wasn't the firm at which I had toiled from 1984 to 1992. However, in the last ten years Morgan Stanley has rebounded, in many people's minds, to be one of the top two full service firms on the Street.

9

MERRILL LYNCH

I arrived at Merrill Lynch in July of 1992 amid some fanfare and puzzlement. Word was out that Merrill had hired a black guy from Morgan Stanley to manage European and UK equity trading in New York and that he didn't have any international equity trading experience of which to speak. My immediate manager, Kelly Martin, and trading counterpart, Anne O'Connor-Mills, were both located in London and were very supportive, given that they had essentially hired me. The senior management in New York (Mike Quinn, head of equities, and Bob McCann, head of U.S. trading) had essentially allowed Kelly to make his own hiring decisions by giving me a cursory interview that was really selling the firm to me. Bob suggested that as soon as I got comfortable, I should start looking for new staff, because the current European and UK trading team in New York was grossly inadequate and probably should be replaced as soon as possible.

My first day on the trading floor with my crew, I was intro-duced to Derrick Williams, a black man, Perter Lau, Asian, Danny and Mike, two Irishmen, and another white Irish employee that I was forewarned would be, "a guy who will definitely be a thorn in your side.'"

I sat myself in the middle of my new crew that knew 100 percent more about the product than I did, which was a definite challenge. Aside from the "thorn in my side," the traders were patient with me and answered my many questions throughout the trading day. I also leaned on Anne in London to augment my learning curve.

A few months into my Merrill stint, I started feeling some resentment from a few of the members of the all-white domestic equity sales and trading force, which seemed to have a bit of a problem with my authority, even though they were in a different department and we only had to interact when one of them had an international stock order. Prior to my arrival, I understood that the domestic sales force essentially dictated what happened on the foreign desk when they had to deal with the crew I took over. There wasn't much respect for the desk, and the domestic salespeople told the traders what the price would be for a bid or offer whenever they got a UK or European order (traders determine prices, not salespeople). This wasn't the case with the international sales force, as they had much more respect for the traders and also understood the nuances in pricing foreign trades (e.g., foreign exchange impli-cations, parity to the home market, etc.). As a result of my pushing back on the domestic salespeople, or as the people of color referred to them, the "Irish Mafia," I gained the reputation of being the dif-ficult black guy. In fact, during a domestic sales meeting, without my presence, someone asked, "Who does this new arrogant black guy think he is?"

I persevered, and with the help of the so-called rejects on the team I inherited, we turned the entire international equity trading group around as a team. The guys came in earlier and left later. We communicated more throughout the day. We helped each other when one was overloaded. We also caught the cycle of international privatizations, as many of the European state-owned companies sold themselves or a portion of themselves to the public in IPOs and secondaries. Prior to my arrival, all these deals were traded off the domestic block desk. I changed that and traded every single UK and European IPO and secondary that came down the pike. Their frequency for at least eighteen months was nearly weekly, which also helped me sharpen my foreign stock trading skills quickly. The efficient, visual, and profitable effort brought major respect on the trading floor, for the most part; there remained a select few who had ill-wishes for the group, even one on my own team, but he was isolated with his negativity, and the other naysayers were mere afterthoughts. I also had two great partners across the pond in my London counterpart, Ann O'Connor, and our boss, Kelly Martin. Ann was acutely efficient, smart, and forward in a skillful, productive way. She and I were able to ramp up the UK and European equity trading operation, with a strong hand behind us in Kelly. Kelly might be the best manager I ever had, simply because he listened and learned before he spoke and acted, unlike many managers I've had in my thirty plus years of working. He wasn't afraid to say he didn't know or didn't understand when he didn't get a concept or a trading strategy, and he gave one the respectable platform to explain what he may not have understood. I always appreciated his level of respect for all, and I carried that tradition throughout my managerial career.

Also, at the beginning of the third quarter, I had one of the true gifts from God, my son, Julian. I couldn't have been happier to welcome a healthy, beautiful, baby boy into the world.

Shortly after Julian's birth and getting my mom and mother-in-law to tag team for my recovering wife, I went to London for a week to meet the trading desk and get further entrenched in the ways of UK and European trading.

When I attended my first floor-wide morning meeting in London, mouths were agape when Kelly and Anne introduced me to all the traders, salespeople, and research analysts. I later learned that many of them had never seen a black trader, and they were surprised Merrill had one in such a pivotal position. A trader with whom I later developed a friendship said, "Derek, you have to understand, we don't even have black policemen or black postal workers here in London! You're a freakin' unicorn, man!"

I managed to ingratiate myself a bit further with the London crew on one end while also becoming an even bigger "unicorn" on the other. Unlike in the states, the London traders went out for lunch and had a few "pops" at the local pub. I looked up one day early in my weeklong stay and saw that most everyone on the trading floor was gone. When I asked one of the stragglers where everyone had disappeared to, he told me to come with him to the pub. I was incredulous that they went out in the middle of the trading day to have a drink or two, followed by a smoke or two, only to return to work an hour later. I learned that since everyone working in the London market went out at lunchtime, very little trading took place. By my stepping out with them, I lost some of my unicorn-likeness, but it all returned when I ordered a ginger ale. I went from being the only black trader in equities in the world to the only person the Brits knew who didn't drink or smoke.

I returned to New York feeling like I had learned an awful lot by being closer to the local UK and European trading, but perhaps more important was getting to know the London trading team. My confidence level, as well as the New York's team's confidence level, began to grow immensely, as we became more relevant and were a more significant part of the firm's trading P & L. Over merely six months, we had helped to raise the profitability of the UK and

European desk over 50 percent. Granted, the markets and volume were in our favor, but, nevertheless, we were prepared to maximize the conditions and associated profitability.

As we waded into the dead of winter, in February of 1993, one morning would prove to be a prelude for what would become the worst terrorist act on American soil eight years later.

On February 26, around lunchtime, as I sat at my desk in the World Financial Center (tower two) on Vesey Street, I felt a massive rumble under my feet. Many of us looked at each other and wondered what the turbulence was. Someone yelled out that it was the technology guys pulling cable under the false floor, where the miles and miles of cable going to all the systems on the desktops lay. I remember thinking that there were a bunch of pythons, not cables, underneath the floor, but I proceeded with my workday without much further thought. Unlike today, where information is instantaneous, we could only rely on news services like Reuters, the Dow Jones, Bloomberg, and a few others to broadcast the news over our Quotron desktop display systems. We received a small note about an explosion in a nearby garage, but not much else.

When I left work around five and walked out onto Vesey Street, I immediately realized that something far bigger than I had previously thought had occurred. Emergency and police vehicles were everywhere. Half of Vesey Street was blocked off. The West Side highway was shut down. A nearby subway stop was closed and forced me to walk a good distance to another subway stop. By the time I arrived home on the Upper West Side, I sensed the city was in a panic. I flipped on the television and saw that a truck bomb had been detonated in the parking garage under the Vista Hotel, below the north tower of the World Trade Center. A handful of people were killed (six eventually died from the attack) and more than a thousand people were injured. I watched the coverage in horror and vowed to never sit at my trading desk again if I felt or heard something like those "pythons" under my feet. I would leave the building immediately and ask questions later. This method of operating served me well eight years later.

Some semblance of normalcy returned to the area a few weeks later, but people were a bit more anxious, knowing the vulnerability of our surroundings. We also realized that the financial district was a target for terrorists, as the plot unfolded during the investigation. I remember asking Danny, a nice, older black man employed many years by Merrill to deliver lunches to the various traders on the floor, what he did on that infamous day. He said, "Mr. D, these white people think I'm a dummy that just brings them their lunches. They think I'm their slave, and I do need my job, but on that day, I got the hell outta here as soon as I felt the rumble. Don't you be a dope the next time something crazy goes down!" I told Danny not to worry, that next time, I'd be right behind him!

Soon after I settled down from the parking garage bombing, I went to London, in late April, and witnessed another terrorist incident. I was in the Merrill Lynch office at Ropemaker Place, in the city' financial district, on April 24, and the world rocked much harsher than it had approximately one month earlier in New York. The Irish Republican Army detonated a massive truck bomb near Bishopsgate, a very popular section of the financial district about a mile away from the Merrill Lynch offices. The physical devastation was unlike any I had ever seen, as glass a mile away was shattered that morning. Fortunately, only one person was killed, but nearly fifty people were injured, mostly due to flying debris. I cut my trip to London short and returned to New York as quickly as I could.

When I got back to New York, after working every single day from mid-1992 to mid-1993, with the exception of a few days off for the birth of my son, the guys on the desk thought that I desperately needed a vacation. I was getting a bit short with them and they unanimously voted that I needed to get away for two weeks. I had passed on four weeks of vacation the previous year, and I agreed that I was long overdue for a break. I made travel arrangements on a Friday, and on the following Monday, my wife, nine-month-old son, and I left for Bermuda. When we arrived, we learned that our luggage hadn't. Making matters worse, our hotel room had peeling paint on the baby's crib—no doubt lead paint! I even got into an argument with the taxi driver as he drove us around to look for another hotel. Clearly, things didn't start off well on my much-needed vacation.

We ended up getting another room in a decent hotel, and I ended up sleeping for a week whenever Julian wasn't screaming, as the thunderous rain outside pounded the island for 5 days! I understand that Bermuda is a beautiful island, but I haven't been back since that trip.

■ ■ ■

The balance of 1993 was relatively uneventful as we continued to put up solid revenue numbers. The team had quickly matured and had found its sea legs. The group walked taller and prouder, and I felt great that I was able to turn around the negative perception of the legacy group and not have to fire anyone or hire anyone to take us to the next level. I was commended for bringing the group together and making a solid and profitable team. As a result of the job I had done and my working relationship with Kelly, my boss in London, he asked me if I had any interest in replacing him as the head of the equity operation, as he wanted to return to the states for a change of venue and raise his growing family on the other side of the pond. I was flattered that he thought enough of me to consider me, but after some thought, I decided to turn down the offer, as, in my opinion, the weather and food both sucked, there were very few black people in professional positions, and I knew my wife would never agree to moving to London with me. Thankfully, Kelly understood and respected my decision, if not my rationale. Besides, I liked the team I had nurtured and molded; they were a fun and entertaining group, and we had gained increased respect, as we were hitting on all cylinders and printing money.

One of the more comical events was during a group effort when all the trading personnel worked together to sell (or buy) a stock by calling other Street broker dealers. On occasion, the entire international equity team would help one of the traders, regardless of what geographical area they traded, and we would all simultaneously hit (sell) or take (buy) a stock at the direction of the trader. His direction might be, "Guys, I need to buy 20,000 XYZ. Please help." One of the more rambunctious, loud, and sometimes annoying trading assistants asked the Latin trader who was seeking all of our help, and said, "I can help. Who do you want me to call?" The trader deadpanned, without skipping a beat, "How about you call Dr. Kervorkian (the suicide assist doctor)?" The trading desk blew up with laughter.

I recall interviewing a possible sales assistant for another department one day, and the young man had a brokerage firm called Stratton Oakmont on his resume. I hadn't heard of the firm and asked him about it and why he wanted to leave Stratton after only a few months on the job. He said he thought they did unethical things and he didn't want to be associated with the firm any longer. I didn't push the subject, and I admired the young man's awareness and concern. He was hired in another department. About three months later, word of this wild brokerage firm, located on Long Island hit the Wall Street circles. A few years later, this firm was on the front pages of the *Wall Street Journal*, and the owner of the firm, Jordan Belfort, became a daily topic of conversation, as fancy boats, fast cars, hookers, cocaine, and outrageous parties with midgets being tossed about were standard fare.

(In 2013, Stratton Oakmont and Jordan Belfort were memorialized in the critically acclaimed movie *The Wolf of Wall Street* after being indicted for securities fraud and money laundering).

Toward the end of 1993, it was time to determine year-end bonuses. My troop had done a commendable job and I thought they deserved a nice bump in their compensation from the previous year. Kelly Martin, my manager in London, had made the move to New York, albeit to corporate finance, and he unfortunately wasn't involved in the compensation negotiations. A manager from New York had replaced Kelly in London and significantly altered my written bonus recommendations without any consultation with me. On the morning of compensation discussions, I received a spreadsheet showing numbers for my five traders that I didn't remotely recognize. I called the new manager to ask if there had been a mistake in the numbers, but he said there wasn't. I was upset and told him he should have called me first to discuss the numbers, but he said those were the numbers and they were what they were. His reasoning was that I had done all the work and that the others were disposable. Infuriated, I called Mike, the head of worldwide equities, to fight for my team. I explained that they'd worked their asses off, had turned around their perceived work ethic, and that I couldn't have done what I did without them. Mike, obviously irritated, told me that if I felt that strongly about them, then maybe I should write them a personal check. We went round and round a bit more, and in the end, I walked out of the office and told the new manager in London that he could communicate the unfair bonus numbers.

After the close of the market, I talked to my traders and told them that when my check cleared, I was leaving the firm. Although I had been paid well for the year, I realized that if this was how they operated, then somewhere down the line, when, perhaps, I was in a vulnerable position, they might screw me as well.

True to my word, when my check cleared a few weeks later, I walked into the head of equities office on February 11, 1994, and told him I was resigning, effective immediately. He was not pleased, especially given that he was leaving that afternoon for South Africa.

I walked out into a foot of snow, with more coming down, and felt like I had done the right thing, even though I hadn't yet secured another job. But the moment felt right.

10

LEHMAN BROTHERS

The events surrounding my departure from Merrill Lynch had left me mentally, emotionally, and physically exhausted. I knew I had done the right thing by resigning, despite friends in the business telling me to ride it out, as that's the way of the Street; however, my ethos is, and still is, we rise together and we fall together. A true team, in all respects, shares *the thrill of victory and the agony of defeat* together. I couldn't fake being personally disappointed with my compensation knowing that the people who helped to make the unit successful and, ultimately me, weren't properly compensated.

My wife was incredulous, even though I had told her of my resignation plans weeks before. She just never thought I'd follow through. But I assured her that I would find another job, and that's exactly what I intended to do.

The week after my resignation, I contacted Don Crooks, my former boss at Morgan Stanley, who had moved from Morgan Stanley to Smith Barney and subsequently to Lehman Brothers, to become the head of worldwide equity trading. I wanted to let him know that I was available. I had stayed in touch with him throughout my career and occasionally consulted with him or relayed information to him that he had requested about foreign markets. The Street was aware of the turnaround at Merrill Lynch's UK and European sales and trading operation, and I was one of the primary architects in that revival; however, I also caught the UK and European markets at just the right time, and luck and timing certainly played a role in the 200 percent revenue uptick. We had become country specific traders at Merrill, rather than being generalist traders that executed trades based upon who was busy and who wasn't. Lehman had similar issues and really didn't have country specialists and, therefore, no continuity of knowledge. By becoming a country specialist, one gets a trading feel for all the stocks listed in that country, a current and ongoing understanding of the related politics that might affect stock movements, a feel for that country's currency, as well as being up to date on the regulatory environment and rules associated with trading of that country's listings.

Lehman was a bit more organized and further along in their foreign equity trading desk development than Merrill when I arrived, but not where they wanted to be. Crooks relayed a scenario to me where one of the senior traders on its international desk went long a ton of Royal Dutch stock, but was bewildered the next day when the stock opened down $2 due to fluctuations in its underlying currency, Dutch guilders. Crooks told me that the desk had dropped $250,000 due to outright ignorance about currency implications. Shortly thereafter, Crooks made me an offer to run the entire international equity trading desk at Lehman. This was a significant step up for me, as this offer included the entire non-dollar world, not just the UK and European desk that I had at Merrill Lynch.

I started the next chapter of my career at Lehman Brothers on April 4, 1994, just a short distance down the hall at the World Financial Center; Merrill Lynch was in Tower Two and Lehman was in Tower Three.

The first thing I did was to meet individually with the traders, to get to know them better and to hear their thoughts on the work we needed to do. I also took the opportunity to let them know that we were in this together, and they appreciated my motto, "We swim together, we sink together."

As we got down to business, once again, the markets cooperated, as volatility and volume were significant. The most important component to having a consistently successful trading operation, putting a profitable one aside, is having employees who abide by risk parameters, are disciplined, and are trustworthy. An undisciplined or rogue trader can bring down an entire desk, or an entire firm, and there have been more than a few instances on the Street where this has happened on both small and grand scales, as we saw with Joe Jett.

After a few weeks into my tenure at Lehman, the culture of the firm became clearer to me. Throughout my career, it was evident that all the firms for whom I'd worked had their own distinct culture. From my perspective, Lehman was the home of the misfits. Wherever a talented person didn't fit elsewhere, especially with the so-called bulge bracket firms at that time, they found a home at Lehman. Merrill was a very Irish firm, Salomon a working-class Jewish firm, Morgan Stanley a very waspy firm, and Goldman Sachs an upper crust Jewish firm. If someone with talent couldn't prosper at those firms for whatever reason, they seemed to end up at Lehman. Very few people I encountered started their careers at Lehman; most of them came from somewhere else.

When I arrived at Lehman, I displaced one of its senior head traders. Management thought he was better suited on the domestic desk, which is where he started, and they ushered him back to that desk upon my arrival. He was more of a producer rather than a leader, and I was expected to be both.

After organizing everyone into country-specific trading units, my next goal was to establish better relationships with our London counterparts, who were the primary personnel with whom we interacted on a daily basis. We used local independent brokers in most other areas of the world, but in the United Kingdom, Europe, and the Middle East, we primarily worked through our London counterparts. One of the major complaints from the U.S. traders was that the UK and European traders *marked up* or *marked down* positions, creating limited profit potential, or worse, immediate losing positions when they were passed to the U.S., given that we tried to run one central book. So, essentially, the trader who traded Italian stocks in New York and the trader responsible for Italian trading in London had a joint P & L book in management's eyes, but due to regulatory restrictions, the two books had separate P & Ls. Each trader understandably wanted to show the profit on his side of the ledger, and the U.S.-based traders thought the London desk took advantage of them and booked the winners on their side and the losers in New York. Put another way, the traders didn't have faith in management that come compensation time, the Italian P & L would be judged as two traders on one book, with both contributing fairly equally, and one trader would be disadvantaged relative to the other when determining year-end bonuses. This was my first hurdle to overcome, but I was confident that I could create the same equitable scenario as I had at Merrill (with the exception of the last year, which led to my resignation); however, it would be an even harder task than Merrill Lynch because I didn't have a trusted counterpart like Ann Mills in London.

I went to Lehman's London office three weeks after arriving at the New York outpost to meet the European management and get to know the traders that I and my desk in New York were working with on a daily basis. When I walked on the trading floor in London, I felt like I was walking on the red carpet at the Oscars, without the customary cheers and hand-waving. Eyeballs focused and bodies turned as I walked toward the office of the head of trading. Most of the traders had gotten input from the London traders at Merrill and knew that I was a black man. Nevertheless, these folks, just like the Merrill people, had rarely seen a black person in a senior role. For the most part, though, I felt respected by my London counterparts, despite walking in on a conversation between two women in which the question was asked whether a trader in London would take orders from a black man in New York. I just nodded my head as they scurried off with embarrassed red faces.

I left London at the end of the week feeling pretty good about the trip and feeling that I had accomplished my goal of instilling some mutual trust in both desks and assuring them that, as a team, we could succeed far better than fighting each other for revenue recognition. I did learn one thing about the English when I got back to New York though. Unlike Americans, or certainly New Yorkers, they are not a very forward people, in that they rarely tell you how they really feel. I was told that they prefer to be subtle and nonconfrontational, and will air their real feelings slowly and on their time schedule.

To prove my point, when I returned to the New York office and briefed the head of trading on what I thought was a successful trip, he told me there was a problem with the book sharing model. I was angry, to say the least, as I told him that no one spoke up at dinner when we discussed the matter, but he reminded me that it was going to take some time to win them over and that they had probably never been in the company of a black guy with authority. He said, "I heard they are still talking about your visit like you came from the goddamn moon!"

Thankfully, my relationship with the London trading desk grew over the next eighteen months, as I made an effort to communicate with them every single trading day, to gain their trust. I shared with them the positives and the negatives, and I think they came to realize I was a straight shooter and called situations as they really were. I also tried to get to London two to three times a year to continue building the cross-border relationship.

On one of my week-long stays in London in mid-1994, one of the London-based traders who traded the Dutch stocks and I were going to Amsterdam to visit the local broker who executed our Dutch orders in the local market. As we entered the Schipol Airport in Amsterdam, I was stopped at customs and asked to step into a nearby office. The Lehman trader threw up his hands in a WTF manner and pointed to his watch, as he stood on the other side of the customs desk. I shrugged and said, "I have no idea what's up."

The customs agent, who spoke English, told me there was a problem with my passport. When I asked what the problem was, he didn't answer. After about ten minutes, the agent returned with two other senior officers, who looked at me in an almost studious way. They asked my name and where I lived, as well as whether I spoke French. I told them I knew enough to get around France. At that, one of the senior officials said, "That's not him. You can go."

By this point I was flustered, as I had been delayed twenty minutes. I asked if they could at least tell me why I was pulled aside in customs. I was told they thought I was Jean-Marie Le Pen, a man who was trying to take France and the rest of Europe down.

Once I got back to the states, I did a little research and learned that Jean-Marie Le Pen was the leader of a far-right group in France called the National Front, the third most popular political party in France behind the conservatives and the socialist parties.

I had considered sending a photo of myself and Jean-Marie to the Schipol Airport customs office because I didn't remotely resemble Jean-Marie!

The Lehman trading desk never let me live that incident down. They routinely asked if they could speak to the "French terrorist" when they called New York. I learned more about Jean-Marie and his antics than I ever wanted to know from the London desk.

■　■　■

My first floor-wide opportunity to really make my mark at Lehman in New York came in October 1994, when the largest IPO from China that was going to be listed for trading in the states came to my desk. The Chinese had recently privatized a state-owned electric power company called Huaneng Power (HNP) and desired to list the new entity on the NYSE. Prior to my arrival, all the big IPO and secondary trading was done off the domestic desks (the listed block desk or the Nasdaq desk), just like it was at Merrill before my arrival. It was really because the two firms felt most comfortable with the personnel and expertise on the domestic desks. I wanted to change that perception from day one, just like I had at Merrill, and I got that opportunity at both firms shortly after arriving.

The opening of HNP went smoothly, and the international desk gained a lot of credibility on the trading floor. I did have to trade the stock off the block desk, due to its central setting on the floor, to allow more room for trading assistant help, if needed, and the room for viewing of the opening and ongoing trading by interested parties internally as well as HNP representatives on the trading floor.

An interesting situation regarding HNP occurred when Lehman asked HNP to "pay up" for the differential created by the volatility of the Chinese yuan (aka renminbi) currency versus the USD, which was HNP's financial responsibility to bear. This differential was commonplace in international deals due to foreign exchange movements. Sometimes it went in favor of the issuer, sometimes it didn't, but this was nothing out of the ordinary. Approximately four weeks after the offering, there was still an outstanding debt owed Lehman by HNP. I asked one of the officials in the finance department of HNP why they hadn't paid the debt, which was multiple millions. He barked at me and said, "We no pay. Currency go against us. We no lose. You lose. You pay!"

I walked over to the Lehman syndicate department with a look of amused bewilderment and told the senior person on the desk about the conversation. He said they were told the same thing.

I believe Lehman had to go through a many months' long legal battle to get their owed money.

■ ■ ■

As the fall and winter of 1994 unfolded, a crisis was building south of the border that eventually led to the Mexican peso crisis. Right before the Christmas holidays, Mexico suddenly devalued its currency against the U.S. dollar, for a host of reasons that caught many investors by surprise. Political instability, rising imports, the North American Free Trade Agreement, and capital leaving the country are some of the reasons that caused this holiday "gift." This devaluation also caused emerging markets around the world to get skittish as well. At Lehman I began to get daily questions from the fixed income division regarding what was going on in the Mexican equity market. On occasion I would get a call from the most senior traders in fixed income. One morning, the head of the corporate bond desk came downstairs and told me to short (a bearish strategy based upon the hope that the borrowed stock goes down and can be bought back at a cheaper price and replaced at a lower cost, representing a profit) as much Grupo Tribasa, Mexico's largest construction company, as possible.

On day one, I shorted roughly 250,000 shares. I reported the sell upstairs to the corporate bond desk and they told me to keep shorting the stock until further notice. I asked if they had quantity, price, or time limits, which is generally associated with any order, and the answer was a terse "no." For approximately three weeks, I shorted between 300,000 and 500,000 shares of stock every trading day. After this time period of aggressively shorting this stock at every instance of a legal plus tick and a lot of inquiry from salespeople and traders alike, I was collectively short about nine million shares, and the stock had indeed gone down. If I were able to buy back the borrowed shares within range, I would have recognized a very nice profit for the firm's account; I just assumed it was the firm account, based upon where I was booking the trade. When I made the suggestion of buying this short back and booking a nice profit if I could buy enough stock back at the lower levels, I was told to keep shorting it. I honestly don't recall how much stock I shorted over a five- or six-week period, but I was becoming concerned that some reporting of the size of the short position was now applicable. I knew that if an entity was long 10 percent or more of a public company, there was a disclosure report. I assumed there had to be a similar report on the flip side, but I never inquired. It was nearly two years later when I somehow found out that Lehman Brothers was hugely exposed to Mexico from a debt perspective, and this was part of a hedge against that exposure. I was never told this internally; I read about it in the financial press. By the way, I never bought the stock back; at least it was never bought back through the Lehman desk while I was there, and I didn't depart Lehman until 1998, some four years later.

■ ■ ■

While the internet emerged in the United States in the seventies, it did not become visible to the general public until the early nineties. In 1995, AOL email became mildly popular. I remember being infatuated with my AOL account, which I still proudly use to this day.

As data input became increasingly more of a necessity, Lehman hired a young man fresh from Rutgers University to input numbers on the trading floor. As our international trading desk began to get more exposure to Latin markets, we realized we needed someone who spoke Portuguese to trade one of the more active geographic regions, Brazil. Diego, the young man from Rutgers, not only spoke Portuguese, but was also truly a square peg in a round hole doing data input. He was engaging, personable, smart, and had a trader's rough and tumble personality. He was a wasted resource doing data input and was no doubt in the wrong position to maximize his potential. I brought him to our desk to trade Brazil and whatever other Latin territories we had neglected.

Diego quickly turned out to be a valuable asset from a trading standpoint, and that he had a very healthy sense of humor was a plus. Every Monday, all the traders waited anxiously to hear of his weekend exploits, which ranged from his interactions with the opposite sex, especially during his summer weekends in the Hamptons. All in all, Diego was a great addition to the team, and he kept us loose, to say the least!

The stress of trading millions of dollars of stock every day and the expectation of consistently posting positive numbers needed to be balanced with laughs and amusement, and Diego was our primary supplier of both, besides being a damn good trader. One of the more entertaining but lesson teaching situations evolved on the desk when Diego assumed no one on the desk understood Portuguese. While speaking Portuguese with the local brokers in Brazil, Diego talked openly and graphically about his female encounters over the weekend. We sometimes got the translations from the local brokers without Diego's knowledge. There was a lovely Latina assistant on the desk that sat near Diego who seemed to always have a quiet chuckle while working on the desk. In my office, I asked her if she was learning and enjoying her time on the desk, and she said that she loved the environment and it was even more special when she could decipher Diego's Portuguese stories. I asked her if she was offended by anything he had said or felt disrespected, knowing how testosterone-filled men can be. I then told her that I was going to teach Diego a valuable lesson on his upcoming birthday, with her assistance.

I called Diego into my office and told him that the young lady understood Portuguese and had finally had enough of his disgusting conversations. As his eyes lit up, his mouth dropped, and he started to sweat profusely when I told him she had gone to the human resources department and filed a complaint, saying that she worked in a hostile environment. As he slumped in the chair, he started muttering to himself, saying, "Oh my God! I'm done! What will I tell my parents? Oh my god! D, it's my birthday!"

"Diego," I said, "HR told me the things you reportedly said!"

Are you kidding me?" he said. "Oh, Derek, what the hell! I had no idea. I wouldn't have said those things if I knew she understood them! I've been saying stuff for months! Oh my God! D, do you know some of the things I said? I'm through! Do you think they'll fire me upstairs?"

"I don't know," I said. "Stay here. Let me ask a few questions."

I left Diego with his head in his hands, moaning. I closed my office door behind me and went straight to the trading desk and told the guys and gals on the desk, who were all in on the joke, that when I bring Diego out for his expected perp walk to HR, we should all wish him a happy birthday. I then went back to the office after a few minutes to get Diego, and he was in near tears. Before I asked him to walk with me, he said, "D, I'm so embarrassed. Is there anything I can do or say to her to fix this? I don't know what the f*** I'm going to do."

"Let's go and maybe they will show you some mercy, but you're in a heap of shit!" I said.

As we exited the office and got close to the trading desk, all the traders stood up and yelled, "Happy birthday!" I think Diego took the happiest dump he ever took, in his pants! Nearly eight years after my bathroom incident at Morgan Stanley with the CEO, Dick Fisher, I was able to teach Diego the same lesson Dick taught me: you never know who is listening or watching, so be mindful and behave.

■ ■ ■

I spent the balance of 1995 close to home, as my wife was pregnant with our second child, our much anticipated and lovely daughter Kara, who was due sometime in December. We were also looking for a weekend home, like many New Yorkers looking to escape the concrete jungle of Manhattan on occasion to maintain our sanity and allow the kids to stretch out a little bit in our personal and safe backyard. In late summer, we began looking in the Hudson Valley, given its easy access from our home on the Upper West Side, the reasonable pricing relative to, say, the Hamptons, and much less traffic to endure. We also thought that because of the lower price point of homes in the area, we might find more racial diversity.

I located a real estate broker in Dutchess County and told him my requirements, one of which was a diverse community. He advised me that I probably wouldn't find much racial diversity, and if I did, it would most likely be in an area that didn't suit my needs. Unfortunately, after looking around in lower Dutchess County, and adhering to a key requirement of being within ninety minutes of the city, he was right, and we ended up settling on a weekend crib with nary a person of color in sight. Fortunately, that mix has changed over time.

The times were exciting for us as a family. We were eagerly awaiting the birth of our daughter Kara, and we looked forward to spending time at our new home in the Hudson Valley on the weekends. Shortly after purchasing the property, I wondered if we had made a critical mistake from a family safety and social standpoint, after an incident with a white, local police officer. As I gassed up at a gas station about five miles from my new Hudson Valley home, I noticed the policeman sitting in the small parking lot of the gas station. As I pulled out of the station, which was located tightly in between the north and south lanes of this active parkway, the officer pulled out right behind me. I accelerated to merge into the 55-mph traffic, which was like playing automobile dodge ball. (In fact, this gas station was reportedly shut down in the early 2000s because of this precarious merging situation.) The officer followed me for three miles to my exit off the parkway. He then followed me off the exit, the two miles from there to my home, and pulled into my driveway. He then shockingly turned his flashing lights on along with his siren. I sat in the car, exasperated in my own driveway, with my three-year old son, Julian, strapped in his car seat in the back. The officer approached the driver's window, with his hand on his gun, and asked me for my driver's license and registration. After I handed him my documents, he then asked me why I pulled into *this* driveway. I told him I lived here. He said, "Since when?" Getting very agitated I said, "Since I bought it." He raised his voice, and I could see this situation going sideways very quickly, as the officer glanced at Julian in the backseat and smirked. The officer then nastily asked me to prove that I owned the home, at which point, thinking solely of my son, I elected to humor him and dangle my house keys in the officer's face. The officer issued me a speeding ticket and peeled out of my driveway. I couldn't wait to get to court a few months later, where I told the presiding traffic court judge that this was pure harassment and most likely racist behavior. I asked the judge how many officers pull cars over five miles after the supposed infraction, pull into the owner's driveway, proceed to alert all the neighbors with a siren and flashing red lights, and ask the driver to prove they live in a certain home? The judge was perplexed as he asked the officer, who had no explanation for his elongated actions, other than to say that he was running the perpetrator's license plate. I told the judge that officers like this are the reason that black people don't trust law enforcement and look at them many times as enemies. The officer's surly actions were unnecessary, over the top, and meant to intimidate and harass. I then told the judge that if anything happened to me, any member of my family, or my property, that the investigation should start with this officer. The judge shook his head, gave the officer a stern look, and then told me to go the window and pay the speeding ticket.

■ ■ ■

For the outside world, the trial of O.J. Simpson brought its own excitement, and it provided for fervent discussion in the workplace. The split between O.J.'s guilt and innocence broke solidly along racial lines in the general public, and I felt this at work as well.

People of color generally thought O.J. was guilty, just like those in the majority who were positive O.J. had murdered his wife and her boyfriend; however, many minorities believed that the majority offenders always got away with crime due to their financial means, connections, celebrity, and skin color. The black community finally had a test case of a black person who had all those characteristics, with the exception of the "right" skin color. We wanted O.J. to be found innocent, primarily because of the many injustices people of color had endured before him, while members of the majority race seemed to be found innocent or received lighter sentences for similar crimes. When the not guilty verdict was announced on October 3, 1995, during the trading day, I think the only two people on my side of the trading floor who were happy were my black coworker, Derrick Williams, whom I had brought over from Merrill, and I. We gave each other a sly high five as the white people on the floor were absolutely disgusted at the verdict and weren't afraid to express it. One could hear a lot of, "You have to be freakin' kidding me," or something similar. For Derrick and I, we felt vindicated that now the other side was finally experiencing the injustice that so often visited our doorstep.

■ ■ ■

Business toward the end of 1995 started to pick up on the international front, as European companies wanted to take advantage of a strong capital market environment and raise capital through a public equity offering before the year ended. I was asked to fly to Europe in November to assist on pitches and provide advice on trading strategies, given that these companies wished to have a U.S.-based stock market listing, along with their European listing. As it was nearly eight and a half months into my wife's pregnancy, I balked at making the trip, even though the firm suggested that if anything happened, they would usher me back quickly. One senior managing director even suggested that because this was my second child, it was no big deal and to just get on the damn plane to Europe. Still, I resisted, and for the first time, I felt that I should develop an exit strategy from Lehman, as my decision to stay local was not met with much positivity. My willingness to assist at any time of night or day via teleconference or video did not soothe any senior concerns much either.

My wife delivered our beautiful baby girl on December 21, and despite it being our second child, I was super glad I was in attendance. By the way, the equity deals got done, and the trading in New York which I orchestrated went smoothly.

■ ■ ■

The Lehman desk is where I had the most laughs in my career, primarily due to the diverse personalities on the desk. I think it's important to have that sort of balance in business, especially one as serious as trading.

Lehman had a strong investment banking franchise in Israel and, subsequently, we traded many of the Israeli stocks in the U.S. as American Depository Receipts. Lehman also played a primary role in bringing Israeli companies to the U.S. equity platform. One such company, which shall remain nameless, had filed paperwork to list their shares in New York in early 1996, after the requisite road shows and investor meetings. A few weeks prior to the U.S. pricing, the CFO would call me every day from Tel Aviv at the four p.m. EST close of the U.S. market to get some color on what had happened market-wise that day. This was not out of the ordinary for a foreign listing, but the fact that the individual called collect was quite amusing to many of us. This company was going to raise a couple hundred million dollars in an equity offering and they were calling us and reversing the call charges!

The night before an IPO or secondary, a pricing meeting of the security offering is held, generally at the lead underwriter's office. I attended these syndicate meetings whenever I was going to be trading the issue so I could get a feel for the investor demand, whether an issue was priced aggressively, and what firms may have a further appetite if they didn't get their full requested allotment.

When I was introduced as the head trader during the meeting, the representatives from the Israeli company present, including the CFO, had a look of absolute amazement on their faces. The CFO asked if I was the Derek he had been speaking with every day. I said yes and asked if there was a problem, but he remained silent. But I knew, as did most in the room, that he was startled that a black man was entrusted with the public unveiling of his company's stock. I had seen that look many times in my life, so, sadly, it wasn't surprising.

The "new issue" was opened and traded the following day, once again without a hitch, and I remained professional, even though I wanted to stick a stock certificate up the CFO's ass.

■ ■ ■

Since I had spent most of 1995 close to home after my wife gave birth to our second child, I had to make up for my lack of travel by going to Tokyo and Hong Kong in the spring of 1996 to visit our offices and meet the personnel in those locations.

I had my first significant taste of an acutely different business culture in Japan. At a dinner with some Japanese businessmen, I was pressed to have some alcohol, as all the Japanese men were smoking and drinking. When they realized that I didn't smoke or drink, the mood of the discussion changed dramatically and the conversation slowed down considerably. When I mentioned this to an American ex-pat in the office the next day, he said that the Japanese rarely, if ever, want the other party to be more lucid than them, and that a level playing field meant that everyone drank and drank relatively equal amounts. He suggested that in future meals with Japanese clients that I somehow get a glass of water rigged as vodka or some other clear liquor to put them at ease. The next time I shared a meal with my fellow Japanese businessmen, I slid the waiter some yen to fill my glass with water from a liquor bottle.

In the fall of 1996, *Black Enterprise* magazine published its second listing of the Top 25 Blacks on Wall Street. The magazine had published a similar list in 1992 for the first time, and four years later, I was included on the 1996 list. I always preferred to stay under the radar when it came to this type of publicity, and for a few days after the publication hit the newsstands, I thought I was in the clear. I realized this commendation wasn't in a mainstream magazine, but, nevertheless, it could become mildly embarrassing, given the mentality of the typical Wall Streeter, even if the publication was buried on the news shelves behind *Business Week*, *Newsweek*, and *Time*.

I was also concerned about professional jealousy in both the majority and minority community, but I was most concerned about the reaction at Lehman Brothers. Sure enough, the magazine wasn't on the newsstands a week and some woman on Lehman's trading floor marched over to the international trading desk I managed and announced, with magazine in hand, "Wow, Derek! I can't believe that we pay a black guy this much!"

The magazine mentioned that to be eligible for the list, a person had to have earned at least $500,000 for the year, including salary, bonus, and stock options.

"Well, you shouldn't believe everything you read," I replied.

For weeks afterward, whenever the question of who was paying for it came up, whether it be lunch, dinner, or charity requests, the response was always "Go ask the rich black guy!"

I was hardly rich, but that didn't matter.

I churned on and took the flack, as I realized that, at some point, the trading floor would undoubtedly move on to another cause to rib, but I vowed that I wouldn't be on the top *anything* list the next time around, if I had anything to do with it!

Toward the end of 1996, a black friend of mine who had previously been on the Lehman sales and trading floor (he was one of only 5 blacks out of approximately 150) asked, my advice on a position that was being offered to him at the firm. He was being offered a position in human resources as a diversity recruiter of talent and my first instinct was to tell him to never give up a production seat for a non-production role. He didn't make the move in 1996 but did years later, only to be severed as soon as the market softened and cutbacks became the order of business.

One never wants to be in a support or administrative role on Wall Street during soft times, as these jobs are the first to be jettisoned versus the positions that actually bring in the revenue.

■ ■ ■

The following year started quietly, as the DJIA surpassed 8,000 for the first time, the S & P 500 hovered around the 700 range, and the Nasdaq Composite went back and forth around the 1,300 level. The quiet at Lehman was rocked in mid-February as the former president, Chris Pettit, died in a snowmobile accident. Chris had been a very popular and revered individual at Lehman and was instrumental in building its strong bond business over a near twenty-year career. He had been forced out of the firm a year before his death, as he reportedly clashed with the chairman of the firm, Dick Fuld. The underground rumor was that Chris, who was married, had an affair with a married woman at Lehman, and the husband of the woman had gone publicly ballistic. To spare the firm further embarrassment, and as punishment for his rumored lack of judgment, Chris was forced out by Dick. At least that's the story as told by many at Lehman.

Unfortunately, sexual pursuits on Wall Street were standard and blatant during this time. It seemed that promiscuity was prevalent in every business where money, power, and drugs existed.

Some of the more outrageous moments included the time I was at Morgan Stanley, when a woman was giving oral sex in the company box during a Giants game, and at Lehman, when a trader was having sex with a woman on a conference room table and not realizing that the audio from a previous meeting between New York and London was still on. Needless to say, the traders in London were jammed into a conference room listening to the encounter and relaying the play-by-play to the trading floor in New York.

The calmness and steadiness of the markets allowed me to attend my first professional golf tournament, and I started at the pinnacle, the Masters in Augusta, Georgia. Lehman had a number of desks that routinely had client outings around sporting events, as did all of Wall Street, and the Masters was the most sought-after event. I was honored to be asked by the head of sales in the international department to attend.

Upon arrival in Atlanta, we were met at the airport by a driver who was carrying a Lehman Brothers sign. He wasn't very friendly, which I found a bit odd, given that he was transporting a group of four guys to the house we had rented. He mentioned that the house we had rented was his brother's home, and I assumed that the car transport was part of the house rental deal. Sitting in the front seat, I tried to make conversation with the driver, but he didn't have much to say. I figured the guy had been shuttling passengers and luggage all day and was tired, so I turned my eyes to the beautiful scenery instead.

When we arrived at our rental home, the driver asked me to wait in the van for a minute. The driver gave one of the other guys the key to the house and helped the others unload their luggage from the van. I patiently waited inside the van, wondering why I was waiting while the others were unloading, but a few minutes later, the driver got back in the van and said, "Sir, I'm sure you're a good guy, but I don't think my brother would want any colored people sleeping in his house. I'm not sure what to do here. You are colored, aren't you?"

I put my head in my hand, and firmly said, "Fuck! I can't believe this shit! Sir, first of all I'm black, not colored. Second of all, are you fucking kidding me? It's 1997!"

The driver, obviously rattled, reiterated that I seemed like a good guy and said he'd call his brother, but I wasn't having it. I got out of the van and walked around the property. One of the Lehman guys walked out to the driveway and asked what was up. When I told him, he said, "Fuck this, we're all leaving!"

I felt bad, because I didn't want to mess up the trip for everyone, and I knew we'd never find another place to stay on such short notice, but just as I was explaining this, the driver walked down the driveway and said his brother was okay with me staying at his house. Part of me wanted to tell this ass-backwards mf to take me back to the airport so that I could take the first plane out of Augusta, but the Lehman guy talked me into staying, saying I shouldn't let an old out of touch racist ruin my trip.

I went upstairs to the last vacant room in the house and felt like pissing all over it, but a calmer head prevailed.

The following day we all went over to the golf course to watch the practice rounds, walk the beautiful course, and buy some merchandise. I broke off on my own, as the only interest I had was to watch a phenomenal young golfer named Tiger Woods.

I settled at the first hole and waited for Tiger to begin his warm-up and practice rounds. As the crowd began to grow, it was nearly four deep when Tiger approached from what I thought was the clubhouse. I also noticed a number of employees clad in white uniforms standing outside near the building, also waiting for Tiger,

I assumed. I overheard someone say they were the cooks, every one of which was black. I found this slightly odd since every other employee, at the gate, the merchandise shops, or the officials, was white.

The hum in the crowd grew as Tiger arrived with his caddy and began warming up, but the moment was ruined when I overheard an older white man say, "I don't know what all the commotion is about. The nigger ain't even going to make the cut!"

I was so infuriated that if I'd had a knife, I think I would have shown this racist how to make the "cut!" Instead, I moved to another spot and tried to enjoy watching the young phenom, but I couldn't really appreciate the moment, given the comment and my inflamed psyche.

After leaving the Tiger crowd, I wandered around the course and stopped at the famed Amen Corner, which is comprised of the 11th, 12th, and 13th holes. With race and racism firmly on my mind, I decided to count the number of black patrons I saw on my walk. By the time I got back to the entrance gate about three hours later, I didn't need to use my second hand to count the brothers and sisters.

I left the golf course disheartened and took a taxi to the local mall just to do something different. Ah, some of my people! My faith was restored when I saw a representative sampling of black people.

The client party that evening was held in a large tent near the golf course, with ample size to fit a couple hundred people. I had lost my fellow Lehman pals earlier in the day, but had told them that I would see them at the event. While in line waiting to get in, I again did my diversity count. Just as I smiled when I saw someone with hair like mine walk out of the tent, someone several feet behind me, and obviously oblivious to my presence (or maybe not), said, "Hey,

Matt, I thought you said there wouldn't be any niggers down here? What the hell is that?"

A number of others in line also chimed in with, "Yeah, Matt, what the hell?"

I'd had enough of this inebriated, insensitive, and racist group, so I left.

Tiger Woods won his first major golf tournament and his first Masters a few days later. I wasn't there to witness his win, but those few days in Augusta left an indelible imprint on my mind regarding the level of blatant racism that existed in some corners of America.

When I got back to New York, it seemed like I had returned from a hostile foreign land. My mother was visiting from Ohio that week and I recall her asking how my trip was, and I told her that I didn't know how she and my dad lived during the fifties and sixties, because having just experienced that same mentality firsthand, I would have been a dead man. But my wise mom told me that if you wanted to live with some degree of comfort and safety in those days, you just had to tune it out.

My mother was basically telling me that during her prime years, if not before and beyond those years, a black person just tolerated racism; it was expected and you just maneuvered through the filthy sludge the best you could while trying to stay safe and out of harm's way. And my very fair-skinned mother caught it from both sides. She endured the normal racism from the majority and a "you're not black enough" scorn from her own people. Being the same complexion as my mother, I have also dealt with that two-edged sword my entire life. My general response to critics, both black and white, about my lack of melanin, especially to white people that love comparing their darker, or tanned, bodies, is, "I'm black where it counts!" That usually stops them cold.

I've also had to deal with some of my own prejudices and biases. I grew up in a blue collar, "hit the bricks if you ain't right" (whatever 'right' means) kind of town. Homosexuality was an absolute disgrace in my town, if not across most of America. I can recall my siblings and I calling each other faggots and my mom threatening to wash our mouths out with soap, not only for using the term but because we didn't even know what it meant! And she was partially right. We knew the term was derogatory, but being gay in Youngstown in the sixties and seventies was a road to being ostracized by basically everyone. We had two gay people in my high school who were constantly harassed, ridiculed, and laughed at by both students and teachers alike.

Billie Wright (aka Billie Holliday, after a reported sex change years later) and Gary Troll were the two *out of the closet* gays in my high school, and they wore it proudly and flamboyantly. More than a few times in the warmer months, they came to school wearing platform shoes, hot pants, and halter tops.

I left Ohio not disliking gay people, but not really recognizing them with the appropriate level of respect they deserved, in hindsight. I left Duke University feeling roughly the same way. I never went out of my way to disrespect gay people, but I did have a dismissive attitude, which is ultimately disrespectful at the end of the day.

My view changed when I met John (I've changed his name to protect his privacy) while at Lehman Brothers. John was my technical support guy while I managed the international equity trading desk. He was a big muscular guy, with a tart sense of humor. He didn't take anyone's nonsense, and gave it right back to the unruly traders when they gave him grief. I got to know John professionally, and he became my go-to guy for any technical issues. His competence was outstanding, and I also liked him as a person. About eighteen months into our professional relationship, John asked if he could talk to me about something. I thought maybe the guys were getting on his nerves, but that wasn't the case at all.

"Derek, I respect you, appreciate your fairness, like you, and value your opinion," he said.

"John, I think the same of you, and don't tell me you're leaving?"

"*Nooo!*" he said. "Well, maybe, but you may be able to persuade me to stay."

I was willing to do whatever it took to keep John on the job, although I told him if there was an offer that paid a lot more money, then I was afraid I'd have to encourage him to go.

"Derek, I'm gay, and I want to come out of the closet."! I can't keep living in denial. Can you help me?"

The look on my face was one for the record books. I'm not sure if it registered with John. He went on to ask if had any idea; I did not. And he wanted to know if we'd still be friends.

In that moment, I felt a major transformational switch go off, and I reassured John that I liked, respected, and enjoyed him thirty minutes prior and his news wouldn't change that. I told him to be true to himself and to be proud of who he was.

It was somewhat hard for me to believe what I was telling him, given my past beliefs, but from that day on, I have embraced and respected people for who they are and who they love. Without even knowing it, John helped me get over a major forty-year prejudice, and from a man who knows firsthand what prejudice feels like, my views were downright wrong.

By the way, John officially came out of the closet shortly thereafter. He thanked me for helping him emotionally and for giving him the confidence and strength to be who he was meant to be.

He said to me once, "I knew if I could get your testosterone-filled ass to accept me, you would have my back and I could handle the rest of these SOB's!" But he was the one who deserved my thanks for helping me rid myself of my own prejudices.

■ ■ ■

One of the more endearing and sensitive moments of my Wall Street career was even more personal, not transformational like the John revelation, but nevertheless a heartfelt moment. I brought my very inquisitive son, Julian, to the job on Take Our Daughters and Sons to Work Day. Julian asked a lot of smart questions his entire life, and at five years old, there was no exception. He sat with me on the trading desk and in rapid fire, asked what this was, what that was, what does that guy do, what are all these wires under the desk, etc. His big question of the day was one that the entire desk heard: "Dad, how do you make money?" I told him we try to buy low and sell high, or the reverse.

"Oh, that's how it's supposed to work?" One of the traders yelled out. "I got it twisted! No wonder I'm down $100,000 today!"

"Where does the money come from?" Julian then asked.

Shrugging it off without providing more intelligent details, I said, "It shows up on our computer screen after it goes through all the wires and stuff."

I turned my head for a second, and when I turned back around, Julian was under the desk. "Julian, what are you doing under there?"

"You said the money came into the computer. I want to see where it comes in so I'm looking at the wires under here."

The entire desk looked at me and just started to crack up, with one of the traders asking, "How are you going to better explain this, Derek? This kid's got you!"

To this day, a few of my former Lehman coworkers warmly bring up the cute incident when they ask how Julian is doing.

■ ■ ■

The financial markets in the summer of 1997 began to show signs of cracking, as the Asian economies, known collectively as the tiger economies, began to unravel due to rising interest rates in the U.S., excessive foreign investment in Asia, and a real estate bubble in many Asian geographical areas. Real estate in Thailand went through the roof and created a bubble that was pricked by its overvalued currency, the Thai baht. The baht was devalued, and other currencies in the region followed, and the Asian financial crisis was full on.

Our international desk got busy as volatility increased, but dangerously there was less volume to get into and out of positions. Every trader knows this is a dangerous combination. After the implosion, where Asian markets and their currencies went down double percentage points, and major economy markets swooned a bit as well, I went to London to get a better feel for the activity in the emerging markets. While there, I heard one of the most hilarious conversations I've ever heard related to a trading desk. The story went that the UK equity market was melting down and the desk in London was way over its skies in terms of balance sheet and capital tied up. The desk was losing a substantial amount of money by the hour and the head of trading asked all the UK traders to pare down their positions. The head trader recognized that liquidity was problematic, but he implored everyone to trim their money as aggressively as they could, even if it meant losing money, as it was expected that the market would fall further going forward. About three hours later, the head of trading came back and surveyed the various traders to see how much capital each trader had pared back. He got to the one trader who had the most capital tied up three hours earlier, 25 million pounds, and asked, "Where is your money level?"

"Twelve million." the trader said.

"Oh, jolly good. Jolly good! What did you sell?" the manager said. "Nothing."

The manager walked a few more steps, but stopped in his tracks and pivoted around like he had been struck by lightning, as he realized what the trader had just told him. The only reason his money was down was because the value of his book had imploded another 50 percent over the last three hours!

After the Asian crisis bottomed out in late 1997, the U.S. equity market picked up steam. In early February, the S & P 500 passed 1,000 for the first time. All seemed right with the western world as financial markets showed significant signs of stability. Merger and acquisition activity in 1997 were at record levels, and early 1998 was no different. Wall Street's dangerous culture of excess had returned on many fronts, as the money was flowing. Drugs, alcohol, philandering, and lavish spending returned in many pockets of the Wall Street population. I personally had one outrageous data point when a former colleague from Morgan Stanley called and requested to purchase my two New York Knicks tickets (I was a thirty-year season ticket holder) when the Michael Jordan-led Chicago Bulls came to town. My first response to his request was something like, "Man, I'm a fan. I go to the games. I don't sell my tickets, and I'm sure not selling my tickets for the Bulls game." He said he had a client coming to town who wanted to go to the game and to name my price. I threw out the crazy price of $3,000 per ticket to merely get my friend off the phone (the tickets had a face value of $300 each), but rather than just hanging up on me, he said he'd call me back in twenty minutes!

Believe it or not, this crazy guy bought the tickets! I banked the $6,000, bought some $50 nosebleed seat tickets near the top of Madison Square Garden from the scalpers outside the venue, and watched the Knicks-Bulls game that night as the most miserable, but $6,000 richer, guy in the crowd!

■ ■ ■

In early April, a shakeup was occurring across the entire Lehman equity floor, as my former boss had been terminated two years beforehand, and the gurus from fixed income had come down from upstairs to run equities. The backstabbing, infighting, and jockeying for power and position was raised to a new level all over the equity floor. I was asked to consider moving to sales trading, and was also asked not to say anything to the current sales trading head who was a friend of mine. My unwillingness to play along put me in a position where I knew I had to leave. I resigned on April 20, 1998.

Once again, I had no clue where my next stop would be.

Mom and Derek in
the early 60's.

In high school in 1974

WILLIAM (DAD) AND QUINCY
(MOM) IN 1973

WITH MY MATERNAL
GRANDMOTHER AND MOM

Junior year at Rayen High School

Being presented with the 1975 Ohio High School Scholar-Athlete of the Year as the North team's representative prior to the North vs South All-Star game

Univ. of Kansas football head coach Bud Moore and the "Kansas Comet" and NFL Hall of Famer, Gale Sayers, in 1975 during a recruiting visit

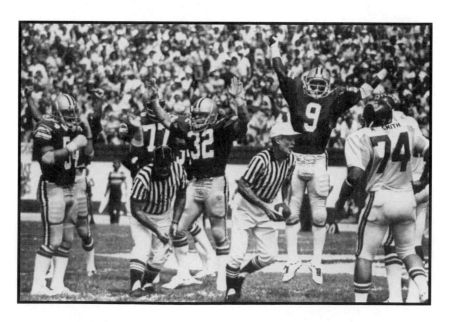

#32 after a goal line stand in 1977 at Duke

Duke University football publicity shot

SPEAKING AT AN
EQUITY TRADING
SYMPOSIUM IN
THE 90'S

NEGOTIATING A TRADE ON THE MORGAN STANLEY TRADING
FLOOR IN 1993

Derek and his Fuqua alumni pals, Owen May and Lionell Parker

The #1 rated Morgan Stanley equity block trading desk in the late 80's. Derek is the last one on the right in the back.

Family at my induction into the Youngstown Curbstone
Coaches Hall of Fame in 2003

The Penn men in the early 2000's

DEREK, DAD, SON JULIAN, AND YOUNGER
BROTHER KARL IN THE LATE 90'S

BROTHER KARL AND
DAD IN THE LATE 90'S

FAMILY AT YOUNGER BROTHER
KARL'S GRADUATION FROM WOOSTER
COLLEGE IN 1990

YOUNGER BROTHER KARL, MOM,
DAD, AND DEREK.

DEREK'S HIGH SCHOOL FOOTBALL COACHING STAFF: HEAD COACH PAT UNGARO, AND ASSISTANTS LARRY SPIRES, CHESTER LEONE, AND RON DEMESKO

OWEN MAY, DEREK, MARIBEL (DEREK'S GIRLFRIEND), AND DAMAN BLAKENEY AT A FUQUA SCHOOL OF BUSINESS SUMMER EVENT

KARA, DEREK, AND JULIAN ON VACATION

The extended Penn family at a reunion in Columbus, Ohio in 2018

Derek, daughter Kara, Mom, and Dad during Dad's final days in 2012

215

JULIAN AND KARA IN ST. THOMAS ON VACATION IN 2015

ALUMNI DAD AND UNDERGRADUATE KARA AT DUKE UNIVERSITY
EVENT IN 2017

Derek with the Duke Blue Devil mascot at the Maui Basketball Classic in 2018

Kara celebrating her Duke graduation in 2018

In Dubai in 2011

Family in London in 2007

In front of the Parthenon in
Athens in 2015

Fuqua B-school pals Daman
Blakeney and Wendell Rayburn
in Red Square in Moscow in 2008

Duke football teammates at game at Duke in 2018. From left to right: Mike Barney, Gene Banks, Mike Dunn, Derek, Larry Doby, Lee Rogers, Rod Sensibaugh, Mike Bennett, and Derrick Mashore.

The Rayen High School football, annual pre-Easter breakfast crew: Maurice Stewart, Gerald Price, Michael Fordham, Derek, and coach Chester Leone

Godsends from heaven, Angelo and Melissa Ciminero, who are Canfield, Ohio neighbors to my 89 year old mother, and treat her like their own.

At the National Museum of African American History and Culture in 2017

11

FIDELITY INVESTMENTS

n mid-April 1998, I walked out of the Lehman/American
Express building, thus ending another chapter in my career
on Wall Street. It wasn't long after that I received a call from a
financial services headhunter who asked if I was interested in managing a significant equity trading organization. I was interested, but
it all depended on what that entailed.

At the time, my son, Julian, was five and a half years old, and
my daughter, Kara, was two and a half. While my children were this
young, I didn't want to be in London, Hong Kong, Tokyo, or anywhere else, that would take up roughly eight weeks out of the year,
not to mention domestic travel, causing me to miss those precious
moments of their development.

The headhunter informed me that the job was primarily for a
U.S.-based trading role and most likely didn't require a passport.
This was a game changer.

The job was with Fidelity Investments, specifically Fidelity Capital Markets, based in Boston. While the job sounded perfect, I wasn't thrilled about going to Boston. Nevertheless, I was willing to interview with the company and see what they had to offer.

I liked everything I heard in Boston, and I really liked the management personnel I met during my visit, especially the duo of Frank Driscoll and Tim McKenna, the two senior managers to whom I would be reporting. The downside was the issue of living in Boston, a place I didn't have good feelings about as a black man.

My dad was a huge Bill Russell fan, the NBA Hall-of-Famer who played for the Boston Celtics from 1956 to 1969. Russell had vowed never to return to Boston after his career was over due to the blatant and omnipresent racism that existed there during his playing days. I recall my dad saying that the same man who brought a city eleven NBA championship rings in his thirteen-year career was called every racial epithet known to man by his hometown so-called fans. He had once shown me an article in which Russell called Boston a "flea market of racism." He also said that early in Russell's career, someone broke into is home and scrawled racial insults on the walls and defecated in his bed.

My dad not only admired Russell for his basketball prowess but also for his defiant *I'm not taking this shit* attitude. Russell took every opportunity he could to point out injustice and racism in Boston, and for a lot of black men, Russell was their national mouthpiece.

This was 1998, however, nearly thirty years after Russell's tenure in Boston, but the stench of racism in the city still existed. I had known Boston to be very segregated, based upon numerous business trips during my then fourteen-year career, and had been told that if your last name didn't start with Mc or your direct ancestors didn't get off the Nina, Pinta, or the Santa Maria, forget about being comfortable in Beantown.

Tim McKenna and Frank Driscoll both were sympathetic to my racial concerns and graciously didn't try to change my mind, yet they asked me to think about it and to bring my wife to Boston to see if she could "stomach the place."

A few days later, my wife and I took the Delta shuttle up to Boston and had dinner with Tim and Frank and their wives. The dinner was lovely, and both my wife and I thought this opportunity could be a good one if we could just get over living in Boston.

The next day, we looked at a few great schools for the kids, but when we asked about racial diversity at the schools, heads were lowered. We had a realtor take us to various houses in neighborhoods the realtor thought we'd find comfortable, but while the homes and neighborhoods were beautiful, when asked the question about racial diversity, the comment was generally, "You'd be the first or second blacks in the neighborhood."

After a long day, and a lot of thought, my wife and I came to the joint conclusion that a move to Boston would not be happening. The next morning, I let Tim know that while I loved the people I met and really wanted the position, my wife and I came to the agreement that we had no desire to move to Boston.

I thought that was the end of the recruitment, but Tim surprised me by saying, "If I could swing you staying in New York, where, quite frankly, most of our financial risk is with our Nasdaq trading and market-making operation, could you commit to coming to Boston whenever needed?"

My answer was a resounding yes!

On June 15, 1998, I started my journey with Fidelity.

The Nasdaq trading group was on a dark and dank floor of a building at 14 Wall Street, right across from the NYSE. The trading group had a manager that Fidelity had soured on, and I had to co-exist with the legacy manager until he moved on after some legal skirmishes between him and Fidelity. Surprisingly, the manager didn't get in my way as I reshaped the group from a strategic, technologic, and personnel standpoint.

After meeting individually with each of the twenty traders, the administrative staff, and the support staff in this roughly thirty-person office, I determined a few courses of action. We needed to solidify our order management system (OMS), which routinely broke down. Second, we were making markets in very few names relative to our manpower capacity, and in my view, we were missing a ton of potential revenue in many stocks in which we weren't making a market. We weren't even trafficking in the entire Nasdaq 100, for starters; however, we couldn't bring on more volume without settling down our OMS and reducing the frequency of outages and intraday trading mishaps.

After a few deliberations with our OMS provider, we gained some technological confidence in ramping up our volume and the number of stocks we traded. We hit the sweet spot at the right time, as the dot-com era blossomed and any stock with a .com at the end of its name became hot. Our volume exploded threefold, as we started making markets in over 1,000 stocks, up from a couple hundred only a few months earlier. Volume in the overall market exploded as well, and brought tremendous volatility, which is the dream combination for a trader: volume to get in and out and volatility to hopefully catch the rises and falls correctly during the trading day. Despite a 4 percent drop in the equity market as the Russian ruble crisis in August raised its head, we charged on and took advantage of the volume and market dislocation. Our profitability quickly doubled, and by the first quarter of 1999, we were in a significant hiring mode, as the market climbed higher and brought along the requisite volume and volatility.

Our immediate success was halted in the spring of 1999, as one evening I got a call at home from the managing agent at 14 Wall Street, saying that a bathroom in an adjacent office had a water pipe burst, and the water had seeped into our server room next door. My first thought was, *what are we doing with a server room adjacent to some hundred-year-old plumbing?* When I arrived at the office, I knew we would be out of business for a few days, if not longer. When I made the call to Boston, management was already on the effort to get us a twentieth century, or even better, a twenty-first century office.

■ ■ ■

We got the office back up and running in a few days and began to hurriedly plan our new office at One World Financial Center, where Fidelity already had a substantial operations related presence.

I nearly didn't make the transition to the new office. One rainy morning around 6:30 a.m., I was walking up a deserted and slightly dark Broad Street, near the NYSE and the Wall Street office, after getting a hot chocolate from a nearby coffee shop. I had my umbrella in one hand and my drink in another as a young man with an umbrella large enough to fit a basketball team under approached me. I expected that as I walked past him, he would move his umbrella slightly to the side, as I did. Unfortunately, the young man's ginormous umbrella hit my umbrella and nearly knocked my umbrella out of my hand. I quickly turned around, as did the young man. As I stood there, the man walked to within two feet of me and purposely hit my umbrella again. I was about to drop my umbrella and drink and deal with this young thug, but something told me that for this 100-pound, 5'3" miscreant to so boldly approach my 6'1", 250 pounds, he had to be packing a weapon. I smartly just smirked and turned around and walked away. After I got about ten steps away, I heard something fall to the ground amidst the noise of the raindrops. I turned around and saw that the thug had dropped a revolver, and he smiled at me as he picked it up and placed it back in his waistband. I got to work thinking that I could have been on the cover of the *New York Post* the next day: WALL STREET EXECUTIVE FOUND SHOT OUTSIDE NYSE. UMBRELLA AND HOT CHOCOLATE ONLY CLUES.

The Nasdaq trading crew I inherited at Fidelity was an eclectic bunch, but I did inherit some good traders. Fortunately, I also inherited a solid head trader in Tom Stones, someone with integrity, someone I could trust, who was also disciplined.

On every desk I have taken over to manage, there has always been a trader who either operated in the regulatory gray zone or simply had no discipline and tested the firm's and my trading parameters.

On a three-day weekend trip to Miami, I learned that a trader in New York had violated a few trading limits. We had single stock limits, long and short limits, overall book limits, and overnight capital limits, and this particular trader had violated the first three limits. On top of that, he had the audacity to be defiant when the head trader told him to get back under the limits. When I spoke with the head trader around the close of business on Friday, he had reduced the violator's positions for him. I told the head trader that I would deal with the offender on Monday, which I did. I called him into the office and asked him what part of the limits discipline he didn't understand and why he didn't follow the direction of the head trader and cut his position when told. His response was that he thought the limits were horse shit. I fired him on the spot. An undisciplined trader is a recipe for insolvency.

After the head trader and I got the core group of traders all rowing in the same direction, and they all understood that "limits are limits," and we recovered from the flood, we began to hurriedly plan our new office at One World Financial Center.

■ ■ ■

In late 1999, we moved into a beautiful space in the World Financial Center. It was a first-class trading floor and allowed us to double our employees and triple our revenue. I couldn't hire traders and support staff fast enough.

I did my best to hire competent traders, but one of them turned out to be regretful. A young black man had come to us as a temporary worker. He was hardworking, reliable, personable, and conscientious. His manager let me know that he would be an excellent hire if an opportunity arose.

I eventually met with the young man, at which time he told me he was trying to make something of his life, at the ripe age of thirty, and just wanted a chance to perform and prove his worth. I referred him to our human resources representative, and he was offered a permanent position in a matter of days. Unfortunately, only after two weeks on the job, which was going well, a human resources representative from Boston called to let me know that we had to terminate the young man because he had a record as a felon.

I was floored but pushed back, asking if we could give him a chance, especially since he was doing a great job and just wanted to make something of himself.

While I waited to hear back, I called the young man into my office and asked him what the felony charge was; it was an assault from when he was twenty-one years old. He had spent a few weeks in jail, and since his release, he had been bouncing from one menial job to the next. His job at Fidelity was the best job he had ever had and he truly wanted to keep it. He became emotional and begged for a chance to prove himself. I told him I'd fight to keep him.

The HR rep called the next day to tell me that Fidelity had a firm policy of not hiring ex-felons, and certainly not ones who lied about it on their job applications. She suggested that I could appeal

227

to the firm's Chairman, Ned Johnson, but I had a less than 1 percent chance of Ned approving the young man's continued employment. After all, Fidelity wouldn't even hire someone who had declared personal bankruptcy.

After speaking with three other senior people at the firm, the consensus was the same: Ned would never approve.

Telling the young man his fate at Fidelity was one of the hardest conversations I've had in my career. Through his tears, I told him that he could use me as a reference going forward, and I gave him a few pointers as to how he should present his checkered past to a future employer. As he walked out my office, he said he was probably headed back to a life of crime because he felt like he had paid his dues, but society was going to keep its foot on his throat for eternity and that he wouldn't be able to get a decent job if he had to reveal his felonious background.

I nearly broke my hand pounding my desk after the young man left my office, as I felt powerless to help him. I vowed never to hire anyone until he or she passed all the required background checks and were officially stamped OK TO HIRE.

Shortly after our move to the new trading floor, I received a call one evening that nearly undid the office. Fidelity security asked me to come to the office the next morning at 5:30 a.m. My first thought was that I hoped it wasn't another flood, not in our brand-new space. But the Fidelity security officer assured me it wasn't and, instead, said that it was personnel-related and reiterated that I should arrive by 5:30. He wouldn't expound on the subject. I didn't think much of it, and, obviously, it wasn't an extreme emergency; otherwise, the security guy would have asked me to come in immediately. The operation was printing money, so it wasn't like they were shutting down the office. Besides, human resources would have most likely made the call to me, not security.

I arrived the next morning in the dark at 5:30. When I walked in the office door, there was an FBI-looking guy waiting for me. (Fidelity reportedly hired ex-FBI guys for their security team.) I asked him what was going on and he asked me to follow him into a secluded conference room on the trading floor. When I walked in, there were five other FBI-looking gentlemen sitting at a long table with laptops in front of them and hard drives at their feet. They explained that someone in the office had complained about online pornography being displayed on desktops and circulating in and out of the trading floor. They asked me if I was aware of this occurrence, which was obviously against company rules. I told them that I wasn't aware of this unsavory activity. The head guy said, "Well, at the very least, we know the porn didn't come from you and you didn't receive or send any, because we checked your hard drive." Overnight the security team had come down from Boston and spent the last eight hours looking at every employee's in-box, sent-box, and hard drive. I asked how many people were involved, and they said ten. I was floored. I had no idea this was happening on the floor, and I had even made mention of not receiving and sending unsavory material on the firm's computers weeks before, when Fidelity sent out the policy regarding computer usage.

The head security officer then told me that when the ten employees in question came in around 7:30, to escort them, one person at a time, to the conference room. I wasn't to tell them anything other than some people wanted to talk with them. At 7:45, he asked me if Exhibit 1 was in the office, and if so, to bring him to the conference room. When I retrieved said person, as we walked toward the conference room, he asked what it was about. I simply told him to just tell the truth and be honest. When we entered the conference room, I sat down in the back of the room, and the security guy asked his subject if he looked at porn on his Fidelity computer. Exhibit 1 said he absolutely did not, that it was against firm policy. The security guy told him he was glad he knew the policy, but that he obviously didn't abide by the policy. The security guy then pressed a button on his laptop, and up popped a scandalous sexual video. Exhibit 1 froze for a second and blurted out, "That's not on my computer."

"Oh, indeed it is!" the security guy said. "And you have been terminated. The gentleman over there will escort you out of the building and we'll send you your belongings."

I just sat in the back of room with my head in my hands.

When I walked Exhibit 2 toward the room, he also asked me what was up, and I told him the same thing: Just tell the truth.

The security guy went through the same line of questioning, and, once again, the employee said he didn't look at porn in the office or even at home. Boom! The computer screen popped up and a guy and a gal were fornicating. "You've been terminated."

Three more employees suffered the same fate, but the last five were spared, as they confessed when asked if they looked at porn in the office. I believe the terminated employees called the desk from the outside and told people what was going on. I guess they relayed that they had lied to the officer about whether they had looked at porn in the office, and maybe they should have initially fessed up or heeded my advice to tell the truth, even though I didn't know if coming clean up front would save them. As it turned out, if you admitted to the transgression, you were put on probation and your year-end bonus was eliminated, but you were allowed to keep your job. We lost some good people, and others were wounded, but we managed to persevere. I don't think anyone on the trading floor looked at anything non-financial on their computer for quite some time.

■ ■ ■

To celebrate Fidelity's great revenue for the year (tripled), we had a holiday party at Chelsea Piers. It was our way of welcoming the holiday season in style.

The band, the food, the drinks, were all superb. At one point, I even took to the mike to sing "Brick House," by The Commodores.

Midway through the party, as I was *working* the dance floor, the enjoyable evening thus far took a bit of a turn, when I noticed some commotion near the food tables. My wife ran over and yelled something in my ear that I didn't hear, so she screamed, "Danna's choking!"

I hurried over to my friend's wife, who was holding her throat and turning blue. Everyone was standing around in a panicked state. Her husband was trying to dislodge something in her throat with his hand, but I pushed him aside and performed the Heimlich maneuver. After about three hard pulls, a piece of raw beef the size of a Post-it flew about six feet across the floor! To this day, whenever my friend has an argument with his wife, he jokingly says, "If you didn't perform the Heimlich in 1999, I wouldn't be dealing with this shit!"

■ ■ ■

The year 2000 proved to be a major inflection point in the finance world, especially in the world of equities. The internet craze, the tech bubble, and the dot-com bubble all came crashing down after the Nasdaq Composite peaked on March 10, 2000, at 5,048. Within one month of the peak, the Nasdaq Composite had fallen 25 percent, as nearly every stock that was internet-related or had the suffix .com was taken to the woodshed. Stocks like Amazon went from $73 in mid-March to $15 by the end of the year. Companies like

Pets.com went out of business within a year of its IPO. Companies that depended on advertising for their revenue had to seriously rethink their business models, as their valuations rapidly imploded. The carcasses of .com companies were everywhere, as investors discarded every speculative tech stock as well as some very established ones. Many companies merged to stay relevant, if not just alive. Tech was a bad word, causing investors to flee to established industrials, which helped to keep the overall equity market afloat.

Given that the operation I was managing in New York was a Nasdaq operation, our performance suffered in line—thankfully, not linearly—but significantly enough with the tech-heavy Nasdaq implosion. We persevered and made money where we could and tried to limit our losses and exposure. We also used the downturn to build some "smart keys" so that we could enter and exit positions quickly. For instance, we created a technology solution to buy or sell entire industry sectors within a manner of seconds. This helped us when, for instance, a semi-conductor company came out with bad news and the entire sector would get smashed. We developed a methodology to hit the exit door very quickly and beat most of our competitors to the few bids in the market.

■ ■ ■

It has to be mentioned that during my first three years at Fidelity, the New York Yankees totally dominated the Boston Red Sox, winning consecutive World Series championships in 1998, 1999, and 2000. I was elated!

Walking onto the trading floor at the World Trade Center in Boston, talking smack or, worse yet, wearing my Yankees gear, got me more than a few looks. I think if they could have, the Boston-based employees would have tossed me in the Boston Harbor! But they would have to wait until 2004 to return the favor.

12

9-11

The morning of September 11, 2001, was very routine for me, my Fidelity coworkers, and probably for most of the rest of the people in lower Manhattan going about their business. As usual, I held my floor-wide 8:30 a.m. Tuesday meeting on the trading floor of Tower One of the World Financial Center. These meetings were attended by nearly all one hundred people in the office on the fourth floor.

It was my job to address the group and go over the trading financials, operational issues, compliance updates, human resources concerns, and any other general Fidelity Capital Markets or company-wide Fidelity Investments news. Our meeting generally lasted fifteen to twenty minutes, unless there was a significant issue that needed to be addressed at length.

As I stood at the front of the room with my back to a south-facing window, we heard a loud boom at 8:46 a.m., and our building seemed to shake, ever so slightly. We also heard what sounded like a giant metal empty beer keg hit the ground. I stopped mid-sentence, as we all had a look of WTF on our faces. When I looked out the large window behind me, I saw small pieces of burning paper-like debris floating in the air. This window only provided a view of the southern part of Manhattan, whereas the World Trade Center (WTC) was northeast of our building, and this window didn't provide a direct view of any of the WTC complex of seven buildings.

Remembering my experience in 1992, when I stupidly stayed in Tower Four at Merrill Lynch till nearly 6 p.m., after the World Trade Center parking lot bombing early that afternoon, I immediately ordered everyone out of the building.

Everyone headed to the exit right outside the office entrance door, as I stopped by my office very near the entrance and quickly grabbed my phone, wallet, and address book; I locked my briefcase and left it behind.

When I got to the stairwell exit, our employees were halted and stacking up, as a security guard stood in front of the stairway door telling everyone to please go back to their areas until further notice as to what was going on. I personally don't recall doing this, but more than a few employees told me later that I physically picked up the security guard and set him aside as I continued to lead my employees down the four flights of stairs.

We exited the building directly on West Street (aka the West Side Highway) and could immediately see the gaping, fire-filled, smoking hole in the North Tower of the WTC. There was a collective "oh shit" from me and the Fidelity personnel, as many of us held our hands over our mouths while trying to figure out what happened.

I called my boss in Boston and asked if he had heard anything, and if so, what were the news reports. He told me the news was all over CNN and that reports were that a plane flew into the tower. I told him it must have been a small private plane that lost its way, but he said reports were that it was a Boeing 757. I was just about to tell him that there was no way a 757 could fit into that building when I lost my signal and my phone service went dead.

The hundred or so Fidelity personnel and others who flowed from the WFC just stood there looking up at the North Tower, trying to find as much information on the circumstances as we could, given that internet and phone services were quickly dwindling.

We started counting the floors downward, as many of us knew there were 110 floors in the two twin towers. The damage to the North Tower (Tower One) appeared to be between 10–20 floors below the top level, or in the 90th to 100th floor section. One person close by suggested that the inhabitants of those floors, assuming they weren't immediately killed, could get to the other side of those floors and take the stairwell down to a level where they could take an elevator down to the ground floor. We also tried to figure out what firms were on those impacted floors, but no one really had a good grip on the occupants. I thought of one of my best friends, Owen May, whom I had known for seventeen years since we went to business school together at Duke, who had a small boutique investment banking firm in the WTC, but I couldn't remember in which tower his firm was or on what floor.

As we stood in stunned awe and bewilderment, approximately fifteen minutes later, we all heard a sound I'll never forget: that of what sounded like a massive revved up Indy car in combination with the sound of a rocket ship being launched from Cape Canaveral. As my eyes tried to locate the sound, I looked up and saw a full-sized jet flying rapidly toward the South Tower (Tower Two). My first thought was that this plane was some sort of reconnaissance effort or perhaps it was bringing water or some type of fire retardant; however, I quickly realized this jet was flying far too fast to do anything positive. As people nearby started screaming when they realized this plane was going to exact more devastation, the plane's wings became nearly vertical as it screamed toward the South Tower. When the plane hit at 9:03 a.m., the deafening noise and violent, disgorging explosion was such that it made you freeze as your mind and body tried to process what your eyes, ears, and psyche had just witnessed.

We didn't have long to internalize what had happened, as all hell broke loose and everyone started frantically running amid screams and expletives. My only thought was to get away from tall buildings, as it appeared to me and others that tall buildings were the target. Everyone realized now that this was some sort of attack, not two misguided planes on this crystal clear, warm September day. Most people began running south. I ran north, thinking that by running south you would be quickly land-locked, with the meeting point of the Hudson River and East River less than a mile away at the southern tip of Manhattan. As I ran past the South Tower and got closer to the North Tower, one of my employees who was running with me stopped, and I stopped with him.

"Chris (Cahill), what are you doing? We need to get the hell out of here!"

"Derek, my brother is in that building!" he said. "He works for Cantor Fitzgerald!"

(Chris's brother, Tommy, was on one of the floors the plane had fully penetrated. Cantor Fitzgerald occupied the 101st to the 105th floors, and, unfortunately, Chris's brother perished that day).

I tried to reassure Chris that maybe he would be okay, but that we had to get away from the area, as deadly and dangerous debris was falling to our right from the two buildings. As I ran with Chris, the name Cantor Fitzgerald hit me again, as I recalled that one of my other best friends, Calvin Gooding, worked for the firm. As I thought about whether Owen or Calvin were in danger, I also thought that with all the tall buildings around, perhaps another plane was on its way, so Chris and I needed to vacate the area.

I lost Chris in the crowd as I continued to sprint north, up the West Side Highway, while avoiding small pieces of debris in the air and on the ground. Other people peeled off and headed for various boats and ferries on the adjacent Hudson River to head to New Jersey. After a good half mile sprint, straight up the highway, I stopped and turned around just in time to see people hanging out of the windows of both towers. Shortly thereafter, as I caught my breath, people began to leap from the North Tower windows. I couldn't comprehend how awful the conditions must have been in those towers for someone to make the decision to leap out of a 100-story building, obviously ensuring a violent death. I watched at least ten people jump and hit the ground in less than ten seconds. Fortunately, I couldn't hear the thud of the ground contact, but I did see a flume of human and other debris as the bodies hit. In my view, what I saw was more than any human being should ever have to witness. When I saw two people holding hands as they jumped from the building, I nearly threw up my breakfast. Before the couple could hit the ground, I turned around again and sprinted north.

As I got near the Smith Barney/Citigroup building in the Tribeca neighborhood, there were what seemed like thousands of people huddled behind a police barricade watching what was going on a little over a mile away. I slowed down to a light jog, intent on getting further north to maybe catch a subway on Canal Street to get to my home on the Upper West Side of Manhattan. As I was hurriedly wading through the crowd, I ran smack dab into Owen, whom I had come to regard as a brother since our business school days. The fact that I ran into Owen had to truly be divine intervention, for a host of reasons. First, if I had gone two feet to the left or right, given the number of people standing there and given my mental state, I probably would have missed him. Second, Owen was poised to go down to the North Tower, where his firm was located on the 87th floor, to hopefully meet his employees as they exited the building. Prior to my arriving, he had spoken to his office manager, who was hiding under her desk. Owen had told her to get the hell out of the building and that he would meet them downstairs.

I told him the police wouldn't let him get anywhere close to the building, as they were rapidly closing off access as I ran up the highway. Still, he was determined to get to his people, but I grabbed him and told him it was getting worse down there and suggested we go to my place on the Upper West Side; there, he could try to connect with his people.

Owen had gotten a late start to the day as he overslept. (The fact that September 11 was the first day of school for many in the tri-state area also saved many parents who were late getting to the Towers that day). As he normally did, Owen was driving down the West Side Highway when the planes hit the towers. Due to the then uncertainty of what was taking place, Owen had been forced to park his car and stand outside the police barricade, where he watched the smoke pour out of the two towers.

When we got to Owen's car, he once again wanted to head south, to the towers, but once again, I implored him to come to my house, because, as I said, "It's crazy down there."

Little did either of us know that things would get considerably worse.

As we drove up a very crowded 11th Avenue, I turned on the car radio to the local news station, WIN-1010. We learned that another plane had apparently hit the Pentagon and that the country was under attack. It was also reported that many planes were in the air, and that the FAA had ordered all planes to immediately land at the closest airport. It was reported that more hijacked planes were headed to Washington, DC.

Owen and I rode in stunned silence as we inched along 11th Avenue toward my home, hearing mini-explosions behind us, coming from Lower Manhattan, and a cacophony of sirens and alarms all over the city. Approximately twenty minutes into our challenging journey, I looked back toward downtown and all I saw was a big black mushroom cloud of smoke covering all of Lower Manhattan. I told Owen it looked like a nuclear bomb had gone off.

When we arrived at my home, my mother, who had been visiting my family for the past week, nearly fainted when Owen and I walked through the door. My wife had been frantically trying to call me, but all cell phone service was down, so they were understandably panicked.

The television was tuned to CNN, and when Owen and I glanced at the screen, around 10:45, we didn't see the towers. Almost simultaneously, we both said, "Where are the towers?" My wife informed us that they both fell. Owen nearly collapsed, and I just put my closed fists to my forehead, and said, "No, no, no!"

As we both slumped down in a chair, my next thought was to get my kids from school and then try and get out of town, perhaps to our weekend home in the Hudson Valley.

Owen decided he needed to get across the George Washington Bridge to his home in New Jersey to tend to his family, so he left. I told my wife that she should go and get our son, Julian, from his school, St. Hilda's & St. Hugh's, on West 114th Street, and I would go and get our daughter, Kara, from Brearley, a private all-girls' school cross town, at 83rd and the East River.

I realized traffic would be next to impossible going across town and that riding my bike would be faster, so that's what I did. The school had understandably not wanted to panic the young girls and hadn't told them of the tragedy downtown, even though when you stepped in the school, you could see the concern and trepidation on the teachers' and administrators' faces.

I checked my daughter and her friend, whose mom was working, out of her kindergarten class, and then, since the girls hadn't gotten to eat their lunch yet, I walked the bike alongside them to Central Park, where we sat on a bench near the reservoir.

The girls skipped around as they ate their lunches, totally, and understandably, oblivious to the tragic event downtown. In fact, as I sat on the bench, trying to be joyful with the two girls, a woman jogger coming from the reservoir trail asked me if I knew why all the sirens were blaring and where the emergency vehicles were going in Manhattan. I told her she should probably go home and check the news right away.

When the girls and I got home, my wife and son had already arrived. Knowing that we wanted to get out of the city, I checked on the best exit routes. Navigating was going to be difficult, as bridges and tunnels were being shut down either by the authorities or by bumper-to-bumper traffic. I realized that the best decision was to stay in our nondescript, nineteen-story building.

We did our best to entertain the kids and keep them away from CNN, but my son, who was nine years old at the time, had a decent idea that the city had been attacked; he just didn't know the magnitude of the tragedy. I assured him that we were all safe, even though I had my doubts, as the news reported a few commercial planes were unaccounted for, and F-15 and F-16 fighter jets were loudly buzzing over Manhattan.

It was a restless night for me, as internet and phone service were intermittent. I tried getting in touch with my friend Calvin numerous times, but to no avail. I finally reached his wife, LaChanze (a Broadway actress), on September 12. She told me that Calvin was missing. She said he had reported to work as normal on September 11, but hadn't heard from him since. I felt like a knife had been shoved deep into my stomach, as I feared Calvin had been killed in the attack. I was hopeful that he had gotten out of the building or, by some miracle, was not in the Cantor offices at the time the plane crashed through the top floors of Tower One.

Whenever I closed my eyes to rest, I had visions of Calvin in unimaginable distress, or I heard a fighter jet in the air, or heard a siren. On one occasion, I heard a bloodcurdling scream from the sidewalk on Amsterdam Avenue that caused me to go to the apartment window and look down, but it was all just in my head.

I watched the clock tick by tick the night after the attacks, with CNN on in the background. Thankfully, the rest of the household could sleep. I realized that unless you witnessed the tragedy first-hand, the impact wasn't quite as great when you saw it played out on television, even though every Manhattan resident could certainly smell what became known as the *burning pile* in Lower Manhattan.

In the immediate days after September 11, things began to settle down just a bit, with the exception of still not hearing a word about Calvin's fate.

My anxiety level was pretty high at this point. I remember standing on the nineteenth floor of my apartment, pensively staring out the window toward the Hudson River, when a slow-moving United Airlines jet proceeded south down the Hudson River. I don't know if my paranoid imagination was messing with me, but it seemed this crawling, fairly low flying plane was measuring up a building to hit. My anxiety quickly rose, as I broke out in a sweat and slightly urinated on myself. Just as I was about to lose it, CNN came on with a live shot of the plane proceeding down the Hudson. The commentator said that residents shouldn't be alarmed, as this plane was full of grief counselors and was coming from Chicago to assist the families that had lost people in the attacks. I went to the bathroom and took a long, hot shower, as the tears streamed down my face.

Over the ensuing days, I was consumed with getting the Fidelity business up and running again in our Boston office while I continued to check with LaChanze to see if any news on Calvin had surfaced. Owen had thankfully accounted for all but one person in his office, as they heeded his advice and miraculously got out of the North Tower before it imploded. Very few people were allowed to get anywhere near the WFC office, and, quite frankly, I had zero desire to go downtown amidst the death and destruction; however, on or around September 17, I was asked to go down to the Fidelity offices to see how badly our fourth-floor office had been damaged. I got official approval to go into Lower Manhattan.

The closer the taxi got, the more toxic and pungent the smell became. When the taxi dropped me off, about three blocks from the site, I came upon the eeriest sight I'd ever seen, even to this day. From street level, the pile looked like a movie backlot. I saw what seemed like hundreds of workers pulling debris on the pile back and forth, backhoes in action, and I was hopeful I wouldn't see any bodies unearthed. I immediately thought that working in such close proximity to this smoking mess couldn't be healthy, so I pulled my jacket up over my nose.

Upon entering the WFC, I saw that the inside of the building was filled with workers tossing debris aside, amidst broken glass and mounds of dirt and dust. I took the stairs up to the fourth floor, to our office, which looked like a Halloween setting. Everything was coated in about two inches of heavy, black dust, and paper and computer-related equipment was strewn about. The windows at the end of the office that faced the WTC complex had had been blown out, and most of the furniture had been tossed about.

I walked the floor and went to the window to get a different perspective on the pile. From this perspective, the pile was more massive than I had thought, but then again, there was 220 stories of building stacked up.

I simply couldn't believe that these two massive towers, the two tallest buildings in the Western Hemisphere, had been knocked down.

After some reflection, I went to my office and was very disturbed by what I saw. The locked briefcase that I had left in my office when we fled some six days earlier had been pried open, evidenced by marks in the leather from that of a large screwdriver or a crowbar of sorts. I couldn't imagine who could have done this, given that I was told that the only people who had access to our offices were police officers and firefighters.

I looked around the office further and realized that the place had been ransacked, and it didn't have anything to do with the blast that most likely came through the floor when the towers imploded. This led me to check a number of the adjacent offices of the other senior executives, and their offices had been turned upside down as well.

What I found was disturbing, so I walked back down the steps to the lobby and spoke with the security people who were allowing access into the building and asked them about the ransacking situation. The security guy at the desk just shrugged his shoulders at the question. Another security guy, with whom I'd become friendly over the previous two years, motioned to me to meet him around one of the columns in the lobby. He told me that a number of firefighters came with their big, wide boots and large pocketed coats, and left with them filled with laptops and anything else they could fit. He said that everyone on site knew about it, but he didn't want to be known as a snitch. He said they also cleaned up in all the stores below the WTC too.

I found myself in utter amazement at this revelation, because it was hard to understand how anyone could take advantage of such a horrible and tragic event.

Feeling a bit dejected, I went upstairs and got my briefcase, brushed it off, and proceeded back downstairs. I tried to balance my disgust at the advantageous thievery with the heroic efforts of the firefighters. Nothing of tangible value was in the briefcase; there were only some files and papers that could have led to some identity theft, but I wasn't concerned about it. I was well aware of all the brave firefighters who perished going up into the burning buildings to save people that would implode on them, and I was aware of the courageous firefighters who perished on the ground when the buildings came down upon them. I was also aware of New York's finest doing an incredible job as well during the worst tragedy on American soil. I filed these negative memories away, for the most part, until the writing of this book.

I'm sure that New Yorkers, and America in general, believed that the heroes of the day, the courageous firefighters and police officers, carried out their duties in an exemplary fashion, given the severity of the tragedy that befell our country on September 11, so I chalked up what I'd learned as just a few bad apples potentially ruining the reputation of the many.

■ ■ ■

I finally received the sad news from LaChanze that there was evidence that Calvin had perished in the attacks on September 11. I believe his parked car was found demolished in the garage at the WTC. I also vaguely recall that a phone call had taken place from or to Calvin after the plane hit and that someone had spoken to him while he was in the building, but this was hearsay, and I never had the nerve to ask LaChanze if the call actually took place.

During my commutes to and from Boston, in an effort to get the Fidelity business back up and running in Boston, I had the opportunity to visit LeChanze. What made everything so much sadder was that she and Calvin had a nineteen-month-old daughter at the time, and she was eight months pregnant with their second daughter.

I missed my friend, and I regretted that we never got the opportunity to spend time together at my place in the Hudson Valley. We had thought about going the weekend before September 11 but decided instead that the following weekend might be better, and now those plans would never come to fruition.

■ ■ ■

My team and I worked feverishly to get the New York trading business functioning again on the Boston World Trade Center sales and trading floor. All of the essential personnel came up to Boston and spent many weeks in the Fidelity-owned Seaport Hotel, which was walking distance from the office. When I wasn't in Boston, I was in New York trying to assist our corporate location people in looking for new space for a trading floor.

I would have thought that given the tumultuous times, race relations would have been put on the back burner, so to speak, but, sadly, that wasn't the case.

I went looking for suitable short-term or long-term office space in the New York metropolitan area. On suggestion by Fidelity's real estate people, I checked on two spaces in Jersey City. After a real estate agent showed me the first space, he stepped out to make a phone call. Twenty minutes had gone by and he still wasn't back, and I realized I was going to be late for my second appointment, so I set out to find the agent and let him know I had to leave. I heard chatter coming from one of the offices, and when I got closer, I heard him say, "They sent some low-level nigger over here to look at the space, so they're probably not serious."

Rather than confront the individual, I left the building and never saw the agent again.

As I was walking to the next appointment, I was incensed for not having said anything to the man, but if I'd done so, my next appointment may have been a Jersey City jail cell for a felony.

We eventually found a short-term space that a vendor was willing to lease to us for a few months. The corporate location people had found a larger, permanent space at Harborside Place in Jersey City where the firm decided to move all of its non-branch New York operations, but the build out for this location would take months. The vendor's temporary space would be helpful so that the New Yorkers could get back to their homes and families and not have to spend the work week in Boston; however, the vendor's space could only accommodate about a third of our current staff. Management recommended we eliminate some headcount for two reasons: first, the current staff level wouldn't fit in the short-term space, and second, the revenue had fallen nearly 90 percent due to our being out of business for a time and the business being limited because of the negative effects of 9-11 all over the Street. Trading volume had also shrunk dramatically. Human resources personnel and senior management came to New York to explain the reason for the downsizing, although there was a general understanding among the troops of why the layoffs needed to happen.

I spoke at the meeting as well and reinforced that we needed to save the business and that, unfortunately, the only way to do that was to reduce our expenses. We also had to get some portion of the business back up and running in New York.

Senior management and I turned over our list of recommended firings to human resources. Meanwhile, I continued running the business from Boston and prepping it for the move to our lease space in New Jersey; human resources personnel returned to New York to carry out the terminations. I assumed HR would talk with each person independently prior to firing, but I learned they were told as a group, and I found this quite insensitive, especially given that many of them were still rattled by the horrific and personally painful events of September 11. I vowed to never give the job of terminating someone who reported to me to someone else.

■ ■ ■

The attacks on our soil on September 11 will forever leave an indelible mark on our country. We learned to cope with new rules put in place to increase our safety, including air travel, new and improved identification, and building construction requirements. I'm grateful to have lived through that perilous day, and mourn those who gave the ultimate sacrifice. We will never forget.

13

PICKING UP
THE PIECES

Anyone who witnessed and experienced what I did on 9-11 most likely looked at life through a different lens now. From that day forward, I pledged to follow the trite saying *live each day to the fullest* in earnest. My thoughts were that if I had the time, financial wherewithal, and wouldn't put myself or my family in any type of harm's way, I was going to do whatever I desired. I had watched my dear friend Calvin, only thirty-eight years old, put his life on hold for something greater in the future, only to lose it on that infamous day. I vowed to learn from his death about delaying the spoils of life.

Once business at Fidelity was back up and running, with part of the operation relocated in Boston and the balance in New Jersey, I returned my attention back to the selling of our condo that we had listed in the spring of 2001. Surprisingly, after about five months of viewings and two broker-only open houses, we still had no firm bids. Our broker, Bill Marshall, a middle-aged, successful white broker, took me out to lunch to discuss another sales strategy. He said the condo was priced right and was in superb condition, and that it was unique because it was a new style townhouse in a condo complex. Bill made a suggestion, though, that stung a little. He asked me to take down the family photos hanging in the hallway. I had read that potential buyers like to envision a home as their own and that personal photos and objects can sometimes cloud that vision, so I had no problem with the request. What bothered me was that he said a few prospective buyers asked if the owners were minorities or black.

Regardless, I took the photos down and, coincidentally or not, we received a full-price offer within a week, a few weeks prior to 9-11; however, my real estate agent had forewarned me that the prospective buyers might try to renegotiate the price, given the events of 9-11, or, worse yet, cancel their contract altogether and forfeit their 10 percent good faith deposit.

I was fine with taking their 10 percent, but I certainly wasn't going to reduce the price. If necessary, we would just relist the property.

In the end, the buyers, a British couple, decided to go ahead with the purchase at the agreed upon price. The female of the buying couple said she had dealt with IRA bombings in England all her life, so the terrorism in lower Manhattan didn't faze her much.

When we bought our condo, the search for finding it was relatively easy. We knew it wouldn't be our forever home. Finding our next home would require a more thorough search, as my hope was to find a home in which my family and I would live for the next twenty years or so.

Once again, Bill helped us in our search, but I soon realized finding our next home wouldn't be as easy as finding our last.

Bill had given me a selection of listings, and I picked a few co-ops on the Upper West Side to check out first. Bill told me to forget about three of those buildings, though, as I wouldn't get past the co-op board, despite my income and credit rating. When I pressed him on the reason, he told me that no black people lived in any of the three buildings and my family wasn't going to be the first. I was stunned. I felt like my dad must have felt when he was trying to buy a home for his family in Youngstown, Ohio, in the sixties and he was told that the home was pulled off the market, only be sold to a white family a few weeks later.

Bill then steered me away from co-ops and, quite frankly, I had zero desire at that point to live somewhere where people of color weren't welcome. Condominiums were the way to go, even if their occupants may not be welcoming either, but at least I wouldn't have to be given the thumbs down by some co-op board simply because of my race. With a condo, I hoped the primary thing that would matter was how much "lettuce" I had in my wallet and whether I was willing to give it up.

With Bill's assistance, I found a lovely apartment near Columbia University, on Broadway and 109th Street, and after my wife approved, I put down a deposit.

The three-bedroom apartment was in a rental building that was being converted into a condominium after extensive renovations. We were very happy and excited with the find, the price, and the location. I brought in a window treatment firm to measure the windows for shades so that shortly after closing, we would be able to move in and have some privacy; there were a lot of windows in the apartment. We also took our six-year-old daughter and nine-year-old son to see their future rooms.

A week went by and my deposit check still hadn't been cashed, so I called Bill to let him know. He said everything was in order and that I would soon be getting a closing date because the apartment had been fully renovated and was ready for occupancy.

Another week went by and Bill called to tell me that our apartment, along with a number of other apartments, was sold to an investor by the sponsor. I was irate and in total disbelief.

I told Bill he needed to fix this situation immediately. He said the investor had insisted on my apartment, as it was considered the jewel in the entire building. I said, "No shit! That's why I selected it and immediately put down my 10 percent!" I told him I wanted to talk to the CEO of his firm, Barbara Corcoran, immediately.

A day later, Barbara Corcoran called me from London while I was sitting at my desk. I asked her how this could happen, and she told me "It's not an official deal in New York state until the check is cashed." I told her that was utter bullshit and that it was no wonder real estate agents have the reputation they do as swindlers and cons.

She didn't seem to care that I had sold my current apartment, ordered window treatments for the new one, visited the property with my kids, and made substantial preparations to move. She casually said there were lots of properties in Manhattan and that her agency would find us another one.

We went back and forth on the matter until, exhausted and even more infuriated, I hung up.

Bill later called to let me know that these things unfortunately do happen every now and then, but that did little to soothe me. I called my attorney to see what recourse I might have, but he told me the same thing Ms. Corcoran did, that in the state of New York, if not elsewhere also, a real estate deal is not official until money changes hands.

My family was disappointed, to say the least. I didn't fire Bill, because I knew him to be sincere and knew he was looking out for my best interests, so we continued our search. We again hit a few snags along the way, but, eventually, came upon a new development on the Hudson River called Trump Place. The building wasn't going to be completed for at least eighteen to twenty-four months, but we had the opportunity to design our own apartment, within reason, if I got the builder the plans before they reached my desired apartments on the twenty-ninth floor. My plan was to put two, two-bedroom apartments together. My design was agreed upon by the builder, and a few weeks later, the purchase of apartment 29CD was official! Within the next two years, we would be moving into our magnificent new home.

■ ■ ■

The equity market in the first quarter of 2002 continued its recovery from the September 11, 2001, implosion, as first quarter earnings projections from corporate America exceeded expectations. The market battled many ill winds, such as the December 2001 Enron bankruptcy and its outrageous accounting fraud. The ripple effect was far, wide, and deep. Enron's fiasco also led to its accounting firm, Arthur Anderson, to fail after eighty-nine years in business. Light was further shined on the remaining accounting firms that comprised the so-called Big 5, as the remaining four firms were forced to go back to the drawing board to analyze their practices of auditing corporate clients. The earnings reports in the first quarter of 2002 were met with more skepticism than probably any time in modern history.

A huge issue that affected the capital markets, specifically equities, was the decimalization of stock prices that started in the spring of 2001 and was fully implemented in 2002. The complete switch from fractions to decimals ran roughshod over equity revenue, as .01 cents became the lowest pricing variable instead of .06 cents (1/16th with fractions), or the most common fraction of 1/8th (12.5 cents), which existed since the NYSE was founded in 1792.

The revenue shock was substantial to equity operations around the Street, but we held out hope that the added volume and turnover would fill the pricing revenue void.

By the end of March, equity prices began to slide. The bloom had already come off the internet explosion rose, and over the next few months, the DJIA lost 25 percent, the S & P 500 27 percent, and the Nasdaq 32 percent. Amid recession and deflation concerns, $7.7 trillion was lost. I saw a quote in the press that stated that "in March of 2000, 500 shares of JDSU (i.e., JDS Uniphase—a company that manufactured optical communications products) would have bought a Porsche 911 Carrera, (my all-time favorite car). In July of 2002, 500 shares of JDSU would finance a 1990 Dodge Omni Hatchback with 100,000 miles and no air conditioning!"

From 1995 to mid-2001, the internet bubble had pushed up the Nasdaq Composite index fivefold, but by late July of 2002, it had all come tumbling down. The accounting scandal of the telecommunications company WorldCom, on the heels of Enron and a few other smaller company accounting scandals, was the final nail in the coffin, as WorldCom filed bankruptcy in July, which represented the largest bankruptcy in United States history. Arthur Anderson was also the auditor for the company's $4 billion fail, as WorldCom reported expenses as investments and reported income rather than a substantial loss.

Due to the seemingly daily obliteration of companies in the internet sector, as well as investor confidence concerns due to enormous scandals at WorldCom, Enron, and Tyco International, my professional life on the trading floor was anything but routine. I encouraged all of our traders to take their allotted vacation time, regardless of what was going on, because during this time, I especially needed every single trader to be alert and focused. Individual company stocks were blowing up regularly and the trading risk was exceptional. I always had a policy that all my coworkers should take all of their vacation; in a few cases, I gave some of the traders more time if it was warranted. The last thing I wanted on a trading desk was a mentally or physically exhausted trader making million-dollar decisions.

I followed my own "everyone needs a vacation" advice and took my family to the Hamptons for a week. I didn't expect to encounter more racism in the process. There was a mix-up with the studio cottage I booked, which I learned while I was waiting to check in at the desk. The couple before me had been given the keys to my rental, while I was given the keys to a two-bedroom rental. The clerk knew I was angry but ran after the other couple to let them know he'd made a mistake in giving them my keys. During the exchange, I heard the woman say, "You gave our upgraded room to some uppity nigger? That's terrible!"

I was incensed and wanted to verbally assault the woman, but my wife and kids had just stepped inside to use the restroom, so I kept my mouth shut. When we got to our cottage, my wife asked why I was so quiet. I wanted to tell her that I was tired of being black, was tired of being called a nigger, but instead, I told her that I was just plain tired.

Just another day in the life of a black man. Thankfully, the rest of our vacation was pleasant and restful, despite my calling into the office every day and violating my own rule: No work calls when you're on vacation!

Back in Manhattan, I was faced with another real estate dilemma. The one-year lease on the rental apartment we had moved into was ending in August, and I had to make a decision on whether to lease for another year. I called the builder at Trump Place and asked whether they could give me an estimate on when our apartment might be ready, as I didn't want to be on the hook for an entire rental year if the apartment was going to be completed in six months. It was probably a moot point, because the rental probably wasn't going to let me lease for less than a full year, but I figured it was worth asking the question. When I explained my dilemma to the builder, much to my surprise, he told me that since I was buying from them, my family could move into one of their rentals on Riverside Boulevard; they'd give us a month-to-month lease.

In late August, we moved into a penthouse apartment, the only rental available with three bedrooms, and we got it at a reduced rate.

I learned a valuable lesson here: you never know what's possible unless you ask!

As if my family's two moves in the last twelve months weren't enough, the Fidelity Capital Markets business was also prepping to move from our post-9-11 makeshift digs to its new location, Harborside, in Jersey City, New Jersey. We moved on October 25, just as the equity market sputtered. The DJIA closed down for the year 16.76 percent, while the tech-heavy Nasdaq Composite crashed 37.6 percent. At one point in the early part of the fourth quarter, it felt like Nasdaq stocks were going to zero. Thankfully, our P & L remained solid, as we played the downdraft well and were set up for a hopefully prosperous 2003.

14

LIFE AND NEAR DEATH

At the onset of 2003, the United States, if not other nations as well, was focused on weapons of mass destruction, specifically those that were reportedly in Iraq. The leader of Iraq, Saddam Hussein, and the terrorist group responsible for 9-11, Al-Qaeda, were discussed daily on the news and in newspapers across the country. President George W. Bush and his administration were publicly preparing for some kind of interaction with Iraq, if not an all-out war. This left the financial markets skittish and choppy for most of the first quarter.

Also of note in early 2003 was the financial corruption at Tyco International, a security systems company, specifically by CEO Dennis Kozlowski, to the tune of $600 million. It left the investment community stunned. To a much lesser degree, Martha Stewart was in the news on suspicion of insider trading, for which she received an eventual indictment. On the back of WorldCom, Enron, Arthur Anderson, and others, investors understandably showed little patience for any financial chicanery.

■ ■ ■

As I had done throughout my entire Wall Street career, I made sure I exercised regularly to relieve stress, which was a derivative of the volatility of the business. I also attended sporting events (I was a thirty-year season ticket holder of the New York Knicks, from 1987 to 2017), concerts, and the theater, to divert my mind from capital markets. At one point in my adult life, I was a season ticket holder of the New York Knicks, the Yankees, the Jets, and the New York Giants, all at the same time. After all, what's the point of living in New York City if you're not going to take advantage of what the City has to offer.

One of my favorite entertainers was smooth crooner Luther Vandross. Whenever he was in the New York City area, I tried to make sure I attended his concerts. On February 11, he performed at Radio City Music Hall; I took my then eleven-year-old son, Julian, with me. Sadly, after his concert the next evening, he would never perform at Radio City Music Hall again. He suffered a severe stroke in mid-April and was never the same after. I felt fortunate to have seen one of his last performances. He passed away in 2005.

In the early eighties, I had an intense desire to see the iconic actor Yul Brynner perform on Broadway in *The King and I*. Brynner had been in the role some thirty years, and after putting off buying tickets all those years, I finally decided that I would buy tickets when my parents visited in August 1985. Unfortunately, Brynner left the production in late June and passed away in October. I was so disheartened, because Brynner was one of my father's favorite actors, and I was looking forward to sharing this experience with him. If I had the personal *9-11 mandate* in the eighties that I had post 9-11, to not put off what I wanted to see or do if I could afford it, be safe and respectful about it, and had the time, I wouldn't have missed the Brynner performance in *The King and I*. To this day, I follow the 9-11 mandate.

■ ■ ■

Toward the end of the first quarter of 2003, the stock market became even more wary, as the verdict that Iraq had weapons of mass destruction was reached and talk of a war with Iraq was just a matter of time. Unfortunately, from a professional standpoint, I had taken off to St. Thomas with my family the week of March 15, as it was the kids' spring break week, but my work timing couldn't have been worse. On the evening of March 19, President Bush announced on national television that a bombing raid by the U.S. and coalition forces had commenced and troops would follow after the bombing. I remember sitting at the outside bar at the resort and glancing up at the television. I nearly spit out my ginger ale.

I immediately called our equity head trader, Tom Stones, and told him to contact all the traders and have them come in early the next morning, as we all anticipated a very violent day when land troops would move into Iraq. Fortunately, he had already rallied the team. I thought about going back to New York, but I knew our people in charge were quite capable of handling things, so I stayed in St. Thomas.

The morning of March 20, the market opened sharply down but managed to recover throughout the day, despite substantial volatility created by the various rumors that Saddam was captured, or Hussein was killed in an air raid, or Saddam's troops surrendered, or the U.S. suffered substantial casualties.

In our risk meeting, which I called into from St. Thomas, we discussed staying light, meaning tying up and using as little capital as possible. The volatility was pretty substantial, but two things were pretty readily apparent by the end of the day, if not certainly by the end of the week: this war was going to be a lot longer than a few days, as many expected, and the market would be quite volatile, probably until Saddam was captured or killed. Despite the volatility and longer war concerns, the U.S. equity market gained 8.4 percent that week and got substantially overbought in many professional investors' views. This 8.4 percent gain was the best weekly performance since 1982 and was understandably led by strong performances in the defense and bio-tech (for bio-terrorism) sectors. The construction sector was also strong, but I never quite figured that out. I guess there was an expectation that once the U.S. forces and their bombs finished demolishing Iraq, we would turn around and rebuild the country. In hindsight, I guess to some degree that did happen, but at the time, I didn't see the rationale for the early and immense strength in the sector.

I was back on the Jersey City Fidelity trading desk on Monday, March 24, just in time to witness the DJIA give up a good chunk of last week's euphoria and trade down 307 points (3.6 percent), its worst drop since a 4.1 percent drop on September 3, 2002. The other two major equity averages, the Nasdaq Composite and the S&P 500 were down roughly the same. The reports and video footage of U.S. casualties made traders a bit more skeptical of the highly expected victorious outcome, and given the previous week's historic performance, substantial profit-taking was warranted. It also didn't help that a video of Hussein predicting many American soldier deaths, whether the video was live or prerecorded, also made the Street pause for a minute and realize that this war effort was going to be more than a quick skirmish. Our trading desk came into the day very light and in good shape from the previous week from a P &

L perspective, but that Monday it looked like the market was going to zero. We took a hit on the trading desk, but, fortunately, it wasn't one to put us out of business. Once again, we lived to fight another day.

After a few weeks of choppy markets, the U.S. equity market began to slowly climb that proverbial wall of worry, as the coalition forces slowly but surely took over Iraq. The market became somewhat immune to the war and began to turn its attention to local matters. I did the same, as two significant events in my life occurred over the summer. In late spring I learned that I had been inducted into the Youngstown, Ohio, Curbstone Coaches Hall of Fame, due to my high school football career and continued athletic and perceived professional success post-high school. The ceremony was held in mid-May, and my family, local friends, former high school teammates and coaches, along with about 1,500 other sports fans, attended the event. I was truly honored to be recognized and to be able to say a few words to the audience regarding my induction.

This event was also attended by a few Big Ten conference coaches, most notably from Ohio State and Penn State. I met the son of iconic Penn State head football coach, Joe Paterno. Jay Paterno was the Nittany Lions quarterbacks' coach in Happy Valley, and I struck up a conversation with him after the event. He asked me how a linebacker with the last name Penn didn't end up at Penn State, the school known as Linebacker U. I never gave Jay a good answer, but he asked me to come to an Ohio State versus Penn State home game as his guest at Beaver Stadium that fall. I took him up on that offer on November 1, for a showdown in front of 108,000 fans. I was never treated better by a near total stranger. When Julian and I arrived after a four-hour drive from Manhattan to State College, we went to the ticket booth to pick up our game tickets. Included in the game ticket packet were two tickets to attend a pre-game brunch with the parents of the game's high school recruits. I thought it was a mistake, unless Jay was thinking that my thirteen-year-old son might potentially be a notable football player in a few years. I guess Julian would first have to start playing football to see if that was a realistic possibility. After the brunch, Jay, who was preparing to play their biggest rival, brought Julian and I down to the football field to meet his dad, the one and only Joe Paterno. Mind you, Joe was also preparing to coach against his biggest rival. Nevertheless, Joe insisted on taking a few photos with Julian and me. I begged off the photos, knowing that he was terribly busy, but he insisted. He did ask me why I never visited Penn State thirty years before as a recruit, but I didn't have a good answer for him either.

After a few photos, we were escorted to 50-yard line seats, sitting amongst some Penn State administrators.

The game was exciting, the crowd was definitely energized, but top-ten ranked Ohio State pulled the game out with about one and a half minutes left by scoring a touchdown and an extra point. They won, 21–20. As the saddened home fans were about to file out, someone from the football staff showed up and escorted Julian and me back down to the field and toward the Penn State locker room. The staffer told us to come into the locker room, and I resisted again, knowing how I felt about visitors in my locker room after a loss. The staffer insisted, so we went inside and listened to Coach Paterno tell his players to keep their heads up, despite the loss and despite the fact that the team was in the midst of a most unusual five-game losing streak. Players were hurt that a major upset was in their grasp and slipped away.

I nodded to the staffer that we were uncomfortable and wanted to leave, so he escorted us out and over to a room to listen to Coach Paterno's post-game press conference. In the press conference, Coach was very magnanimous toward the Ohio State Buckeyes and their coaching staff and said that his team would lace them up next week and try and get a victory to end their losing streak. No

excuses, just matter of fact. As we walked out of the press conference, the staffer handed us some travel food for the long ride back
and some Penn State paraphernalia. I thanked Joe and Jay and told
them I truly appreciated the over-the-top hospitality and that they
had a fan for life, even though I was a natural born Buckeye fan. I
had never been treated better.

I was heartbroken when the Penn State assistant coach Jerry
Sandusky, the coach who recruited me out of high school (I turned
him down for a recruiting visit), took down the whole program
with his child molestation scandal in late 2011. Coach Paterno was
severely tarnished behind the scandal and passed away in January
2012. The cause of death was officially lung cancer, but I think the
unofficial cause of death was a broken heart. I shed a tear when
I heard he passed away and reached out to Jay and expressed my
condolences.

Months prior to the Penn State game that fall, we closed on our
newly built condo. We moved to the expansive home on June 28.
For me, the next time I moved, I hopefully would have a toe tag
identifying me.

As we got everything sorted in our new home, life continued.
Julian began school at St. Hilda's & St. Hughes, and Kara now had
to trek completely crosstown from one river, the Hudson River, to
another river, the East River, on the Upper East Side of Manhattan
to the Brearley School. I myself was trekking across the Hudson,
via ferry, to the Fidelity office in Jersey City. In the non-freezing
months, this was a very calming and pleasant commute. In the
midst of a harsh winter, it would become a dodge-the-ice-floes
commute for the ferry and was less pleasant.

On August 14, residents in the northeast, including us on our
Jersey City trading floor, were experiencing a normal humid August
afternoon when around four p.m., all the lights went out and all the
computers and anything with a plug went dark. I stepped out of my

office, as I heard a number of traders exclaim, "WTF" and "You've got to be kidding me!"

Having experienced 9-11 firsthand, we thought that some sort of terrorist attack had taken place again, as rumors quickly spread that half of the United States was without power. We couldn't turn to an iPhone or smart phone then for immediate information, as neither platform was introduced until June 29, 2007. We had televisions all over the trading floor, but without power, they were rendered useless.

Thankfully, the outage happened right at the end of the trading day, so trading was only interrupted a smidgen at the close. As I looked around the trading floor, it was obvious that there was substantial anxiety amongst the troops. I told everyone to get home and we would communicate later that evening, after we had more information. I made a few calls to friends in the Midwest with my Motorola flip phone, only to find out that people in Ohio were without power as well. At that point, my anxiety level grew as well.

I walked over to the Jersey City ferry pier to jump on a ferry back to Midtown Manhattan, but found hundreds of people waiting for the ferries, which ran approximately every twenty minutes. The disposition of the crowd ranged from hysteria, panic, and crying, to calm, relaxed, and laughing.

Nearly two hours later, I was able to get on a packed ferry back to Manhattan. From there I walked from 34th Street to my apartment on west 70th Street, in high humidity, and up twenty-nine flights of stairs. When I got upstairs, a bit winded, carrying a heavy briefcase, and soaking wet with sweat, my wife said, "We need some batteries for flashlights. Can you go get some?" If looks could kill!

We learned that the blackout was due to a software bug in the alarm system in an Akron, Ohio, control room of FirstEnergy. The power system reportedly got overloaded as energy became too concentrated in too few power lines, after a few other lines shut down due to some interference from trees. Fifty-five million people in eight states and Ontario, Canada, lost power. Some got power back late that evening; some didn't get power back for two or three days. We were fortunate to have power restored at work the next day.

■ ■ ■

Over the next several weeks, the US. equity market continued its gradual stair-step ascent. Our traders worked out of the late spring revenue hole, and we started to get back on budget in the fall. On occasion, the market responded to some Iraq war news or some corporate news about a public company's accounting methodologies, but it was fairly orderly.

During the kids' fall break in October, we decided to go to Aspen, Colorado. None of us were skiers, but we had a fractional ownership in a time-share there, so we decided to take advantage of it. We landed at the Denver International Airport in the evening and rented a car for the 220-mile drive to Aspen. Our car wasn't equipped with a GPS system, but I had a paper map and the route looked pretty straightforward. The drive was uneventful until we got to a portion of the route called Independence Pass. I recall there being another route to Aspen, but the quickest route was to take Independence Pass, through the Rocky Mountains. We passed an open gate to the Pass, which I found a bit odd. Why would this supposedly major road have a gate? Within minutes, we were climbing the Rockies, and every five minutes, we started encountering more and more snow flurries. About five miles into the trip up the mountain, the kids woke up and started asking the usual questions, like where are we, and are we there yet? My wife noted that the snow was starting to get pretty heavy and asked if I could see. I told her yes, but, honestly, I was thinking of turning around, because visibility was getting worse the higher we climbed.

We only encountered one car coming toward us in the first fifteen minutes, as we began to go slower and slower due to poor visibility. At one point, as we rounded a corner, we were able to see that we were not only on a narrow two-lane road, but if we veered too far to the left, we would end up at the bottom of a very deep gorge.

Shortly thereafter, we found ourselves in a white-out. I wanted to turn around but was afraid I didn't have enough room to do so safely. At this point, we were approximately halfway through the thirty-two-mile route, and it seemed like we had reached the highest point in the road (12,095 above sea level). Thankfully, we started our descent; however, visibility was still extremely poor, so I opened the car door and tried to drive with one eyeball looking at the ground, with the other focused on what was in front of me. When I looked out the door, I could see that we had veered over into the other lane and were about ten feet away from the cliff edge. I quickly jerked the steering wheel back the other way and the car slid just a bit, causing a collective "Wow!" from the car passengers

It took us two and a half hours to get down the mountain, but we made it in one piece. When we checked into our hotel, I told the clerk about our adventure, and his eyes lit up in astonishment. He asked why we were on Independence Pass, as it was supposed to be closed at this time of year. Apparently, the gate shouldn't have been left open. The clerk said many people had died on this route in the past, and it was generally closed at the first hint of frost.

The next day, we drove over during the daylight to get a view of a portion of the pass from ground level. When I saw how narrow the road was and how deep the falloffs were, I realized that God clearly had the wheel the previous night. We took the long way around the Rockies back to Denver Airport at the conclusion of our trip.

■　■　■

Upon returning to New York after our trip, I attended a few games of the New York Yankees versus Boston Red Sox American League Championship Series (ALCS) at Yankee Stadium. The Yankees had dominated the Red Sox in nearly every important do or die series in their history, and I was lucky enough to see their present do or die game seven.

Through seven innings, the Red Sox dominated the Yankees with eventual Hall-of-Fame ace Pedro Martinez on the mound. It was looking like the Red Sox would finally break their losing streak and move on to the World Series, as they led 5–2 going into the bottom of the eighth inning. The Red Sox manager, Grady Little, failed to take Martinez out of the game as he tired, and the Yankees managed to scrape up three runs to tie the game before Little took Martinez out. The stadium was literally shaking as the Yankee fans roared with excitement, at the unexpected development. The next two innings were incredibly tense as all the fans and players reacted dramatically to each and every pitch. In the bottom of the eleventh inning, the most unlikely hero, Aaron Boone, who had only five hits in thirty-one at bats in the ALCS, stepped up to the plate. On the first pitch, Boone took the Red Sox's knuckleball pitcher Tim Wakefield to deep left field, and the stadium exploded. The two women seated a few seats down from my friend and me, wearing Red Sox caps, cried. One of the women screamed, "Debbie, they freakin' did it to us again! I can't freakin' believe this!" I have to admit, I was overjoyed at their reaction as they hugged each other in sorrow.

I couldn't wait to get to Boston the next week after the exciting Thursday night game. The World Series would be starting on Saturday, and if the Boston office had been open on the weekend, I would have been there in a heartbeat.

When I strolled across the trading floor in my Yankees jacket, I could feel the scorn, but I didn't care! One person finally said, "I hope the Marlins (the Yankees' World Series opponent) kick your ass!" (They did).

The mood quickly shifted, as it was time to meet the new boss of a major division of Fidelity, which included Fidelity Capital Markets. After the close, I began to see the writing on the wall regarding an exit date on my career at Fidelity. That realization came when I met a longtime Fidelity veteran, who was taking the reins. In her first introduction to the troops, she said, "I'm smart, I'm tough, and I'm funny!" The mutterings in the audience weren't kind. The more she spoke, the more I was convinced that she and I wouldn't mesh well.

On my flight back to LaGuardia, I thought about what was next after Fidelity.

When I arrived back in Manhattan, I received what seemed to be a notice to come down to the Taxi and Limousine Commission (TLC) and state my case, based upon a complaint I made earlier in the year regarding a New York yellow cab refusing service to me. Since first moving to Manhattan in 1984, I had visited the TLC at least eight times, if not more, to complain about taxis purposely passing me by and not stopping to pick me up. So far, I was undefeated versus the taxi drivers. This visit was prompted by the same complaint: I was standing on a Manhattan corner, about three feet into the street, with my hand up. A cab went right past me and picked up someone at the other end of the block. I never wanted to say it was because of race because, quite frankly, other than my coarse hair, I could easily pass for a white person, certainly at a quick glance.

At the meeting with the TLC judge, I presented my case, and then the driver presented his. The driver claimed his *available* light wasn't on and he wasn't looking for passengers at that time, nor was he driving on that street. The judge then asked for the driver's trip sheet, and low and behold, it showed a pick up at 7:15 a.m. on said street and a drop-off at 7:35 a.m. in Midtown. Case closed. The driver was fined $200 for non-pickup.

Before leaving, I told the judge, in front of the taxi driver, that I had no interest in coming here, taking up my valuable time, and inflicting economic harm on these, most likely, economically struggling taxi drivers, but this injustice needed to stop, and I was just doing my best to make that happen.

I walked out of the courtroom 9–0, but I certainly didn't feel victorious. I was sadder that I, and I'm sure other people of color, still had to deal with this nonsense.

■ ■ ■

In the United States, economic growth in the third quarter of 2003 reached levels that it hadn't approached in nearly twenty years, and the stock market ran with this growth into the fourth quarter. Our trading desk put up good numbers in the most normal trading patterns that we had seen since the invasion of Iraq. We had the holy grail of trading: some volatility and substantial volume, combined with trading discipline.

In late November, I went to Rio de Janeiro for four days to attend a friend's bachelor party. I had always wanted to see Rio, Copacabana Beach, and, of course, the beautiful Brazilian women. The fourteen-hour trip, with a quick stop in Sao Paulo, was well worth it, both good and bad. The good part was the diversity of women, who ranged from white skin to jet black skin, with unusual eye and hair color combinations; however, the beaches were dirty, reportedly from the tides bringing back untreated wastewater from discharge pipes that were far out in the ocean. The poverty level was also disturbing, as the streets were littered with the homeless and panhandlers, and many of the "homes" were nothing more than lean-to shacks, not far from the main business district.

One of the saddest, most disturbing things I encountered was that of the housekeeper of the apartment we rented offering up her own teenage daughter for sex if the guys wanted to indulge. I didn't speak Portuguese, but I think I made it clear to her that I thought her actions were wrong and sick. I didn't want to judge her and her motivations, certainly given her perceived economic state, but I was sickened by her offer.

I found Rio to be quite dangerous, and the guys and I made a pact to never go out alone during our stay. One night we went to a McDonald's, around the corner from our apartment, across from the beach. When we got there, a bloodied American was sitting at a corner table. I asked him what happened, and he said that a band of kids had beaten him up and taken his food and wallet. He said it happens all the time and that, generally, they let you go unharmed if you give them the money. I wondered why anyone would keep coming back for that sort of punishment. Just like the young man said, though, when we left with our bags of food, out of the thin night air came a band of about six young kids screaming Portuguese at the three of us in a violent manner as they tried to surround us. We met crazy violence with crazy violence, New York style! We started screaming back at these kids, who couldn't have been more than twelve to fifteen years old.

I picked up a broken bottle and started my own verbal assault while daring one of them to come closer to me. When they realized we were willing to fight back and wouldn't be an easy target, they backed off.

This incident reaffirmed our pact to never travel alone while in Rio.

■ ■ ■

Back on the home front in New York, the Christmas holidays were in full swing, and our building held a Christmas party in the beautifully decorated lobby. As I stood in the lobby with my family, listening to some soft holiday tunes, eating some cookies, and drinking a beverage, there appeared to be some commotion near the center of the lobby. My inquisitive eight-year-old daughter, Kara, pulled us over to the scrum and there was Donald J. Trump. Our condo was located in a six- or seven-building development known as Trump Place (in 2017 and 2018, this name was removed from the various buildings). Trump was at the party to interact with those who lived in the development that bared his name, if only for marketing reasons. Kara pushed her way into Trump's orbit and put her hand out to shake his. Knowing Trump was a germaphobe from reading Page Six of the *New York Post*, I pulled Kara back slightly to give Trump an out; however, Kara insisted he shake her hand. Trump somewhat reluctantly did after Kara firmly stuck her hand out again.

■ ■ ■

The equity market closed 2003 strongly, as the DJIA closed up a whopping 29.3 percent, after three years of declines after the internet bubble burst in 1999 and 2000. Bonuses for 2003 were decent, but the trend of bonuses going down 10–20 percent each year after 2000 was intact and becoming an annual expectation.

15

MISCHIEF AND COMICAL MISHAPS

Early 2004 was a digestion period after the DJIA got back three years of negative returns in one year. The world was in a much calmer state, despite terrorism still being on the rise in nearly every corner of the world, and new security protocols became standard, for everything from corporate buildings to airports to sporting and entertainment venues. I, however, managed to poke a little hole in said security measures.

In early February, through a special promotion by American Express, I was lucky to secure a ticket to the Grammy Awards in Los Angeles, at the Staples Center. American Express provided a wonderful two-day program, which included a MusiCares auction, a small music concert on February 7, and the Grammys the following evening. At the auction, I was intent on making the winning bid for a pair of bongos signed by one of my favorite musicians, Carlos

Santana. I hung around the bongos all night long to make sure my bid was at the top of the sheet, but just before the auction ended, Hugh Hefner, surrounded by a bevy of well-endowed blondes, walked into the covered auction area. He nodded and said hello as he walked by, and, in return, I said, "Hugh, you are the man!" to which he replied, "No, I'm THEE man, and don't you forget it!"

Unfortunately, my little interaction with Hugh Hefner made me take my eyes off the bid sheet, and I didn't win the bongos!

The night of the Grammys, American Express bused us to the event early, so that we could watch the celebrities arriving and walking the red carpet. I wandered off a bit and somehow ended up standing next to Billy Bush, of *Access Hollywood*. Perhaps it was the tuxedo I was wearing, or maybe my build, but he thought I was his assigned security person. He asked me to please keep the paparazzi and fans a few feet away as he interviewed various guests as they came down the red carpet, so I played along. "No problem. I got it." He even asked me to watch his station when he stepped away for a minute. While Bush was gone, an official security tandem came by and stopped to check me out. I had seen them earlier and realized I didn't have an earpiece like they had. Thinking my ruse was up, I pretended I had an earpiece and held my finger in my ear and began talking to myself. One of the security guys said, "He must have that new, really small earpiece and his own setup with *Access Hollywood*, and just as he said it, Bush came back and said, "Thanks, man. Now, let's get this party started!" I guess I could add security officer to my list of career accomplishments!

For the next ninety minutes or so, I watched as Billy Bush interviewed some of the entertainment world's elite, including Carmen Electra, my all-time favorite band, Earth, Wind, and Fire, and the one and only Beyonce, who was set to open the show with Prince.

Through all the excitement, I had lost my American Express group, who had probably entered the arena long beforehand. I had an entrance ticket but was concerned that if I went through the general admission entrance line that I would miss the Beyonce/Prince opening. Just as I walked to the VIP entrance to see if I could slide through there, 50 Cent (aka Curtis Jackson) and his crew rolled up. He and his posse basically bum-rushed the entrance, and being stuck in the middle of the melee, I got waved in with everyone else!

I found my group in the American Express luxury box, and they shared with me that they had witnessed me pulling off my "security detail" for Billy Bush. They laughed hysterically.

So much for post-9-11 security!

A few weeks after playing Hollywood security guard, I got a strange call from Fidelity's corporate offices (I don't recall if the call came from human resources, compliance, or security, but it wasn't from anyone I had ever spoken with before). The first question they asked me was whether I went to either the 2002 or 2003 Super Bowls in New Orleans or San Diego, respectively. It was known around Fidelity that I had attended a few Super Bowls, but I had only attended Super Bowls in Miami, up to that point. I told the caller that I had only attended one Super Bowl while at Fidelity, and that was in 1999, in Miami. The person then asked me who I went with and who paid the expenses for the trip. I told the person I went with a friend and we both paid a hundred percent of our own expenses. I thought the call was odd but chalked it up to perhaps compliance just doing a random check to make sure no company or industry violations had occurred. Later that year, it hit the national press that an employee of the brokerage firm Jefferies had spent millions entertaining Fidelity traders with lavish gifts, bottles of wine, Super Bowl trips, trips to Wimbledon, and various exclusive golf outings. The craziest assertion made in the press was that on some of these chartered flights, there was midget tossing! This followed on the heels of the email and porn scandal, and I heard Chairman Ned Johnson understandably hit the freakin' roof. I know from a later conversation with Ned on one of his semiannual visits to our New York trading floor that reputation was extremely important to him. I assured Ned that the porn scandal was the first and last incident under my watch that would besmirch the firm.

■ ■ ■

By mid-year, I always felt tired, day in and day out, regardless of how much I slept. I had recalled hearing a few years earlier that Katie Couric's husband was tired every single day and chalked it up to his flying cross-country on a regular basis. Her husband, Jay Monahan, was in his forties, as was I now, and I never forgot his story of finding out he had advanced colon cancer and, unfortunately, died nine months later. The first thing I did was have a colonoscopy, which came back clean. I felt better mentally, but physically I was still tired most of the time. I consulted my general practitioner, and he suggested that I get a sleep study done. Sure enough, the sleep study determined that I had a mild form of sleep apnea. The sleep technician told me I never got to so-called REM sleep, which is where you get the really restful sleep and have dreams. I was surprised he mentioned dreams; apparently it happens often during REM sleep. I couldn't remember the last time I'd dreamed.

I was fitted for a CPAP machine and have used one ever since. I dream every night now.

■ ■ ■

In the late summer of 2004, I took my travel CPAP machine and went to Hong Kong with the Fuqua School of Business on one of their international summits for board members, administrators, and any alums who wished to travel on the subsidized trips. The trips were meant to get to know fellow alums, administrators, faculty, and staff, while also learning about the locale we were visiting. The school also tried to visit places where the business school or Duke University had some sort of vested interest from an academic standpoint. (Other trips over the years were to Paris, Geneva, Prague, and Venice.) Generally, whenever there was an international summit, my B-school pal and fellow board member, Owen May, and I visited another major city in the same region as the summit. After the Hong Kong visit, Owen and I headed to Bangkok, Thailand. We went upscale and stayed at the Mandarin Oriental in Bangkok, along the banks of the Chao Phraya River. We went downscale and visited what I found to be the greatest imitation goods shopping in an outdoor market called Patpong. Every single designer, luxury goods item imaginable (e.g., purses, suitcases, watches, clothing, etc.) was knocked off here. When I saw the imitation goods, I thought Louis Vuitton, Hermes, Patek Phillipe, Mont Blanc, Nike, etc., should be really upset at the pervasiveness and quality of this merchandise. I picked up a few items that fooled everyone back in the States.

Back at the hotel, I wanted to get an official Thai massage that I had always heard about. I knew I would obviously get the real thing; no imitation like the goods at Patpong. The concierge set up the massage session for me and told me that I had to take one of the boats across the river to their massage facility. I went down to the river and jumped on the first boat I saw that was going to the other bank. The boat let me out directly across the river from the hotel, and I walked down the alleyway looking for a massage sign. Little did I know there were numerous massage places, and I went into the first facility where I saw a massage sign. The woman at the front desk escorted me downstairs and motioned to me to get undressed and get a shower, and then she left. Even though I showed up sparkling clean, as I would for anything close to a massage, I figured this was their custom, so I may as well follow their instructions.

277

When I came out of the shower, there was a beautiful young lady in her birthday suit waiting for me. Once again, I was like, well damn, maybe this is how they do it. She approached me and rather forcefully grabbed my appendage, and I immediately recoiled as far as I could move without creating a painful separation. I then realized that I wasn't in a place to get a body massage. I was in a house of prostitution! I gently unfolded the woman's hand and quickly put my clothes on as she muttered Thai. The naked beauty left, and as I was tying my shoes, the lady who escorted me to the room came in and, in broken English, asked, "What wrong?" I told her that there must have been a mistake. I wanted a massage, not sex. She said, "You no like?" She then made the screwing motion with her hand and middle finger. I quickly walked around her and jetted back up the steps past a strong man who was coming down the steps. I don't think he realized that I was the client, trying to escape, as I think I got out of the house of ill-repute just in time.

Now, I'm back in the alleyway and, thankfully, not being followed by the brute, looking for the proper Mandarin massage venue. After a ten- to fifteen-minute search, I found the Mandarin massage facility on an adjacent road. I was now twenty-five minutes late, and the greeter at the Mandarin massage facility somewhat angrily told me that I would have to reschedule. I told her that I had gone to the wrong venue and that was why I was late. She didn't seem to understand, so I used the hand signal that the woman at the prostitution house had used on me. This exhibit only infuriated her, and she motioned for me to go back to the hotel and work it out with them. With extreme frustration, I went back to the river, jumped on a boat, and went back to the hotel concierge. When I approached the desk, the concierge read me the riot act. In near perfect English, he said, in a very stern manner, "We don't do that here! Our massage therapists are professionals, not hookers!"

"Wait a minute!" I said. "I initially unknowingly went to the wrong place, which was a whorehouse. I showed up late to the Mandarin facility and she told me I had to reschedule. What are you talking about?"

"You asked her for sex!" he said.

I now understood that the Mandarin lady misinterpreted my hand gesture explaining the prostitute and why I was late, thinking that was what I was requesting. The Mandarin concierge now understood what had transpired and he apologized profusely. He then rescheduled me for an hour later and explained to the Mandarin massage lady what had happened. Phew! I was sitting in the lobby area when Owen came down and asked how the massage was. When I told him how it had gotten all screwed up, he laughed his ass off. As I sat in the lobby, I also realized that the entire desk staff at the Mandarin had heard about my mishap and were grinning at me as well.

■ ■ ■

The stock market was eerily quiet all year, as politics seemed to be the focus in this presidential election year. There wasn't much concern amongst Republicans that incumbent George W. Bush wouldn't defeat the Democratic nominee, John Kerry; however, there was some concern, given the hanging chad incident in 2000.

It seemed like the stock market was in a wait and see mode through the summer, up until the November election, and the year thus far was quite boring. I took advantage of the docile market and took my auto enthusiast son to see the Brickyard 400, a NASCAR race at the Indianapolis Motor Speedway thru another American Express event. It was my bad that I bought the wrong tickets; my son wanted to go to the Indianapolis 500, not the Brickyard 400, but given his intense interest in cars of all kinds, he was just as excited to go to this event.

Julian and I enjoyed all the pre-race events, including the time trials and dinner at famed steakhouse St. Elmo's. While at dinner, a mature white man from New Orleans befriended Julian, the youngest member of the Amex group, and gave him his racing hat. He also schooled us on various racing tidbits and customs over the two-day event, as he was a NASCAR enthusiast and had attended many races in his lifetime. He was also impressed with my twelve-year-old's knowledge of NASCAR and racing in general. At the end of our very pleasant and informative two days, the white gentleman pulled me aside and told me what a good kid I had. Unfortunately, he added, "I've never met any colored people like you." When I sarcastically asked him what kind of colored people he had met in the past, he said the ones that weren't too bright, unlike my son and me. He actually thought he was paying us a compliment, but once again, I walked away shaking my head. Julian also made note that out of the reported crowd of 300,000 people at the Speedway, we could count the number of people of color on our four hands. I reminded Julian that auto racing was truly a white sport, maybe the whitest sport of them all.

■ ■ ■

A few weeks before the November presidential election, the stock market started to heat up just a bit. After close to nine months of calm waters, the market had built up a base of confidence and created some pockets of opportunity to trade; however, given the limited volatility and only moderate volume, the trading desk was challenged for revenue. This scenario helped to grease the skids for the leader of Fidelity Capital Markets to hire two senior people from Citigroup to come in and run Fidelity Capital Markets after terminating my friend, former head of fixed income and then head of Capital Markets, Craig Messinger. I knew of the two individuals she hired, and I once again knew that my life at Fidelity would be short-lived. I also knew that these two hires would quickly blow themselves up, given their cowboy-ish ways versus the conservative ways of Fidelity. I decided to stick around and watch the grenade go off.

The guys didn't bother me too much, as the business I ran was sort of on autopilot, but as they created chaos around the firm, many of the long-time Fidelity people started taking bets and laying odds regarding how long they would last—it was less than eighteen months. They reportedly approached Fidelity Chairman Ned Johnson and suggested he move all of the Capital Markets personnel to New York and also suggested buying another medium-sized broker dealer to augment what we had. Word has it that Ned threw them out of his office after their presentation, and they were gone within a few weeks.

■ ■ ■

George W. Bush was reelected in November without issue, and the market got a little wind behind it. The DJIA closed the year up 3.1 percent; the Nasdaq Composite rallied strongly in the fourth quarter and ended up 8.6 percent; and the broader market index, the S & P 500, concluded up 9 percent.

16

REFLECTION

Like so with many others who witnessed the events on September 11, 2001, I was forever changed, in many ways. Aside from the mental anguish and recovery associated with such a tragedy, I adopted a different approach to life in general. I vowed to live every day to its maximum and to do and see everything I wanted if it was within my means. I also decided to visit family and friends I cared about whom I hadn't seen in the last year or two. Losing my friend Calvin provided the impetus for my new outlook.

Calvin once told me that he and his Broadway actress wife were going to bust their asses and work as much as they could, and save as much money as they could, so that by age fifty, they could move to the West Coast and chill for the rest of their lives. He rarely took a day off from work, as a day off to him meant a lost opportunity to shine brighter and earn more.

Once or twice a year, a couple other Wall Street friends and I would go on long three- or four-day weekends to take in a few sporting events somewhere in the country. Calvin would join us late Friday night or early Saturday morning because he didn't want to miss work. I respected his work ethic, but many times I told him the job would be there when he got back, but he wasn't having it. Tragically, he never got to enjoy most of the fruits of his labor, as he died at 38 years old. At his funeral on October 2, 2001 (it was actually a memorial because there wasn't an actual body), I spoke at his wife's request. I talked about the kind of man Calvin was and how much he loved his wife, baby, and the one in the womb. I also relayed how much fun Calvin and I had at work and how he kept me in social check while we worked in the same department at Lehman Brothers prior to him leaving for Cantor Fitzgerald. I was the head trader on Lehman Brothers' international equity desk, and Calvin was an institutional salesman covering Latin America. We interacted and watched each other's back, as we represented 40 percent of the black faces on the approximately 200-person trading floor. Calvin was very conscious of race at the job and this was evidenced one day when we were discussing Microsoft founder Bill Gates in an informal group discussion as we sat at our various stations on the trading floor. One of the young white female sales assistants innocently asked, "Who is Bill Gates?" I saw the look in Calvin's eyes and I signaled to him not to respond congruent with the look of bewilderment on his face. Calvin immediately got up and walked off the desk, and the next thing I knew, my cell phone was ringing. I answered and Calvin sternly asked me to come back to a nearby conference room. I walked into the conference room and Calvin nearly assaulted me, as he aggressively stepped toward me.

"D, what the hell?" he said. "How did this clueless woman get a job on the desk? We got Ivy League brothers and sisters that can't sniff Wall Street, and this woman gets a job in this department? My eight-year-old cousin knows who the hell Bill Gates is!"

After I gathered myself, I said, "Man, you know how this works. She's a nice, good looking young lady with the right connections. She wasn't hired for her smarts, and she is only a sales assistant. I didn't hire her."

"This is total bullshit, and you know it," he said. "I know smart black and brown people that would kill for that lowly sales assistant spot to get their foot in the door!"

I didn't disagree, but I reminded Calvin that this is their ballgame, their field, and their bat and ball.

Calvin left in a huff and said he was going for a walk.

On the stage at Calvin's memorial service were three other speakers, one of them being Howard Lutnick. Howard was Calvin's college friend and boss and the CEO of Cantor Fitzgerald at the time of his death. Calvin had left Lehman in late 2000 or early 2001 and was doing well at Cantor working for Howard. Howard was spared from death because he, like a few chronicled others, was late arriving to work because he dropped his young son off for the first day of school. Cantor lost 658 employees, which was two-thirds of its New York-based workforce. Howard also lost his brother that infamous day and was obviously hurting deeply, as was everyone who knew Calvin or any of the other people who died in the attack.

At the conclusion of the service, someone I didn't know approached me and said, "I didn't know Calvin or anyone else who died, but I wanted to come here and have these poor people I didn't know brought to life in their death. Thank you for doing that, sir. Sorry for your loss of what sounds like a great man and friend."

I welled up, walked to my car, and sat in the parking lot sobbing for thirty minutes before I drove back to Manhattan from the Brooklyn church.

■ ■ ■

After September 11, I remained at Fidelity Capital Markets for an-other four years, but my mindset about life in general was different now. I was more cautious, more aware. I made sure I knew the exits of every multi-story building I entered. I made sure my phone was always fully charged. When I flew, I booked a seat as close to the front as possible so that in the event there was a rush to the cockpit, I could get involved. The tragedy of that day also played a role in the dissolution of my marriage. The one significant time in my life when I needed emotional support from my wife, it was nowhere to be found, and I never forgave her for the lack of it. Of course, there were other issues, but this was the beginning of the end, so to speak.

■ ■ ■

In early 2005, a management change at Fidelity and a different busi-ness focus led to my departure. A division head that I felt had racist tendencies on top of misandry, with a particular, if not perceived, disgust for ex-jocks, struck the trifecta for me. Life at Fidelity had gone from pleasant to dismal for me, and when the decision was made to throttle back the risk-based equity trading business, I couldn't have been happier. I stuck around to help the dismantling before I took the ferry from Harborside back to the 34th Street dock for the last time on July 1, 2005.

I immediately began my search for employment, but wanted to try another industry if it was feasible. My search ranged from commercial real estate to professional sports administration. My most interesting job unearthing came at the NFL, when I met with then COO, Roger Goodell, and talked to him about the possibility of managing the NFL's European League. The offer never came to fruition, and I was concerned about moving my family to Europe anyway, especially given the increasingly fragile state of my marriage. In the end, it was probably a good miss, given that the NFL shut down the league in June 2007.

For the balance of 2005 and early 2006, I worked on a weekend home we'd bought in the Hudson Valley years ago, visited friends and family, and traveled around the world, just like I vowed to do. I traveled with either my children, a friend, or by myself, as my wife had a fear of flying—yet another issue that factored into our marriage deteriorating.

■ ■ ■

In 2006, America learned that three members of the Duke University men's lacrosse team were indicted for the rape of one of two strippers hired for an off-campus party. The fact that the two strippers were black and the accused students were white inflamed the situation even more. There were other factors in play as well, including the Durham working class versus the elite university, as well as the juxtaposition of the perceived rich athletes versus the, perhaps, exploited strippers. Also in question was the disparity in legal defense. The University was faced with an unprecedented set of bad circumstances, and whatever way it turned, it was going to be harshly criticized.

I was asked to participate on Duke University's ad hoc Culture Committee to address the culture of the university and, to some degree, represent athletes while also providing an additional voice of a person of color. Beyond the agreed upon fact that the lacrosse players made a huge error in judgment by inviting the strippers, there was very little agreement on who was telling the truth and who was lying, what the university's public stance should be, how it should address the administrators, alumni, and current students, and what approach the university at large should take to keep it functioning amidst the negative attention. That a group of Black Panthers arrived on campus to demonstrate didn't help the matter.

Over the course of our weekly meetings, I was among the minority who suggested that we not rush to judgment in the case, because some things just didn't add up in my mind. Also, I believed the guys were solid kids who just made a terrible error in judgment by inviting the strippers to their party. I drew shaking heads and disgust when I suggested that these kids weren't necessarily privileged or wealthy brats, as they were perceived by the general public. Privately, I offered to a few committee members that if a rape did occur, someone on the lacrosse team who was there that night would have broken their silence by now, two months later, after such intense scrutiny.

The situation was getting intense, with parents of some of the lacrosse team members taking up residence in Durham to look after their offspring. I talked to one athlete who said, "Mr. Penn, do you think I want my dad down here up my ass? If I knew something different than what we have already stated, I would have said so, and I could have done it anonymously."

That sealed it for me, and, fortunately, for the athletes, the North Carolina attorney general dropped all the charges in April 2007, and the district attorney was shortly thereafter fired and disbarred.

I was personally pulled from both sides of the situation, as some members of the black and brown Duke community were puzzled that I supported the so-called white privileged, arrogant players prior to them being found not guilty. My general response, which sometimes got heated on both sides, was based upon a pursuit of the truth while not rushing to judgment. A few black Duke alums who didn't agree with my assessment called me an Uncle Tom. My response was that I hoped they'd never become the victim of a rush to judgment before the facts are exposed. One of my fellow alums eventually apologized for the characterization after the case unfolded. I understood their ire, the same as I hoped a few of my white friends understood why I was ecstatic that guilty-ass O.J. Simpson walked, even though most black folks, including me, believed he was guilty of double murder.

17

EARLY DAYS AT PERSHING LLC

After my Fidelity tenure, I took a year off and subsequently landed at Pershing LLC in June 2006. A few reasons played into my decision to return to the Street and go to Pershing. First, the head of what later became Pershing Capital Markets, Craig Messinger, was my former colleague at Fidelity who managed fixed income there; he eventually headed up all of Fidelity Capital Markets and became my direct manager. We had a mutual respect for each other and shared a similar skill set. Second, I arrived at Pershing because the gentleman who previously held my position got caught up in an email scandal, as well as reportedly "dipping his pen in company ink" with a subordinate. Last, I was available.

I was surprised to find a handful of people of color in significant positions at Pershing. I had worked at two previous firms where I was within the top two or three of the highest-ranking people of color in the entire firm, but Pershing had senior black and brown people in sales, operations, compliance, and finance. I was warmly welcomed by the majority of people of color, who were very happy to see someone who looked like them on the trading floor. Supposedly, Pershing had never had a trading floor salesperson or trader of color above the vice president level. I came in as a managing director and was responsible for a decent chunk of the firm's revenue.

The first order of business, as the head of equity sales and trading at Pershing was to get a handle on a bloated equity market-making operation. The security industry's change from pricing equities in decimals rather than fractions in early 2001 had financially gutted equity trading street-wide, and Pershing was relatively slow to reduce their market-making related expenses in light of the reduced revenue opportunity. Pershing had roughly thirty traders making markets in about 600 stocks. The profitability had been reduced between 5 and 10 percent each year after the onset of decimalization in February 2001, and upper management was reportedly toying with shutting down the operation if we didn't get it turned around quickly. Consequently, within four months of my arrival, I had to pare down the trading desk to about fifteen traders. Concurrently, we also needed to beef up our order management system (OMS), which had been very unreliable and went down far too often. We were processing less than eight million shares per day and needed to at least quadruple that volume, in my view, to have a chance to get firmly back in the black. We also needed to automate many of the trading processes so that we could handle more volume with fewer people; thus, with the significant help of our quantitative development team, we were able to create our own proprietary trading system, a system we nicknamed PEMM, for Pershing Electronic Market-Making. The primary architect of this PEMM system was a ridiculously smart, large combination of Herman Munster/Lurch-looking individual whom I was certain was either an idiot savant or had Asperger's syndrome, or both. He had a supreme mathematical and computer coding mind, but sometimes forgot to wear socks. He was terribly awkward socially, but his expertise put us on the map.

The slimmed down trading operation settled in well fairly quickly, due to our technology additions, as the equity market proceeded to march upward as the Federal Reserve slowed down its interest rate tightening policy that started in June 2004. After seventeen straight increases, four of which came in the first half of 2006, the Federal Open Market Committee held rates steady at its August 2006 meeting. As a result of the fiscal policy change, by October, the equity market had surpassed the record it had set in 2000, on October 19, Ironically, one of more infamous dates in financial history in1987, the DJIA closed above 12,000 for the first time, at 12,011. Despite giving up 5 percent of its gains toward the end of 2006, the DJIA was up 16.3 percent, at 11,407 for the year. This performance was also despite the yield curve being inverted the second half of 2006, portending an economic recession.

The market-making operation showed promise, and senior management at Pershing gave us some more rope to hopefully expand the revenue stream while keeping a cap on expenses.

In 2007, recession talk was quite common, as the former Fed chairman Alan Greenspan warned of a recession shortly after he left his post in late January. Existing home sales had peaked in February, and the U.S. economy was working on two consecutive quarters of negative GDP, the commonly accepted definition of a recession. On February 20, after a poor durable goods number, the U.S. equity market dropped more than 400 points, 3.3 percent and 4.7 percent, from its all-time high of 12,786. That hellacious day, the DJIA closed at 12,216, and our trading desk survived, thanks to our fortified OMS and nascent proprietary trading engine. The downtrend was the biggest U.S. market loss since the World Trade Center terrorist attacks, with the Asian markets hit twice as hard and European shares also suffering greatly. By March, the housing slump was worsening, and word began to spread around the Street that many hedge funds had invested heavily in mortgage-backed securities. To add insult to injury, it became known in the industry that hedge funds had also deployed significant leverage using derivatives, which would only magnify their losses if these investments turned further south.

In April, the R-word (recession) was on the tip of every talking head's tongue, and the definition of a recession was full blown at this point. Home sales hit another pivot point lower as equity markets worldwide grew more and more nervous. By August, the U.S. market had swooned approximately 10 percent from their mid-July highs. During mid-August, the largest mortgage lender in the U.S., Countrywide Financial, added rocket fuel to the anxiety, as it announced a liquidity crunch and tapped a $11.5 billion line of credit. It also didn't help that there were reports in the marketplace that a major hedge fund was on the verge of a collapse. We speculated as to whom that hedge fund was, but we were in a "sell now, ask questions later" mode, so the identity of the troubled financier didn't really factor into our decisions. I fielded calls from senior management at least once a day asking what kind of shape we were in, besides keeping my direct manager on the trading floor abreast of developments. Overall, my manager and senior management were confident in our discipline and communication, and they knew that if something significant had gone down on the desk, they would have been informed first. I learned early in my career that no one likes surprises. Our mantra was to go home as *light* as possible with our capital every night because the likelihood of an overnight surprise somewhere in the world, or a preopening news bombshell, was extremely high.

One of the more apparent observations was that the financial world was very connected internationally. Concerns about mortgages, especially sub-prime mortgages, were getting world-wide attention. About the only positive distraction from the financial markets was the summer introduction of the first Apple iPhone, which Wall Street swooped up to watch their portfolios melt down.

In the summer of 2007, I met two of the most impressive and influential politicians in modern history. I was invited to a fund raiser for then Illinois Senator Barack Obama at the home of cosmetics guru Bobbi Brown, in northern New Jersey. At the event, I ran into a fellow former Duke athlete, and Obama assistant, Reggie Love. Reggie introduced me to Barack, who said, "Oh no, not another Duke guy!" Reggie mentioned there was a Duke graduate at every campaign stop or fundraiser, and he made sure to introduce them to Barack. I was quite impressed with Mr. Obama's dignity, grace, and charm, and he was an eloquent speaker.

I also met former Secretary of State Colin Powell when he was a guest speaker at Pershing's INSITE Conference in Hollywood, Florida, in early June. Pershing had set up an opportunity for some senior personnel to meet with Secretary Powell before his presentation. When I walked into the room, I had one of my hands in my pocket, as I typically do. Secretary Powell immediately zeroed in on me and asked me to take my hand out of my pocket. I found the request a bit odd, and he saw the puzzlement on my face. He then explained that he was a career military guy, and military guys always wanted to see everyone's hands at all times. I told him I'd never thought about that. He said that in his line of work, you had to think about those things. A little later on, as I was getting something to drink, my hand unconsciously ended up back in my pocket. Secretary Powell walked over to me and tapped me on the shoulder and repeated a little more forcefully, "Sir, please keep your hands out of your pocket or I'm going to have to ask you to leave." Embarrassed, I pulled my hand out of my pocket and walked around the conference room for the rest of my visit with my hands in the air, almost in the same fashion a doctor who had just scrubbed before going into surgery would.

■ ■ ■

The economy worsened considerably in August and prompted the Fed to lower the federal funds rate half a point. This aggressive move, albeit a needed one, served to wake up the few stragglers who thought this market implosion was a short-term situation. Banks had stopped lending to each other, and a structured product called a collateralized debt obligation, or CDO, became part of the Street lexicon, even though most of us, certainly us equity practitioners, had never heard of a CDO. This asset-backed security is a product that allowed banks to repackage pooled mortgages, or nearly any other asset for that matter, so that they could be sold to investors in the secondary market with supposedly less risk, due to the diversification of the pool. One of the senior Pershing managers, who was less familiar with the world of trading, asked me if I had any CDOs in our portfolio. I answered him using some pretty colorful language, but, in a nutshell, I told him they were credit instruments and that I'd just found out what they were myself.

■ ■ ■

The fall season in the financial world was anticipated to be treacherous, so I planned a late August trip to Paris and London and a return to the states on the Queen Mary with my family. I wasn't expecting the trip to provide the rest and relaxation I desired, but given the state of my marriage, this trip would probably be the last time we would vacation together as a family. I was at least excited about exposing my children to a different culture.

Our trip started in my favorite city outside of the States, Paris. I had visited the City of Light many times on business, but just a few times as a tourist, and I was looking forward to sharing all this city had to offer with my family, especially the kids, from the outstanding architecture, to the beautiful museums, to the quaint specialty shops, to the croissants and hot chocolate.

In Paris, I was in my element. What I loved was the warmth Parisians showed black people, from us regular folks to famous entertainers and authors, dating back to the fifties. French people have a reputation for being standoffish and cold, according to many Americans, but I never experienced any chilliness on my visits. Generally, I was treated better in Paris than I was in New York. No one called me the N word. No one followed me around in a department store. No one questioned my intellect. Paris was refreshing in this way, and it's a major reason why I've returned so many times. I generally stayed at the wonderful Le Bristol Hotel in Paris and got to know the concierge. One visit, I asked him where the "nasty Frenchman" characterization came from that I always heard in the States. The concierge said it came from New Yorkers who came to Paris and bossed them around like they were second class citizens in their own country, but the Parisians always tell them to get lost! He said that Americans from other cities don't boss them around so much and black people treat them with much respect and warmth, so they return that respect and warmth.

I immediately recalled how Parisians welcomed black entertainers like Josephine Baker, Eartha Kitt, Billy Eckstine, and Nina Simone when they weren't wholly accepted in the States in the fifties, sixties, and seventies. Black authors like James Baldwin were also embraced by the French, evidenced by him moving to Paris where his race and homosexuality were more palatable.

After a beautiful stay in Paris and a side trip to Disneyland Paris, we took a Eurostar train from Gare du Nord Station in Paris to Waterloo Station in London. We hired a guide to take us to all the sights in London (i.e., Westminster Abbey, Buckingham Palace, the British Museum, St. Paul's Cathedral, Trafalgar Square) over five days, with some shopping wedged in between. After a few days with our family, our guide grew more comfortable with us and asked the typical *where are you from, what do you do, what race are you* type questions, and once he realized I was black, as was my family, he exclaimed, "Wow, you guys are the lightest black family I think I've ever bloody witnessed!" I then asked him why he asked me what our race was and why that was of interest to him, and he said, "We don't see many multi-person American black families here." I just shook my head and instructed him to take us to the London Eye.

Despite having a great time with the kids, I knew on our cruise back home that my marriage was over, at least as far as I was concerned. I made the best of a poor situation and had just focused on making sure the kids enjoyed what was most likely our last vacation as a family.

■ ■ ■

Despite all the financial terror circulating the world going into the fall of 2007, the DJIA continued its ascent, and peaked on October 9, 2007 at 14,164, and then hit an intraday high of 14,198 two days later. One of the first signs of major trouble headed for the world of finance was the mega Swiss firm, UBS, reporting losses of $3.4 billion from sub-prime, mortgage related loans. We wouldn't see the peak DJIA levels of October 9, 2007 again until 2013.

By the end of the year, the Fed was in continued motion of cutting interest rates for the third time in 2007 and announced the Term Auction Facility, which provided loans to banks to hopefully give banks more comfort in making loans to each other. This liquidity move by the Fed was desperately needed, as liquidity dried up everywhere, while the home foreclosure rate doubled in a matter of months. Our equity trading desk came out relatively unscathed for the year, especially compared to the reported trading carnage that surrounded us on the Street. The oddest thing was, the carnage was only rumored. No one really knew how bad anyone's situation was because everyone kept their cards as close to the vest as possible, outside of what was learned from earnings, or lack of earnings, reports. The Street always smells blood, and when the blood flows, the participants gang up like hyenas on a wounded wildebeest on the Serengeti; however, the bloodletting was only rumored. Very little was actually confirmed about Wall Street trading desks and hedge funds. The DJIA closed the year up 6.4 percent, at 13,178, while the S&P 500 was up 3.5 percent, and the Nasdaq closed up the most, at 9.8 percent. Oil was also a winner, as it closed up considerably per barrel from the previous year, coming within striking distance of $100 in November. In hindsight, the Street should have anticipated what was coming in 2008, but most, including me, thought at worst that 2008 would be a flat to small down year, given the late 2007 momentum and perceived turnaround.

18

THE FINANCIAL AND PERSONAL CRISES OF 2008

Most of the first quarter of 2008 was death by a thousand cuts for the equity market. Every day it appeared that negative news sapped whatever upward energy the stock market could muster, but there were no huge dislocations of note on the downside on any particular day. Home foreclosures and unemployment were expanding, and print and television programs had daily stories of personal and corporate hardships due to a rapidly slowing economy and dissipating credit. The financial sector also was smarting, and stories of shrinking Wall Street bonuses and job elimination were in all the Wall Street rags.

On the personal front, I was dealing with my own hardships away from the stock market. My father's only sister, Mae Etta, was 87 years old, never married, a very private individual, living in Crown

Heights, Brooklyn. I was the only relative who lived within close proximity, so I routinely checked in on her and made sure she was okay. If I didn't have dinner with her out somewhere, I used to drive to Crown Heights every so often, which, at the time, was a Jamaican drug-infested area. Each time I visited, I prayed I wouldn't catch a stray bullet or that my car would still be curbside, with all four wheels, when I returned from her fifth-story walk-up apartment.

I hadn't been able to reach her for a few days in the summer of 2007, so I decided to pay her a visit. She didn't answer when I knocked, but I heard a faint voice inside. I immediately called 911, because I didn't have a key and couldn't get in touch with her super.

When the ambulance arrived, we broke down the door, and found her lying on the floor in her bedroom. She had suffered a stroke, but, fortunately, she was still conscious and reasonably con-versant. I followed the ambulance to Kings County Hospital and was totally unprepared for the carnage I witnessed in the emergency room. Patients were lined against the walls on stretchers, and all the examination rooms were full. There was blood on the floor and blood on the stabbing and shooting victims waiting to be tended to. As I walked around the emergency department hallways, I noticed that every patient was a person of color. I remember thinking, *what are we doing to our own people?*

Two hours later, when my aunt still hadn't been seen by a doctor, I pressed one of the nurses to please check on her as she'd been lying in the hallway far too long. She said, "Welcome to Kings County Hospital! It's just another Friday night in the hood!"

My aunt's health deteriorated rapidly, and by early 2008, she was placed in an assisted living home on the Upper West Side of Manhattan. I visited her every other day, even as her faculties di-minished. Visits with my aunt made me appreciate life all the more.

As if dealing with my aunt's decline in health wasn't enough, I got a call from my father the evening of February 7 that was quite unsettling. His voice was trembling, something I'd never heard before in my life, as he relayed to me that he and my mom had just been robbed at gunpoint in their home. The intruder came into the house through an unlocked back door and accosted my dad as he sat on the couch with an I.V. in his ported arm to address the bladder cancer that he was fighting. The criminal, with a gun to my dad's head, asked if anyone else was in the house, just as my mother came in the room and was startled at what she saw. Both of them were told to lay face down on the floor, and the criminal pressed the cold steel of the gun to my dad's temple. My dad said he believed the next sound he would hear would be the last sound he would hear.

The thug told them to lie there and not move as he went upstairs and took all the jewelry and valuables he could find. When he came back downstairs, he emptied my parents' pockets and took their wedding rings. He told my parents that if they called the police, he would be back to "finish the job."

I told my dad to lock up the house as best he could and then go check in to the local Holiday Inn. I caught the first flight out of LaGuardia to Pittsburgh the next morning and then rented a car for the one-hour drive to Northeast Ohio. A family member who was on the Youngstown police force watched the house after the investigation by the police the night of the incident.

When I arrived, the first thing I did was arrange to have an alarm system installed in my parents' home. I also had bars put on the lower basement windows. The next move was to round up the fellas and figure out who could have preyed on my then 76-year-old mom and 78-year-old dad. My heart sank when my dad told me how the asshole manhandled him and my mother. To say I was enraged was an understatement.

The robber made a mistake a few days later and sold some of the jewelry to a local pawnshop. One of my Ohio cousins called me in New York and said, "Derek, the person that robbed your parents at gunpoint was apprehended."

I returned to Youngstown in early March and bought my parents a lovely condo in a gated community out in the suburbs.

■ ■ ■

On Tuesday, March 11, 2008, Bear Stearns, an 85-yearold investment bank, had its mortgage-backed holdings harshly downgraded. The rest of the Street refused to deal with Bear, especially in the repo market, and by March 13, Bear had gone from a firm with a $20 billion market capitalization two years prior to one with only $3 billion. On Friday, March 14, the firm had to be rescued by the Federal Reserve with an emergency loan. Bear's stock imploded when the market opened on Friday and took everything else with it. On the weekend, it was reported that Bear's market cap was around $240 million, and the firm most likely wouldn't open on Monday. In an emergency meeting over the weekend, the Federal Reserve greased the desperately needed skids and lent J.P. Morgan $30 billion for it to ultimately purchase Bear Stearns for $10 per share. This $10 per share price was up 400 percent from an initial agreement at $2/share, a 93 percent discount from Friday's closing price. Those who thought the market would stabilize on Monday after the Fed's intervention were gravely mistaken. I told our traders to have as little capital as possible tied up over the weekend. It isn't every day that the fifth largest investment bank in the U.S. goes under. In fact, it was reported that the Fed hadn't rescued a firm in this fashion since the Great Depression.

As I looked at the faces of my 30-year-old traders as they exhaled at the close of the market on Friday, I could tell they were shell-shocked. I had personally seen financial carnage in the crash of 1987 and had a number of moments since then when I thought the world was coming undone. But most of these traders had only gotten a taste in the dot-com implosion, and none had really been in the seat to endure what had happened this past week. As they walked out the door, I told them all to get some serious sleep, as come Monday morning, they needed to be ready to rumble.

For the next two weeks, the entire Street was in tumult. Global markets imploded, and every trading desk was trying to be as nimble as possible and keep their intraday balance sheet as light as possible, and they were certainly trying to go home with an unencumbered balance sheet to avoid the overnight and pre-market news known as tape bombs that were affecting markets with regularity.

Our normal $100–125 million intraday balance sheet was purposely cut in half. Our end of day balance sheet was $15 million, a paltry amount for a trading desk. I was very pleased that senior management trusted the discipline of our trading desk and obviously my management and communication. I had worked hard over my career to make those north of me on the totem pole comfortable with my orderliness and steady hand. I never panicked, and they, in turn, never panicked, even though I had my moments where I wondered what disaster was around the corner.

Just as I started to settle into the new normal for this extremely volatile market, my aunt passed away on March 25. I hadn't suspected that she would survive the year, but I didn't think she would pass this soon. I took care of all of her affairs and arranged for her body to be brought back to Youngstown for the memorial service and burial.

When I returned to New York, I stepped right back into action just as the quarter closed. The DJIA closed its worst quarter in five and a half years, down 8 percent, the S&P 500 at a negative 9 percent, and the Nasdaq Composite spit up 14 percent. From the market's high point in 2007, the first quarter implosion was nearly 19 percent.

The second quarter started with a strong uptick, as the major equity averages surged nearly 4 percent as investors and analysts seemed to think that the worst was over and the market was oversold. A stronger dollar, some better manufacturing figures, and announced write downs by a few major European investment banks helped the psyche of the market, as the perception was that firms were putting the worst behind them. Central banks around the world were being aggressive as well, with the Federal Reserve providing backstop after backstop to shore up the U.S. financial system.

In mid-May of 2008, I headed to Europe for another Fuqua School of Business international summit that was being held in Moscow. As I typically did when attending these foreign summits, I visited a few other countries in the region either before or after the summit as a tourist. On this particular trip, I visited Oslo, Copenhagen, Stockholm, and Helsinki before arriving in Moscow.

Oslo is a beautiful city, and one of the highlights for me was visiting Oslo City Hall and the room where the Nobel Peace Prize is announced. In Denmark, I strolled along the longest pedestrian shopping venue in Europe, Stroget Street, and then stopped at the most wonderful amusement park I had ever seen, Tivoli Gardens. While in Stockholm, I hooked up with a business school friend, Daman Blakeney, who was also on his way to Russia for the summit. We spent a considerable amount of time on Gamla Stan (Old Town) Island, shopping at the boutiques that specialized in the glass design for which Sweden is famous. We then went to Helsinki, where I stayed at one of my favorite hotels, Hotel Kamp.

In Helsinki, as I stood in the lobby of the hotel waiting for Daman, who was staying at another hotel, an American approached me and somewhat under his breath asked me what lobby door led to the parking garage. He thought I was part of the hotel's security detail, as he was the head of security for the American rock band KISS. We both laughed a bit when I told him that I wasn't security, and then he shared with me that Gene Simmons was in the garage and they wanted to get him and the band up to their rooms as quietly and secretly as possible. There was a crowd outside the main entrance awaiting the group's arrival, and their fervor and numbers were growing by the minute. I wasn't much help, but we struck up a nice conversation and talked about their tour. He invited me to the band's performance that night at a local venue and the after-party in the hotel's restaurant at two a.m. I didn't attend the concert, as I had other plans, but I stopped at the after-party in the closed-off restaurant. The scene was over-the-top bacchanalian, and I quickly departed, as I had little desire to be in a Finnish jail; however, before I left, I got the name (Igor) and contact info of the Russian guide KISS used during their stay in Moscow prior to coming to Helsinki.

Prior to all my trips out of the country, I consulted BNY's head of security, Tim Masluk, to get security advice I should heed while in that country. He told me that I shouldn't bring anything that indicated I worked at BNY Mellon to Russia because BNY was party to a major money laundering lawsuit in Russia. BNY was reportedly holding a significant sum from the Russians, and Tim mentioned that I could perhaps be held hostage. I nearly canceled the trip after hearing this, but Tim said to just not take a single thing with BNY Mellon stamped on it and I should be fine.

When we landed in Moscow, we taxied over to the gate, and the flight attendant announced that some authorities were coming on board and that everyone should remain in their seats. If I could have gotten my 250 pounds out of one of those small porthole windows I would have, as I broke out into a sweat. Three policemen came on board and one looked directly at me. After a brief pause, he headed past my section, and they handcuffed a man in the back and walked him off the plane. After we deplaned, customs was a two-hour process, and by the time I got to the baggage carousel, my suitcases were gone. I walked around looking for my luggage and fortunately saw through the window that my luggage was about to be loaded into a Moscow taxi. I sprinted to the taxi and grabbed my luggage from the grasp of the taxi driver. I didn't speak the language and didn't bother trying to explain, in any language, as the passenger and the driver merely just looked at me with puzzled faces. I went back inside the dilapidated Sheremetyevo Airport and immediately called the guide the KISS security guy had recommended. Moscow was going to be a challenge, and Igor was going to come in very handy.

When Igor dropped me off at the Ritz Carlton, near Red Square, I met up with a few of my fellow business school friends. I told them that Igor was going to take care of us when we weren't involved with business school activities. As we sat in a restaurant and I told them about my near loss of luggage, we watched out the window as a policeman put a boot on a legally parked car and then took a seat on a nearby bench. About ten minutes later, the driver of the car showed up, had a conversation with the policeman, and pulled out his wallet and peeled off ruble after ruble as the policeman held out his hand. Igor later told us that this was standard procedure for the police, as they unethically and illegally augmented their incomes. Aside from spending time in Red Square and visiting St. Basil's Cathedral, the Kremlin, Stalin's Bunker, and the absolutely stunning Cathedral of Christ the Savior, one of the major highlights was spending hours in the uber exclusive Soho nightclub that Igor got us into immediately while hundreds stood in line. My friends and I agreed this venue had the largest collection of beautiful women we had ever seen in one place. That still holds true to this day for me.

■ ■ ■

The latter part of the summer of 2008 was eerily quiet in our business, even though everyone knew that just under the surface, grenades, so to speak, were everywhere, as the Federal Reserve was scooping up toxic bank debt all over America. By the beginning of fall, the pins on those grenades started to be pulled. Freddie Mac and Fannie Mae were being bailed out by the government with $200 billion in early September, and right behind the bailout of the quasi-government agencies, Merrill Lynch joined hands with Bank of America in a $50 billion transaction on Sunday, September 14. After that came the biggest casualty, as the financial crisis came to a head and revealed its darkest moments to date. On Monday, September 15, Lehman Brothers filed the biggest bankruptcy in history (which stands to this day), as $600 billion in assets disappeared. I'll never forget riding down Seventh Avenue in Midtown Manhattan in a taxi at seven a.m., headed to the train station to go to Pershing in Jersey City, and seeing Lehman employees on the sidewalks with boxes of their belongings. I had a lump in my throat, imagining what work would be like that day. It was indeed a tumultuous day, but we survived.

■ ■ ■

The next day required a government rescue of American International Group, as it couldn't pay off the credit default swaps it had issued against failing mortgage-backed securities and required $85 billion from the U.S. kitty. Lehman had reportedly been counting on a similar government bailout, or some sort of Bear Stearns' type of development, but for many reasons, ranging from leadership arrogance to just the size of the needed cash infusion, it didn't happen, and Lehman was left out in the cold.

On September 17, things got even worse, as money funds lost an unprecedented $144 billion. Credit markets essentially shut down. Commercial paper, municipal bonds, corporate bonds, mortgages, and anything else with a maturity and coupon became virtually illiquid. The equity market was dropping multiple percent each day, as mortgage companies stopped doing business and folded. The financial dominoes were falling and the velocity of their collapse was startling. I sat on the trading desk to solely watch our capital and make sure we stayed as flat as we could. The following day, word that the Treasury Secretary, Hank Paulson, had met with Congress to educate them about a plan to buy "toxic" assets from banks propelled the equity market to post its biggest gain in six years, as the DJIA sprang 410 points and virtually got back all but 39 points of the previous day's losses. Our trading desk enjoyed a near record day, as we fortuitously bought cheap stock from panicked investors early and sold into the day's strength, as the market moved violently higher on record volume. Despite the day's snapback, we were warned that things were probably going to get worse.

Over that weekend, the Bush administration, led by Treasury secretary Paulson, Federal Reserve Chair Ben Bernanke, and Tim Geithner, head of the New York Fed, met with Congress to discuss a $700 billion dollar bailout of mortgage-related assets. Congress was concerned about the enormity of the bailout as well as the idea of bailing out financial institutions that had reportedly behaved badly or, at least, irresponsibly. There was also a major concern regarding how the bailout would play amongst the average citizen in America and what the political ramifications would be. It was also announced that Sunday that Morgan Stanley and Goldman Sachs, the last two stand-alone investment banks, were being converted into bank holding companies, which would give them better access to funding from the feds if necessary. That Saturday was also the day Treasury Secretary Paulson replied that if Congress didn't approve the bailout, then "Heaven help us all."

Late Sunday night, September 21, Heaven's help was summoned, because the Senate voted against the bailout bill. I immediately sent a text to a few of my senior traders to make sure we got in the office early the following day. I turned on the *Bloomberg News* to see that equity futures were down multiple percentage points, the dollar was imploding, and gold soared as a hedge and safety net.

Despite our trading desk enjoying another solid day the next trading session, I personally believed we were three to five days away from a 1929-like depression if Congress didn't pass an aggressive bailout plan.

The rest of the week was quite hairy, as the Bush administration and Congress debated the pros and cons of the largest government bailout in history. Many of my non-financial friends were totally against any bailouts, which I somewhat understood from a taxpayer standpoint, but I warned them that if these financial entities weren't rescued, the carnage would make the Great Depression look like child's play, as $40 billion was lost then, but we were talking of loss most likely north of a trillion here.

On Monday, September 29, Congress voted again to reject the altered bailout bill. Not only did the U.S. equity market implode with its biggest point loss to date (770 points), but global markets also got trounced. The London Financial Times Stock Exchange, better known as the FTSE, plummeted 15 percent. Other markets, like the Brazilian stock market, were down double digits (10 percent). No market went unscathed. Credit markets around the world ground to a halt. Everyone on the Street was not only glued to their trading screens but also to C-Span.

After what seemed like an eternity, as the world melted down daily over the next four days, Congress finally passed a $700 billion bailout bill on Friday, October 3. The bailout bill accomplished a number of things, but perhaps the biggest positive was the creation of the Troubled Asset Relief Program, or TARP. This program saved the U.S. auto companies and provided funds for AIG, as well as ammo to buy stock in many of the troubled financial institutions in the U.S. The overall goal was to provide liquidity into the currently stalled financial system. Many of us thought that after a brief settling, markets would stabilize and begin to recreate a foundation in a matter of weeks after the bailout took hold.

Over the following weekend, things seemed to settle down a bit, but by Monday morning, October 6, all hell had broken loose worldwide again. Banks were still hoarding their limited capital and the financial wheels in the U.S. had only loosened up a smidgen. My trading team and I met with my manager to discuss our strategy, which was basically to not play for a hoped-for bounce after the early anticipated implosion. Well, once again, as market-makers, we were forced to buy more stock early in the session than we had wanted, as the DJIA quickly imploded and was down 800 points. For most of the day, we treaded water while the three major indices hit 2003 levels, but when the market came back strong in the final hour of trading and recovered over 400 of those down points, we once again fortuitously registered a very respectable P & L, as the various indices closed down only 3–4 percent. Foreign banks and their central banks were still weeks behind the U.S. action. European markets closed down between 7–9 percent. Most Latin markets closed down roughly 5–7 percent. Russia, while not a major market, nevertheless closed down a hefty 20 percent. A good indicator of the volatility that day was the CBOE Volatility Index, aka the VIX, which hit a nineteen-year high.

Overall, the month of October was brutal, as the DJIA lost 13 percent of its value. The economy was in dire straits, and 240,000 jobs had been lost just in October. As if I didn't have enough on my plate, I finally made the tough decision to move out of my marital residence and set up camp in a condo I owned in Williamsburg, Brooklyn, overlooking the East River. It was hard to leave my two children, but I felt they deserved a quiet and saner home life than the daily bickering they'd witnessed. Also, from a mental standpoint, I couldn't have a chaotic life at the office and a somewhat more chaotic one at home. It wouldn't have been good for my health.

In November, the situation at AIG grew even more dire, as its tentacles into worldwide financial institutions became even more exposed. AIG became the poster child for the "too big to fail" doctrine, as the bailout for this insurance behemoth rapidly grew from $50 billion to $150 billion. One reckless division of AIG had created hundreds of billions of derivatives that were spread worldwide, and AIG didn't have enough collateral to cover all those derivative bets that had gone wrong. Furthermore, someone at AIG must had been a damn good international salesperson because its product was part of portfolios in nearly every nook and cranny of the financial world. The U.S. financial trio of Paulson, Geithner, and Bernanke felt that a failure of AIG would be catastrophic internationally and perhaps sink worldwide markets and economies, not just stateside entities. The various Fed programs, (i.e., TARP and Term Asset-Backed Securities Loan Facility) put a floor under the markets in late November and, the markets actually rallied quite sharply. The election of President Barack Obama also provided a significant boost to the markets as he announced part of his administration and began to work behind the scenes on tackling the various financial issues that he would inherit in late January 2009.

December started out with a bang as definite recession stories hit the media and the public began to realize how close we came to an all-out depression. On the first trading day of December, the DJIA lost 680 points, or 7.7 percent, while the S&P 500 and Nasdaq Composite tallied losses of 9 percent. At this point the DJIA had lost 39 percent since January1, while the S&P 500 and Nasdaq Composite had lost similar percentages.

Just as investors began to lick their wounds, or count their chips if they played the immense volatility correctly, the morning of December 11, 2008, was a jaw dropper. The FBI announced the arrest of financier Bernie Madoff, of Madoff Securities, and charged him with the largest investor fraud in history, to the tune of $50 billion. Madoff's Ponzi scheme was the last straw to conclude a horrendous year in financial circles, but I found some small solace in this diabolical industry discovery.

While at Fidelity, I sometimes went with our order flow manager to see where we were sending stocks for execution by other broker-dealers in the marketplace. Even though Fidelity traded nearly every security that we wanted, there were significant orders coming from certain clients within and external to Fidelity that were required to be executed away from Fidelity. Fidelity also wanted to keep other broker-dealers "warm" in the event that we had a technological shutdown and had to route all executions away. A third reason to route away order flow was to keep our own internal traders honest and compare their executions and pricing with outside dealers. Once a year, at the very least, part of the due diligence of a firm was to ensure that other broker-dealers with whom we dealt were real entities and not some bucket shop operating out of the back of a garage or in some obscure basement like one of my peers found in Russia while I was at a previous firm. The primary responsibility of this surveillance was for the regulators, but any firm worth its salt should also know their customer or counterpart. Earlier in the decade, around 2003 or 2004, I visited Madoff Securities with our order flow manager to meet the principals and give their operation a cursory look. At the meeting, Madoff provided some documents showing their performance and shedding a little light on their highly profitable strategy. They did this to exhibit to us the soundness of their platform and reveal how they were able to aggressively provide what is known in the industry as price improvement. Essentially, because they traded so well, they could give our clients even better pricing on executions than the rest of the Street could. Better price improvement would logically lead to more order flow sent to Madoff rather than others. The first red flag for me was that the stocks in which Madoff trafficked were the blue-chip stocks, and blue-chip stocks had the least amount of opportunity to make money as a trader due to their tight spreads and massive liquidity. The riskiest stocks, or those with the widest spreads between the bid and the offer price, and those with less liquidity, were the stocks most market-makers would want, not the blue-chip stocks. The only way to make substantial money with this slice of the order flow was to become a portfolio manager, in a sense, and hold positions over a matter of days, if not weeks, and hope for either depreciation or appreciation, depending on your position orientation. When I questioned this strategy, Bernie and his son stated they also incorporated options in their strategy. He mentioned that they also utilized strategies such as buy-writes (buying stock and writing a call position against the long stock position).

I told my manager, Craig Messinger, after that Madoff meeting, that something wasn't right about their method of making money, as one of the Madoff sons had showed us documents that detailed their outstanding trading performance and stellar price improvement. Craig asked to see the documentation, but I told him Madoff collected the documents before we left the meeting, citing they didn't want their investment methodology and performance out in the marketplace. I understood that secrecy, but I never believed in their trading methodology, especially the simplistic buy-write strategy. My boss jokingly informed me that I would have to reverse engineer their process and come up with a better mousetrap to beef up my trading P & L. He chuckled when I told him there was no way Madoff's trading strategy was legitimately producing the kinds of returns he showed me, and I didn't stand to lose any additional order flow to Madoff from a better performance standpoint, but it was embarrassing that their revenue production was so much better than ours.

Almost six years later, as I was sitting in my office at Pershing, watching the market news on CNBC, the anchor announced that authorities had evidence that Bernie Madoff was operating a massive Ponzi scheme at Madoff Securities. He was pumping up his artificial and superior performance by paying off old investors with money from endless new investors. The financial crisis upended the scheme, as old investors requested their money back and new investors were nonexistent and couldn't provide the new capital for Madoff to pay back the old investors.

I knew I was right about Madoff's performance being questionable, and I made sure I respectfully rubbed that in Craig's face.

19

BERNIE "MADE OFF" AND THE STREET GETS AUTOMATED

As the calendar turned and the Madoff situation seemed to unveil a related financial atrocity on a daily basis, Wall Streeters and investors remained skittish, gun shy, and uncertain. Despite the respite over the holidays, nerves were raw, and mine were particularly inflamed, as I was also dealing with an ugly divorce. The one bright spot was that I stumbled into another relationship soon after my wife and I separated.

I began spending time with the real estate broker, a lovely Russian woman, helping me to sell my marital residence. While I wasn't sure whether it was a good idea to start a new relationship so soon after separating, we both threw caution to the wind, and things progressed to a pretty serious level rather quickly.

She was different in a lot of ways, especially when it came to speaking her mind. I remember being out to dinner one evening, and her manner of attire, a sexy dress that hugged her shapely body, garnered the attention of both males and females in the restaurant. Upon returning from the restroom, she overheard a group of black women say, "Who does she think she is? She needs to go put some clothes on! That bitch has one of our men!" Rather than ignoring the comment, my girlfriend said, "Maybe if you treated your men like I do, you might have had him!"

The situation escalated from there, with both sides trading insulting barbs, but I thought it best to leave the tab for our dinner on the table and get out of there before someone got hurt.

Of note, I hadn't dated a non-black woman since 1976, the year I met my black wife at Duke University. The restaurant altercation was a reminder that many black women resented white women "taking" their men, so I had to educate my new girlfriend to be a bit more sensitive to the matter going forward.

■ ■ ■

On January 20, 2009, history was made with the swearing into office of Barack Obama, the first black president of the United States. I, along with most every other person of color in America, was overwhelmed with pride as he took the oath of office. I hadn't cried since election night in November 2008, but tears streamed down my cheeks again at this most historic occasion.

I couldn't have been prouder of America and its citizens for electing this smart, elegant, positive, charismatic man who represented hope and change. While he would inherit an economy on its knees, businesses like the auto industry on the brink of bankruptcy, and wars in Iraq and Afghanistan, he was the man for the job.

■ ■ ■

On March 9, 2009, the three major equity indices—the S&P 500, the DJIA, and the Nasdaq Composite—all bottomed and the bull market began. The S&P 500 stood at 676, the DJIA was at 6547, and the Nasdaq index weighed in at 1268. The stimulus bill that was passed by Congress and signed by Obama began to apply bandages to the very sick economy, even though home foreclosures and job losses continued at a rapid pace.

I felt the job loss and foreclosure scenario personally when I returned to Youngstown for Easter, as I have done every year since I moved to New York in 1984. Beginning in 2003, four of my former high school football teammates (Gerald Price, Mike Fordham, Maurice Stewart, and Fred Saunders) and Mike's brother, Jerry and I have breakfast on the Saturday before Easter, at eleven a.m., at Perkins Pancake House. Sometimes, a few of the other former players and a former coach, Chester Leone, join us as well. I treasure these lifelong friendships, as they also help to keep me grounded and in touch with middle America, which is quite different from what sometimes seems like the fantasy world of New York City.

Even though all of my teammates are doing well, I hear the stories of financial struggles, job losses, murders, and premature death because of inadequate or poor health care. One of my teammates struggled with the goings on of Wall Street, which, at times, greatly affected them financially. I did my best to explain the ins and outs of the financial world, including collateralized debt obligations (CDOs), mortgage-backed securities, TARP programs, and stimulus packages, as well as home ownership, without getting too technical. I also told them that Wall Street was getting all the blame, but there were at least five other entities that should share the blame and are complicit in the Great Recession, but they don't get much press. I said that first of all, let's look at the federal government. The government espoused home ownership and, to some degree, rightly so; however, the federal government indirectly and irresponsibly encouraged non-financially sound people to take on home ownership. The Federal Reserve assisted that dream by cutting interest rates after 9-11, and by 2004, rates were the lowest they had been since the early seventies. Home ownership was cheap, with low mortgage rates, and the doors to mortgage brokers were swung open for all. Cheap money caused mortgage lenders to aggressively seek clients, and many of those clients were not only buying a home on Tuesday that they couldn't afford on Monday, but they were buying two or three homes in hopes of flipping them for a quick profit. Furthermore, the rating agencies were assessing mortgage bundles that they had no idea of the content of those bundles and were very ill-equipped and, in some cases, too lazy or overwhelmed to properly grade those bundles as safe or risky. And, last, Wall Street stepped up to the plate and kept producing these bundles of mortgages, called mortgage-backed securities, that only Wall Street halfheartedly understood the inherent risk. In summation, many homeowners were irresponsible and saw fool's gold. The federal government encouraged everyone to seek home ownership, not just those who could safely carry a mortgage. The mortgage brokers welcomed anyone breathing and with a checking account into their offices to borrow money from banks more than willing to dole out cheap money and play the "quantity over quality" game. And Wall Street provided the platform and the fuel for the real estate bubble.

The guys listened intently and thanked me for the explanation, but one of them closed the discussion with, "I know you bastards (i.e., Wall Street) made out all right!" We all laughed, as they gave the $40 breakfast bill, including tip, to me! I gladly accepted the check, as this same breakfast in New York City would have been four times as expensive.

■ ■ ■

Despite the equity market bottoming in March and hints of the economy gaining some stability, home foreclosures, bank instability, and unemployment continued to dominate the headlines. The equity market continued to climb the proverbial "wall of worry," but every now then, the remnants of the bear market reared its head and reminded everyone that financial market nirvana was a good distance away. During these somewhat turbulent times, I was commuting from Williamsburg, in Brooklyn, to Jersey City each day. At least three nights during the workweek, I managed to get in a workout at the Reebok Sports Club on Manhattan's Upper West Side (now called the Equinox Sports Club). One night, I apparently loaded too much weight on the stack, and when I executed an overhead press on the Life Fitness machine, I heard a pop in my left elbow. I immediately knew I had just made my life more difficult. On April 30, I had surgery at Lennox Hill Hospital to repair a torn ligament.

While in recovery, the nurses, who happened to be black, couldn't have been nicer and more attentive. They asked who was picking me up, and I told them my girlfriend. When my Russian girlfriend arrived to get me, I overheard one of the nurses say, "Can you believe this? We are obviously doing something wrong ... losing a good black man like that!"

I wasn't sure if my girlfriend heard the remark, but she later told me she did. Thankfully, after I schooled her a bit on letting these types of comments slide, she heeded that warning, and we got out of the hospital unscathed.

As I negotiated social situations with a white woman at my side, I began to pay more attention to mixed-race couples in New York City as well as those in my travels. I consulted black female friends to better understand their agita over a black man coupled with a

321

white woman, and I heard all sorts of rationale for their concerns. They ranged from there weren't enough black men for them as it was to the assertion that many black men equate success with having a white woman. And they resented it. I had never had a white girl-friend before, so this was a learning situation for me, even though I often felt that given my lack of melanin, people couldn't necessarily, nor immediately, identify me as black anyway; however, one of my black girlfriends stifled that potential observation. "Man, you walk black, you probably run black, you talk black, you have a black ass, your hair is nappy, and you have general black style! Only a blind, deaf, and dumb person wouldn't know you're a brother!"

■ ■ ■

On June 25, 2009, after doing some shopping at FAO Schwarz, I noticed people crying, mouths agape, while staring at their phones. My phone started buzzing as well, and my first thought was that another 9-11-type event had happened. As I reached for my phone, I heard a young girl yell, "Oh no! Michael Jackson is dead!"

I was a huge Michael Jackson fan, and my heart sank as I read the news of his cardiac arrest on my phone. This music icon's death was a huge blow to the world, but the black community took it especially hard.

■ ■ ■

The daily news of the broken economy, troubled banks domestically and internationally, job terminations, and brokerage firms on the financial cliff became standard news by the fall season. I was hesitant to leave the trading floor for any extended time because I didn't know what would happen next; however, a trip abroad to see some jumpy European clients was necessary.

The financial crisis had its origin in the United States and, as a result, the U.S. had begun to deal with the dumpster fire before the rest of the world reacted. The rest of the world was certainly affected quickly, but they hadn't had a chance to peel the onion to its core as we had domestically and observe directly where all the bodies were and in what cracks they were lying. My mission in going to Europe was to let our clients know that we were financially stable, our technology they utilized to execute their trades through us was sound, and that we would be there for them no matter what. I also hoped to garner more execution business from our current clients.

As was now typical, at one of our client meetings, I was met with, "So, how did you get to be the head guy?" I relayed a little bit of my Wall Street history and got the usual, "I've never seen a black man in a position of such huge responsibility prior to today!" I somewhat smugly responded, "You ever heard of a man called Barack Obama?" That shut it down right there. I once again was reminded of what an ex-pat, white American in London had told me years before about Europe in general and London specifically. He said, "In London, you'd be hard-pressed to find a black postal worker, a black policeman, even a black taxi driver who had the famous *knowledge* credential. Forget about a black person barking orders at a bunch of Brits as somebody's manager anywhere here, and most likely anywhere in Europe." Although I was used to these comments and reactions to my position and success, it never failed to bother me.

■ ■ ■

The year ended strongly from a market performance standpoint, as U.S. equities posted their best performance since 2003. The S&P gained 23.4 percent, the DJIA closed up 18.8 percent, and the Nasdaq Composite exploded up 44 percent. If one were to look at the performance from the March 9, 2009, low, the three indices strongly bounced 65, 59, and 79 percent, respectively.

■ ■ ■

January 2010 started slowly, as investors and market participants digested the previous tumultuous year, with the *bears* feeling that the equity market must experience a pullback, given the outsized gains, and the *bulls* expecting more appreciation as the U.S. financial crisis began to reportedly subside.

At Pershing, we started the year with our annual leadership conference, with this one being held in Secaucus, New Jersey. The event was an effort to look back at the previous year's wins and losses and for senior leadership to map out the direction and expectations for the new year. Pershing prided itself on communication and transparency, and rightly so, in my view. Every year, the firm invited some sort of motivational speaker to address corporate teamwork, stretch goals, or the power of positivity. This year, the speaker was the iconic former Notre Dame football coach Lou Holtz, whom I had met some thirty-five years earlier during my high school football recruitment to college.

A few of the senior leaders of the firm were invited to a small gathering with Coach Holtz before he spoke at the conference. Given my football background, I was invited to the event. I'm not sure Coach Holtz remembered me right away, but after sharing my recruitment story when he was the head coach at North Carolina State, he remembered me. I also took the opportunity to remind him that he still owed me a pair of gloves and a scarf!'

At one point during the gathering, I overheard Coach Holtz ask a very senior person where the name Pershing originated and whether the name had any connection to General Pershing. To this day I can't believe what I heard. The senior person relayed that the firm got its name from one of the founders, who was the son of General "Black Jack" Pershing in World War 1. When asked about the name Black Jack, the senior person went on to say that General Pershing was originally called nigger Jack, because he led black soldiers prior to World War 1, but that name eventually became unacceptable, so they started calling him "Black Jack."

I was dumbfounded and nearly dropped my ginger ale. I had to leave the room for a minute to collect myself. They say time heals all wounds, but the sting of racism never goes away.

I never looked at that person who used the N word the same way again, and, fortunately, I never heard or witnessed any further racist activities by this senior person during my remaining years at Pershing. I eventually chalked it up to too much alcohol, even though I don't generally give people passes for their actions and words due to being drunk. I also came to realize that some people in the majority may not acutely understand how the N word cuts through the heart of black people, especially when it's said by white people. I consider the N word and the C word (a derogatory term for women) as two words that should never be used.

I mentioned the Holtz incident to a few longtime Pershing personnel that I trusted, and they were not surprised. To this day, I like to think that I misheard the unnecessary and horrid characterization, but in my heart, I know the reality.

■ ■ ■

I was now into the second year of waiting for my divorce to become final. By this time, I also realized that many matrimonial attorneys, and certainly our representatives, were borderline crooks, and that the whole system was set up to extract as much money from the couple as possible. There is an unspoken minimum dollar value that many of the attorneys expect to separate from the couple before they actually proceed to try and arrive at some sort of settlement or agreement. The courts are even in on the game, as they require you to visit the courtroom from say nine a.m. till three p.m. for a five- to ten-minute session with the judge. So, the clients sit in the courtroom for hours, while paying the attorneys $600/hour, to see the judge a maximum of ten minutes, to see what progress is or isn't being made. On the way out, another appointment is made for weeks later for essentially a repeat performance of thievery. If you ever get divorced, by all means try mediation rather than give your hard-earned money to these "legal crooks." I also realized early on in the divorce process that the system is set up to nail the male in the relationship to the wall, especially if the male is the breadwinner in the family. First, the judge and her attorney stated that the wife was allowed to continue her lifestyle. When I asked about my life-style, it was dismissed. When my wife presented her financial needs statement, I also whipped out my similar document. No one ever looked at my document. The male is financially screwed the minute the word "divorce" passes the couple's pearly whites.

Just as the attorneys played "take away" with my wallet, volatility was playing give and take in the financial markets, as U.S. stocks gyrated around fifteen-month highs in January, 2010. In February, Greece came into play, as it was feared that the country would default on its debt and the sanctity and rationale for the European Union was called into question daily. European markets began to be the dog that wagged the tail of the rest of the world's financial markets, and traders in the U.S. were looking at European indices before brushing their teeth every morning.

Stocks in the U.S. treaded water, up in the 5 percent range in the first quarter. Conversely, stocks in Greece, Portugal, and Spain stayed in the negative spotlight, as their sovereign default issues continued. In the middle of the second quarter, specifically on May 6, 2010, equity traders experienced perhaps the most insane day in modern day trading: the so-called flash crash, in which $1 trillion of market value was erased, as the Dow Jones sank 1000 points, or 9 percent, in a matter of minutes. The day started in a fairly turbulent manner, as the European debt crisis grew more and more dire, but certainly didn't portend what was about to come mid-afternoon EST. The reason behind what happened that day has never definitively been determined, even to this day, but the cause has generally been pointed at two entities. One reported culprit was a trader in the U.K. who was trading something called E-mini S&P 500 futures contracts, utilizing an algorithm that continually put significant pressure on the security while not actually executing many, if any, trades. He reportedly put outsized sell orders just above the market and gave the impression that there was a boatload for sale. An active seller would see this massive overhang and sell in front of this artificial wave, and this selling would feed on itself. The U.K. trader's algo would then follow the security lower and lower but above the market, still without executing a single contract, in an illegal practice called spoofing. At some point, or at multiple points, the U.K. trader actually bought some futures that he had artificially drove lower and then sold them at higher prices after he canceled his massive offerings and let the contracts appreciate a bit. He reportedly made close to $900,000 that day. The second theory, which I personally think is more credible, is that a large investment firm/mutual fund placed a $4 billion sell order via an automated algorithm and drove the market in the E-minis down to artificial levels, and the automation aspect kept a foot on the accelerator, without any finesse. Other traders and automated programs also responded to this pressure and drove stocks down to some incredible levels in a matter of minutes. For instance, Procter & Gamble, a stalwart consumer goods icon and a component of the DJIA, lost nearly 40 percent of its value in a matter of minutes, trading from the low $60s to a price just below $40. Another corporation, Accenture, had its stock lose 90 percent of its value in fifteen minutes; it remarkably traded at a mere one penny! The market rallied hard minutes later and into the day's close, while recovering some 650 points, to finish down only 348 DJIA points, or 3.2 percent.

The automation of equity trading on the Street was in full force by now. Automated trading systems that required very little human interaction were on every significant desk on the Street. The thirty traders who were in the seats at Pershing years before were now less than ten. The small orders were executed automatically, allowing the traders to focus on the big, capital intensive, difficult orders. Algorithms that were keyed to various financial measures were prominent on every desk. A broad example was if the ten-year bond trades here, and gold trades at this level, and oil at this price, and the S&P' 500 hits X, and the five-day moving average of index Y is here, and the online retail ETF reaches here, then sell all equities in the retail sector. This level of automation preceded and perpetuated this flash crash and continued many months and years later, due to silicon eyeballs rather than human eyeballs and a lack of proper technical governance.

The senior management at Pershing, as well as nearly every friend I knew who owned stocks but didn't work on Wall Street, called me the afternoon of the flash crash to ask what the hell was going on. My response to management was that I hadn't a clue and that we weren't fighting it, as our positions and capital were light. My response to my friends was to not do anything and just let things settle down a bit, because no one had ever seen this before. Management was happy to hear that we had one of our best trading days in history, as we caught the proverbial falling knife and were able to place the knife back in its holder for some impressive trading profits. I also told them that if the market hadn't rallied so harshly that we would have faced more than the usual headache at the end of the session and that we probably would have gotten crushed the next day with our overnight holdings if we couldn't have liquidated our positions after that insane forty-minute *flush* down and *flash* up.

The flash crash experience kept all market participants jumpy for weeks later. Every time the market dipped a bit, it seemed like all the buyers ran for cover, wondering if flash crash 2 was in the offing. This scenario played throughout the summer, and by July, stocks were at their lowest levels of the year. Volume dried up as well, as investors wouldn't commit one way or the other, as competing stories and situations confounded even the savviest participants. Summer months were typically slower, and most everyone on the Street appreciated the down time and lack of activity this particular year. I was no exception, as I took a quick vacation to Paris to watch the final days of the Tour de France before I underwent surgery for an umbilical hernia. My maniacal incline sit-ups at the health club had finally taken a toll, and one day I woke up with a slightly protruding belly button. By the time I returned to unencumbered health and a flat belly button, the Fed's quantitative easing program was in standard operating mode and Fed Chair Ben Bernanke was out on the circuit downplaying recession worries. The Fed's purchasing of assets like bank debt, treasuries, and mortgage-backed securities from its member banks kept a floor in the market, and by the end of August, the equity market was quickly back to two-year highs after hitting 2010 lows only six or seven weeks earlier.

By the fall, I was hit with more personal issues. I closed on the sale of my marital residence in the Trump Place development, and I also dropped my son off at boarding school in New Hampshire, as his relationship with his mom had deteriorated and their coexistence under the same roof became untenable. I also thought his going away to boarding school would help his maturation and reduce some of the stress on the household, where my daughter was also trying to experience some level of civility and normalcy, given the implosion of our family structure.

My son had a rough time at the predominantly white boarding school, but his biggest issues came from the few black students at the school. He told me that one of his fellow black students said, "You ain't no real black with those light (hazel) eyes." His stay at this New Hampshire boarding school was short-lived for this and other reasons, even though he was knocking it out of the park academically.

The last week of the year, I had exciting plans to take my eighteen-year-old-son and fifteen-year-old daughter to Las Vegas for some bonding and some age-appropriate fun, given how tough a year it had been for all of us. We had plans to see Jerry Seinfeld at Caesar's Palace on Monday, Criss Angel and his magic at the Luxor Hotel on Tuesday, a side trip to Hoover Dam and the Grand Canyon on Wednesday, the Broadway hit *The Jersey Boys* on Thursday, and a dinner and celebration at Mix at Mandalay Bay to bring in the New Year on Friday; however, a massive snowstorm in New York and the northeast prevented us from getting anywhere other than a two-day stay in uncomfortable seats at the Delta terminal at Newark Airport. We ended up trudging through the snow in Williamsburg, near my new apartment, trying to make the best of a major letdown and significant financial hit, given that all of the show tickets and celebrations in Vegas had been paid for and were non-refundable. At least the DJIA, S&P 500, and Nasdaq Composite closed on a better note than we did, as they finished 2010 up 11, 13, and 17 percent, respectively.

20

XENOPHOBIA AND RACISM IS EVERYWHERE

The year 2011 was by far the most professionally boring stretch of my then five-year tenure at Pershing. Some macro-events had caused market gyrations throughout the year, but intermittent market implosions and explosions seemed to revert back to the middle after a few market sessions. The Eurozone crisis continued to dominate the headlines, with $100 oil, a near-catastrophic earthquake in Japan, and the downgrading of U.S debt sharing the first page of the newspapers.

I had my own implosions and explosions as well. I started the year with a wonderful, expenses paid, trip with a group put together by a watch company that wanted to further endear some of its primary watch-buying clients. About fifteen of us traveled to an international watch show in Geneva, Switzerland. This trip began in Geneva, and then went to a watch factory in Schaffhausen. We made a few stops along the way but ended the trip in Arjeplog, Sweden, to do some car racing and snowmobiling on the frozen lakes, in weather that could approach minus forty degrees, given its mere sixty miles from the Arctic Circle.

For the most part, the trip was wonderful, but again, I experienced racism up close and personal. None of the observations were new to me, as I had experienced them all in the states before, but it just reinforced how little much of the world had come to accept and equally respect people who are different from themselves.

I would venture to say that nearly every black person has been followed at some point in their life by either a security guard or store employee while shopping. Well, try shaking a security guard at the International Watch Show in Geneva. As I stopped to check out and try on the various high-end watches (i.e., Audemars Piguet, IWC, Patek Philippe, Vacheron Constantin, Jaeger-LeCoultre, Breguet, and Blancpain), I noticed that I had been followed for nearly two hours by security, and he wasn't doing a very good job of camouflaging himself. When I finished browsing and headed out the door of the convention center, I waved at him derisively, and he slyly smiled back at me. A few nights later, after our travel group had gotten to know each other a little better, someone yet again asked how I got into an institution like Duke. I guess they thought I was academically inferior, but the gentleman's wife piped up and offered that black guys get into places like that if they can play football or basketball. Two could play that game, so I told the woman that perhaps her son should have played a sport instead of playing the cymbals in the band.

At dinner the following night, where the French wine was again flowing, one of the more outspoken of the group asked how I got to Wall Street, especially at a blue-blooded firm like Morgan Stanley. My answer was simple: through education, hard work, and a little luck. He then asked whether I had come in through some affirmative action program, to which I responded, "Yep, they affirmed that I was a better candidate than your white cousin who had four hundred years of affirmative action and still came up short."

In Berlin, one of the group members and I went to an upscale retail watch boutique to look at some timepieces and compare U.S. prices for particular chronometers. The person I was with wanted to try on a watch, and he did so on his right wrist without taking off his own watch on his left wrist. When I asked to see a watch and try it on, the salesperson insisted I take off my personal watch and place it in the felt box on the counter. I would typically take off my personal watch anyway, but it was quite obvious to me that the salesperson was uncomfortable with me looking at the watch. I told him not to worry, that I wasn't going to steal it. The salesperson pretended not to understand English even though he had just explained the features of both watches we tried on in near perfect English.

Upon leaving the boutique, my travel buddy was astounded at the subtle, yet obvious, racism on the part of the salesperson. I told him it was par for the course.

But the "fun" didn't end there! Prior to our flight home, we stayed at a hotel in Germany near the departing airport. I went to the lobby to buy a bottle of water and upon returning to my room, my key card wouldn't open the door. I went back to the lobby and asked if they could reauthorize my key card, at which time I was asked whether I was actually a guest at the hotel. I gave the man at the desk my hotel room number and showed him my American driver's license, while mentioning that I had just checked in twenty minutes beforehand. The man then spoke to a porter in German and uttered what sounded like "schwarz" and "nigger" in the same sentence. I thought he was asking the porter to escort the guy who had a build like Arnold Schwarzenegger to his room with the newly authorized key card. When we got to the room, the porter walked in with me and stood there for a minute, as if he wanted to see whether I belonged there. I hadn't unpacked yet, so I guess he couldn't tell if the belongings were mine. In any event, I thanked him and he left. I found the whole situation strange and wondered why the desk clerk hadn't just given me a new key card after I identified my room and provided my ID. Who knows? I just wrote it off until the following morning, when at breakfast, I mentioned the incident to one of the people from the group who spoke German, and I immediately knew from the look on their face that the desk clerk wasn't referring to my poor man's Arnold Schwarzenegger-like frame. The person told me that schwarz meant black and *neger* meant Negro, but when a German said neger, he was very likely using it in the pejorative manner, just like it's used in the States.

It seemed that wherever I went in the world, negative stereotypes, unpleasant perceptions, and downright racism, certainly toward black people, followed me.

■ ■ ■

January was spent determining the previous production year's bonuses. Despite Pershing being the most organized, hospitable firm for whom I have ever worked, it also unfortunately rushed the most important thing that Wall Street managers do for their employees. Maybe it's the fact that the bonus pools have to pass through so many hands and be manipulated and massaged at every level and step. By the time the process gets to the line manager and back to the top, the time frame is ridiculously compressed. Nevertheless, if I were a Wall Street CEO or a CEO in any industry that had a bonus plan, this process would be elongated, even though I do realize that the pool is many times a moving target, based on what revenue and losses happen on a daily basis, right up to the day the numbers are communicated to the troops.

The year was a mediocre one, so the payouts would be slimmer than usual; however, management, including me, had been managing expectations for the last few months so that the skinny envelopes wouldn't be a surprise. In fact, I found there was less disappointment about bonuses when times were rough than when times were good.

By the time the financial press got done writing about the lack of revenue on the Street for any given year and senior management finished their "save your money" declarations, one was just happy to receive anything. I personally believed that the chieftains of Wall Street got together in the fall in a windowless back room in Midtown and came up with a monopolistic game plan to talk down bonuses at their respective firms as well as feed the financial rags and the talking heads with negative compensation thoughts.

■　■　■

After getting past the tough compensation period of January and February, the spring went fairly smoothly, but things heated up in early summer, both professionally and personally. The legacy firm that was left over from the Bernie Madoff scandal, or at least its trading platform, Surge Trading, came up for sale. We kicked the tires on the trading platform but ultimately decided that the technology was mediocre and was made even more so by the association with Madoff. We spent hours looking under the hood but couldn't get comfortable enough to pull the trigger for both operational and reputational reasons.

In mid-June, the senior staff at Pershing went to Hollywood, Florida, for the firm's annual mid-summer conference, INSITE, where the firm's institutional registered investment advisor, wealth managers, and retail clients come for a two and a half-day conference to hear subject matter experts discuss products, platforms, and issues. Regulatory and legal guidance are also on the docket, as are experts in present and future investment products and financial markets in general.

Pershing did an outstanding job of bringing in prominent speakers who provided guidance on motivational techniques and how to work as a team. Many of these speakers also happened to be some of the most influential people in the country. In my twelve-year career at Pershing and/or BNY Mellon, I'd had the privilege of hearing Bill Clinton, George W. Bush, the prime minister of the UK, Gordon Brown, Colin Powell, Condoleezza Rice, Peyton Manning, NFL coach Bill Belichick, Bob Woodward, Fareed Zakaria, Alan Greenspan, Hank Paulsen, and Michael Lewis address the group. This conference is perhaps the finest of its kind and attracts 2,000 to 3,000 clients each summer.

Over the years, I've had the opportunity to serve as moderator on many of the equity investment panels at the INSITE conferences. After one particular session I moderated, a member of the audience approached me and stated he really enjoyed the session and was glad he came for two reasons, one of which was that the content presented was great and that it gave him some ideas about how to improve his equity portfolio. He was hesitant to tell me the other reason until I pressed him, as I said it was important for us to receive feedback so that we could put forth the best information possible in subsequent sessions. He reluctantly said, "It was good to see a black man speak well other than President Obama." I told him he needed to get out more as I walked away shaking my head.

■ ■ ■

I spent a significant portion of 2011 traveling internationally, which is one of my favorite things to do. I was able to fulfill one of my bucket list wishes and attended a championship match at Wimbledon, where I saw Czech Petra Kvitova beat Russian/ American Maria Sharapova. I also traveled to Paris again before returning to work. The summer proved to be slow, so the June RIFs proved to be warranted, given the lack of activity, even though we did have some bouts of extreme volatility in early August, when Standard & Poors downgraded U.S. debt from AAA to AA+ for the first time in history.

It wasn't long before I was packing my bags again and setting off to China and Dubai, this time with the Duke University basketball team, who were playing some exhibition games there. Alumni, Iron Duke donors, and avid Duke basketball fans had been invited to tag along at a reduced cost, so it was a great opportunity to cheer them on as they played some of the host nations' national teams. It was also an excellent way to see the countries up close and personal through an atypical, chaperoned lens.

We first visited Shanghai, a modern New York-like metropolis. In Shanghai, I watched with extreme puzzlement as Chinese residents ate all sorts of insects and slimy things on a stick at various food trucks. I nearly threw up as I watched the locals eat scorpions, cicadas, seahorses, crickets, centipedes, and other disgusting insects, with some of the insects still seemingly hanging onto life. I then understood how some of the animal viruses, like SARS, had been transmitted from animals to humans. Severe acute respiratory syndrome (SARS) was first reported in China in 2002, and I think I was at ground zero. When the 2020 coronavirus—COVID-19—hit the worldwide press, I immediately thought of what I witnessed in Shanghai in 2011, and I recall walking through one of their wet markets and seeing animals that I had never seen before.

A few days later we went to Kunshan, China, where we saw the site where Duke University would later build a satellite campus when it expanded its international offering and academic platform. We concluded our China excursion in Beijing, the equivalent of

Washington, DC, from a vibe and seat of political authority stand-point. The biggest highlight in China was our trip to the Great Wall, where I believe we traversed the Badaling section of the Wall, the section nearest to Beijing. The magnitude of the Great Wall was overwhelming, which was reportedly 13,170 miles long at one time but which only has approximately 5,500 miles existing today. Climbing up the uneven and steep steps to one of the primary land-ing and fort-like areas was one of the hardest physical efforts I've ever endured. When I asked the guide how many heart attacks take place on the Wall, he said, "Probably one every few days."

From Beijing, we flew to the Persian Gulf to Dubai, in the United Arab Emirates. The futuristic city in the desert was smoking hot, but I finally understood what dry heat meant. I didn't sweat the entire time, even though I'm a huge sweater. I inquired how the women could withstand the heat in their dark colored hijabs from head to toe, and one lovely woman told me that their attire is not only cool and breathable, but it acts like a shield from the sun. She also mentioned that their attire allows them to perhaps have fewer undergarments on than one would imagine. I probed no further. We were there during Ramadan, which is the month on the Islamic calendar where fasting, prayer, and reflection is observed for thirty days; however, I did witness some Muslims getting *loose* when the sun went down, but I'll let Allah deal with that.

While in Dubai, I also witnessed the most opulent mall I have seen to date, the Dubai Mall. This massive mall sat at the base of the world's tallest building, the Burj Khalifa, and housed the greatest collection of upscale stores that I've ever seen. It was as if the mall owners went to every country in the world and brought in an out-post of that country's top two or three stores. The aquarium and underwater zoo in the mall were just as startling and unexpected. From the Burj Khalifa, to the Dubai Mall, to the Burj Al Arab Hotel, to the three artificial islands in the desert, to the fancy Dubai

Airport, Dubai appeared to have been created to ultimately impress even the most skeptical visitor. They succeeded with me.

I left Dubai a day early, as reports of a major hurricane (Irene) on the East Coast, especially in the New York City area, surfaced. The hurricane was due to hit on Sunday, August 28, and I returned just in time to batten down the hatches.

The following weekend, while at Duke University for an event, I had some time to kill, so I drove out to Butner Prison, about fifteen miles from Durham, just to take a look at the facility where Bernie Madoff was imprisoned. I drove onto the prison parking lot in my rental car after the gate guard curiously just waved me in without asking any questions. I got out of the car to look at the outside walls of the prison. Just as I'm taking in the enormity of the structure and thinking of Bernie, a prison official drove up to me in his official car and asked if he could help me. I told him that I was just looking and was curious about where Bernie Madoff was going to spend the next 150 years less time served. The official said, "Sir, you need to get the hell out of here right now."

■ ■ ■

The equity market closed the year flat, despite being up 8 percent at one point and being down 12 percent at another point. A lot happened in between January 1, 2011, and December 31, 2011, but just like my personal life, the ups were balanced with the downs, and it appeared as if the status quo had ruled.

21

FREEDOM, FACEBOOK, FATHER

I n January 2012, the U.S. equity market rallied strongly in the first quarter, as the Fed's stimulus policies continued despite major fiscal problems elsewhere in the world, especially Europe. The first quarter performance was the best in fourteen years for the S&P 500 (up 12 percent), but this was merely a setup for major mid-year disappointment. (The DJIA closed on March 30 up 8.1 percent, and the Nasdaq Composite was up 19 percent for the quarter).

In April, my son, Julian, and I struck out to find him an apartment near the college he was going to attend in Queens, beginning in the summer. Knowing very little about Queens, I consulted a real estate broker in the neighborhood, as I wanted to make sure he'd have an easy commute between home and school. Our real estate agent was a Chinese woman, which wasn't a surprise, given that the area near Flushing is heavily populated with Chinese citizens. She took us to see a small garden apartment, where we met the

Chinese landlord. We liked the apartment and the monthly rental price, so I asked for the lease to secure the residence, but as I began to write a check for the first month's rent and the security deposit, the landlord started talking animatedly, yelling, "No check, cash!" I apologized and explained I didn't carry that much cash on me ($2,000) and that my check was good, but this didn't seem to placate him. He then turned to the broker and had a heated conversation with her in Chinese, and she then apologized to me for not telling me the landlord only dealt in cash. The situation continued to get out of hand, with the landlord pulling the lease out of my hands and tearing it up into little pieces, at which time I heard him mutter the N word. At that point, I told him to go to hell and tore up my check in his face.

My son had a hard time believing what had just happened, but I, unfortunately, was quite used to it. We found Julian another apartment in another part of Flushing.

■ ■ ■

After four long years of lining the lawyers' pockets, my divorce was finally official, and, ironically, the official divorce date fell on our wedding anniversary, May 2. Karma or poetic justice, I thought.

On the flip side, the third largest initial public offering in U.S. history, Facebook, hit the radar. The hotly anticipated IPO was due to raise over $16 billion, offering 421 million shares priced at $38/share by the lead underwriter, Morgan Stanley. On May 18, at approximately 11:30 a.m., the IPO opened after being severely delayed, and nearly 82 million shares traded in the first 30 seconds; however, a monumental technical problem with the Nasdaq trading platform caused absolute bedlam, as investors and traders didn't know if they had bought stock, sold stock, whether there was an execution, or what the price was. It was the biggest clusterfuck in trading history by nearly every participant's estimation. And, the problems of the trading day, where a record 460 million shares traded on day one, continued for at least another few weeks, as firms futilely tried to sort out what they bought, sold, and at what price. It was estimated that the Street firms and broker dealers lost $500 million over this period, and I personally think that figure was light.

At Pershing, we had our problems as well, as we tried to determine what prices and executions our customers were owed or not owed. Even though we had no significant capital exposed, certainly relative to the firms that actually traded the stock on a principal basis, we had reputational and regulatory liability that had to be addressed for clients that entrusted us with their orders. After a week of analyzing spread sheets and running programs to decipher what was legitimately owed to our clients, we finally closed the book on this debacle. Other firms that were major market-makers in this IPO suffered huge losses, with one competitor, Knight Securities, reportedly losing $35 million. There were reports of other firms losing similar or multiples of that amount, with UBS claiming that it had suffered $350 million in losses. What was supposed to be a big payday for the Street turned out to be an unmitigated disaster due to the Nasdaq system problems. Nasdaq later had to fork over a mere $42 million in restitution to affected broker-dealers.

By June, the first quarter equity market gains were all gone. The debt crisis in Europe, especially Greece and Portugal, provided daily worldwide concerns. Global economic measures were percolating, and the U.S. first heard the term *fiscal cliff* from Federal Reserve Chair Ben Bernanke. Essentially the fiscal cliff was the soon expiring of previously approved personal tax cuts and a reduction in government spending. The theory was that this double whammy at the end of the year would have sent the recovering economy into another tailspin and ratchet up the unemployment rate again quickly. Fortunately, Congress was able to come to some bipartisan agreements before the year ended, but mid-year, these issues were dominant.

By July, I was due for a significant vacation. I was burned out from the first half of the year, but, more importantly, my dad's health was failing. His bladder cancer had progressed and he was now on dialysis, as his kidneys had failed. I traveled to Ohio a few times to see him in 2012, but each time I left, I wondered if that visit would be my last to see him alive. I cried all the way to the airport each and every time I left him and my mom in Canfield, Ohio.

Despite my dad's waning health, my now Italian girlfriend (things didn't work out with the Russian girlfriend) and I decided to go to Europe to visit my daughter, who was studying in Spain for the summer. Before meeting my daughter on the Mediterranean coast of Spain, we went to Madrid and stepped right into the midst of Spain's celebration of their European championship in men's soccer. We may as well have been in Times Square on New Year's Eve, as a major party took place right outside of our hotel at the Plaza de la Cibeles. From there, we flew to Seville, rented a car, and drove to see my daughter in Conil, Spain. The towns of Tarifa, Marbella, and Malaga were next on the route before we caught a flight to Casablanca, Morocco. After a few nights in Casablanca, we took a car service 150 miles to Marrakech, which outside of seeing my daughter, was the highlight of the trip.

By September, the Federal Reserve had started its third round of quantitative easing (aka large-scale asset purchases) to push long-term interest rates lower and to inject liquidity into the financial system. Market participants began to firmly understand that the Fed was going to be the backstop for the financial markets whenever they were distressed, and the equity market began to climb. The probable reelection of President Obama was also on the horizon, and the market began to recognize that the Democratic policies put in place were taking hold. The markets became stabilized while allowing for enough volatility to create the best of both worlds for the trading community.

Just as my professional life had started to somewhat normalize, my personal life came undone in October. My father's condition worsened and he had to be hospitalized. On October 5, I took my son and daughter to see my dad in hospice. He was lucid and able to sit upright in a wheelchair while I fed him, but I think he hung on long enough just to see me and the kids. I knew when I left that I would never see my precious father alive again. Sadly, he passed away on October 13, at eight a.m. My rock, my barometer, my standard bearer, was gone.

To get my mind off of the loss of my cherished father, I decided to click off another of my bucket list items and go to a Green Bay Packers home game in Wisconsin. My girlfriend and I made our way to Wisconsin and took in a University of Wisconsin versus Michigan State game on Saturday, and on Sunday, we drove to Green Bay to see the Packers beat up on the Jacksonville Jaguars, winning 24–15. While the venue and atmosphere were great, my attention quickly turned to pending Hurricane Sandy, quickly approaching New York and the East Coast. Flights to the East were being canceled and coastal inhabitants were being told to move cars to higher ground and tie down anything outside that would move.

We left the Packers game and headed straight to the airport, where we got a flight to Detroit, and then luckily got the last flight that day to Binghamton, New York, the only flight headed anywhere near NYC. The flight was so turbulent that we wondered if we had done the right thing. It didn't help that a woman behind us screamed the last half hour of the flight. We landed with one of the wings nearly hitting the runway, but, thankfully, we were safe on the ground, evidenced by everyone on the plane clapping. We were lucky to rent the last car available, a large SUV, which turned out to be a good thing, because on the 155-mile trip from Binghamton to my Hudson Valley home, the winds were so bad that a lighter vehicle would have been blown off the road.

Fortunately, my home sustained minimal damage, with just a few downed trees and some rain spouts that had to be reattached.

The next morning, we drove the rental to LaGuardia Airport, where my SUV was parked. The majority of the cars were under two to three feet of water. I had parked on the fringe of the parking lot, and that area was higher, so the water level was only about halfway up the tire, thankfully.

The streets along the drive back home from LaGuardia were eerily quiet, and I wondered what I'd find when we got to my place. What we found was the complex's underground garage water level to be almost level with the adjacent East River. Cars were floating in the garage. While I was grateful that my car hadn't been left in the underground garage, I was more grateful that my apartment hadn't sustained any damage in the storm.

■ ■ ■

Toward the end of the year, I invited my mom and my younger brother and his wife to New York for the Christmas holidays. We all needed a lift, especially my mom, who was still grieving the loss of my dad, after his four-year battle with cancer; however, the week in New York for them turned out to be the updated version of the Jack Lemmon film *The Out-of-Towners*. Everything that could go wrong, did go wrong. My mom passed out on Sixth Avenue from dehydration and partially fell in a public fountain in twenty-degree weather. She then got the flu and had to basically spend the week in her hotel room. My brother had just had knee surgery in Ohio before he came to New York, and he developed a terrible staph infection and had to lay up in his hotel room the entire time, in agony. His wife tended to him and my mom, and I was hopeful they'd be able to salvage part of their trip, but they ended up going back to Ohio early, and I was left holding the tickets to the Radio City Music Hall Christmas Show, *Evita*, and Knicks and Giants games. I guess it was an appropriate way to close out a very bad personal year. Conversely, the U.S. equity markets turned in a stellar performance, as the S&P returned 13.4 percent, the Nasdaq Composite 15.9 percent, and the DJIA 7.3 percent.

22

EDUCATING WHITE FOLKS

D espite 2012 ending on a sour note, I had much optimism personally and professionally going into early 2013. On the personal front, the dissolution of my marriage and the daily agita associated with those acrimonious legal proceedings was over. My daughter, Kara, was also beginning to focus on colleges for admission in the fall of 2014.

Duke University continued to play a prominent role in my personal life, as I continued my participation on the Fuqua School of Business Board of Visitors; I also attended a few football and basketball games every year, with a relevant official reunion thrown in when applicable. In late January, the university celebrated its fifty-year anniversary of blacks being admitted to Duke. The weekend-long event was done extremely well, and I let university President Dick Brodhead and his wife, Cindy, know how proud I was to be a Dukie, especially a black Dukie. I only wished that

I could have reported back to my late father how tremendous an event it had been, given his initial concern nearly forty-years earlier about my attending a school in 1975 that had only admitted blacks in 1963, the year the first five black undergraduates enrolled. Some of those original students attended the weekend anniversary celebration, and their stories were enthralling, because aside from them, the only other people of color on campus back then either had a broom in their hand or a hair net on their head.

The stock market posted a quarter for the record books. Two of the major equity indices appreciated double digits (DJIA 11.9 percent, S&P 500 10.6 percent, Nasdaq Composite 8.2 percent) in the first three months of the year, as the stock market recouped levels of five years ago, primarily helped by the easy money of the world's central banks. Cash on the sidelines since the financial crisis being deployed, share repurchases, and steadily increasing corporate profits also played a role in the first quarter upward explosion. The trading environment was also excellent, as the basic maneuver was to come into the market in the morning long and ride the upward wave.

With things on the work front going well, I was able to devote more attention to my two precious kids. Like every high school kid concerned about getting into the college of their choice, the admissions process adds another level of anxiety. My daughter was no different, as she worried about whether she would be selected by any of her school choices. Our meeting with Kara's high school college advisor at the prestigious all-girls school, Brearley, wasn't the most pleasant of experiences. The counselor intimated that our daughter, despite what we thought was a very impressive academic and extracurricular performance during her twelve years at the upper eastside school, wouldn't have much luck getting into any of the upper echelon schools. I was shocked, and immediately thought of my father and how he used to say that the "system" always tried to sell us short. When we got home from the meeting, I reassured my daughter that a great school is where you feel comfortable, where you can thrive, where you can learn under ideal circumstances, and where you can be happy. I had no doubt she'd get into one of her top three choices, and she nearly made me cry when she said, "Dad, she (the counselor) is trying to kill my dreams." I became even more determined to do everything I could legally and ethically to make sure she got into whatever school she ultimately desired, even though I felt her scholastic resume should kick open a few select doors on its own.

While Kara's multi-year ramp to college was unfolding, her travel soccer team participation provided some great quality time for us. One of our more interesting trips was to Commack, Long Island, where we encountered a true racist. One woman, whom I believe unfortunately was a parent of one of the local Commack team players, was upset at the physical play of our superior Manhattan soccer team. She started with a chant of "Go back to Manhattan." Then it was "Your team is the United Nations!" I assume this communication was due to the fact that the Manhattan team was as diverse as New York City, as Kara's team had at least four or five ethnic groups represented. After a particularly hard check by my faster, stronger, and physically larger daughter, the Commack woman finally unleashed what I believe she had wanted to say all along. "Referee, call a foul on that nigger!" A pall came over the crowd as the "nigger" word seemed suspended in the hot summer air of Memorial Day weekend. I took a deep breath and walked over to the woman and said, "You stepped over the line. Now you have to deal with me." I wasn't planning on getting into a physical altercation with the woman, but I wanted to let her know that her vile language couldn't continue. She said, "I'm going to get my husband. He'll deal with you," to which I replied, "I'll be waiting right here.

The other parents of the Manhattan team players who were present quickly encouraged me to seek out law enforcement, as they were concerned that the racist might return with a weapon and/or her husband. None of us wanted any drama, but I told them that sometimes drama is created for you and one must deal with it head on. I decided against involving the police; for one reason, the only police I saw were hundreds of yards away, directing traffic and parking, and, quite honestly, being a black man, I didn't necessarily trust the police. Second, I was angry enough that I wanted to mix it up with the racist and her husband. Third, as any black man will tell you, interacting with the police, even for mundane reasons, can quickly go sideways.

I had watched which way the woman left the soccer fields area and assumed she would return the same way and that I would be able to see if she returned with a weapon, much less her husband. Sure enough, about twenty minutes after halftime, she returned with a rather large male accompanying her. I could tell there was no visible weapon, even though there could have easily been a concealed one under the rolls of fat on both of the approaching t-shirt-clad mastodons. Those around me cleared out, even though I marched out to the duo to, hopefully, avoid putting anyone else on the sidelines in harm's way. The woman was pointing at me as I approached the two of them.

"Bobby, he's the nigger that assaulted me!" she said.

"First of all, I'm not your nigger! Second of all, I didn't assault you. *You* insulted me, which is what I think your dumbass means, and the entire crowd with your nigger bullshit. Third, we can sort this out right now and see who walks away from here."

Big Bobby looked at me, looked at her, and said, "I don't want any part of this. Let's go."

As he turned and walked away, she said, "Aren't you going to do anything to this nigger?"

"Did you see how big he is?" he said. "I ain't messin' with him!"

When he turned and walked away, I sent him off with a message. "Bobby, get yourself another wife before she gets you hurt! She ain't worth it."

As I watched them walk in the distance, they got into their own skirmish. She smacked him, and he retaliated by punching her in the back of her head.

When I went to work after the holiday weekend and the unfortunate event, I relayed the story to a few coworkers who either lived on Long Island or grew up there. As soon as I mentioned Commack, all of them said they weren't surprised, given the geography. One of my white coworkers told me that Commack was "white trash heaven" and that they wouldn't take their white kids to a tournament there. He said, "Derek, we have more non-white people on this trading floor than they see in a year out in Commack!" I try to not generalize and negatively paint an entire community because of one or a few ignorant people, but, nevertheless, we eliminated this Long Island community as a future tournament destination.

■ ■ ■

On April 17, the Associated Press's Twitter account was hacked and a tweet was sent that stated President Barack Obama was hurt in an explosion at the White House. The equity market instantly dropped 150 points; however, the market quickly rebounded when traders learned the tweet was a hoax. Nevertheless, this activity put everyone on notice that the market was very vulnerable to these false statements, and given the high frequency nature and electronification of the market, with algorithms and automated programs, everyone had to be more on their toes than usual. A trader had to react even quicker and had to determine the veracity of the information before reacting. Easier said than done.

In late April, I visited a few universities in North Carolina with my daughter, including Duke, Elon University, Wake Forest, and Davidson College. Aside from Duke, none of the other North Carolina schools struck a chord with her. She later visited some top-rated schools in California, as well as NYU, in her own backyard. Time would tell.

■ ■ ■

The third and fourth quarters of 2013 were dominated by the feud between President Obama and the Republicans as the White House tried to institute the Affordable Care Act, also known as Obamacare. This feud led to an October shutdown of the government by the Republicans in an attempt to primarily stop the funding of the Act. The stock market reacted daily to comments from both sides of the aisle, which provided significant volatility, 50 percent of a trader's dream. Our principal trading troops played this masterfully and rode the strong performance of the equity market in the third quarter. Our agency sales and trading desks also processed heavy volume, which added to the coffers. The DJIA gained 1.5 percent, the S&P 500 gained 4.7 percent, and the tech-heavy Nasdaq Composite gained a whopping 10.8 percent. We had also installed more automation into our principal trading platform to allow our traders to focus on the larger orders and positions and also allow us to move into and out of strategies at the click of a mouse. Our head quant primarily toiled alone, typically in a room with minimal or no windows, for eight hours a day, while drinking colas and eating sandwiches brought from home. As I previously mentioned, he was "special," but he was a serious money maker up until his strategies and methodologies began to wane and then stop working altogether a few years later.

In early November I returned to Duke's Fuqua School of Business for our semi-annual Board of Visitors meeting. I had been on this board (as of this writing, I am an emeritus board member) since 2004 and thoroughly enjoyed participating and assisting the dean and the school in making the institution the best it could possibly be. The board was, and still is, comprised of many influential business leaders, ranging from CEOs of Fortune 500 companies, to hedge fund leaders, to marketing, legal, and operational gurus of prominent companies. One of things I enjoyed most serving on this board was to learn how the majority think about issues and concerns. This doesn't necessarily mean that people in different places on the color spectrum don't come to the same conclusions, but how we get there can sometimes be a very different course. At any particular board meeting there are approximately thirty to forty members, with only four to six people of color. The gender breakdown was roughly even, but the racial breakdown was less than optimal, and the dean and the administration were very well aware of the disparity and were taking steps to address it. At this particular board meeting, I had a chance to elaborate on the different thought processes that most black people have relative to the thoughts of most white people when it came to charitable contributions.

Educational institutions rely heavily on charitable contributions, and Duke University, despite its $9 billion endowment, is no different. Furthermore, The Fuqua School of Business's individual slice of that overall university endowment is only $270 million and puts the business school at a significant financial disadvantage relative to B-School peers like Wharton, Stanford, Dartmouth, Northwestern, and others. Fuqua's peers can offer fatter salaries to administrators and professors and offer bigger and more scholarships to prospective students, among other things. So, at nearly every meeting, Fuqua's financial position, relative to its peer group, is often discussed. At this meeting, the board was presented with a breakdown of where the most logical contributions were coming from: alumni. Understandably, the older alumni were contributing more than younger alumni. Alumni from Wall Street were contributing more than those alums who had chosen employment in the nonprofit sector. Alumni who had received scholarships and other non-debt funding while at Fuqua were giving back more than those who didn't receive any financial assistance, with one exception: alums of color. One board member rightly, but somewhat tartly, suggested that those who had been granted scholarships should feel a stronger obligation to give back. As a quiet, and slightly uncomfortable, pall came over the room as the minority alum group was somewhat outed, I raised my hand to hopefully provide this individual, and the white room in general, with some minority insight and perspective.

I began with the fact that minorities are just as charitable as the majority but for different causes and at different levels. I didn't want to get too deep into the subject matter, but I started with the fact that, historically, the most important charities to blacks were their churches and other family members who were impoverished. I said there were very few black people on this earth who didn't have a close family member or members who weren't struggling financially. So, if it came down to providing charity to Fuqua or family, family was going to win every time. I offered that this doesn't mean that the majority population also don't have impoverished relatives who need financial assistance, but their situations are generally not as dire and deep as those for people of color. The poverty rate amongst blacks was twice as high as the majority, and high wage minority earners, like the people of color in the room, were probably the first people in their family to make six figure salaries, so our resources are stretched further because the assistance to our impoverished family members is most likely a solo, rather than a multiple family member, effort. I also offered that one must understand that minorities are playing nearly insurmountable catch-up on the financial curve, and outside of Oprah Winfrey and one or two other blacks, generally don't have the same level of resources as the majority. In the back of my mind, I heard my dad's words: "Son, they have a four-hundred-year head start. We'll never catch up as it relates to the depth of our wealth relative to theirs, but we have to start somewhere. You have been allowed to participate, so it may as well start with you and your generation."

When I finished my explanation, there was a long pregnant pause, because I think most of the board had never heard or thought about this perspective, least not from me, and they didn't know whether to follow up with a comment or wait for the dean to move to the next subject on the agenda. I wasn't sure if what I said resonated with anyone until we had a break from the meeting and several board members thanked me for my perspective out in the hallway.

■ ■ ■

The balance of 2013 followed the script of the first three quarters. Equity markets shrugged off Washington budget concerns and shutdowns, and my work at Pershing continued on an upward trajectory. The various trading desks for which I was responsible were cranking out the numbers, and the year progressed to the holidays on auto-pilot. On the personal front, I sold the apartment I owned in the Williamsburg section of Brooklyn and moved into a rental apartment on the Upper West Side of Manhattan. This put me closer to my kids and health club, and it allowed me to leave my car in the garage and commute to work. I also received the best housewarming gift I could have imagined a few days after moving into my new apartment: Kara was accepted to Duke University's freshman class in August 2014. Job well done, honey. Job well done. Hallelujah!

23

MY LAST GOOD YEAR AT PERSHING

I n 2013, the equity market closed extraordinarily strong, as the DJIA clocked in its best year since 1998, closing up 26.5 percent. The broader market index, the S&P 500, had its strongest performance since 1997, exiting on December 31 up 29.6 percent. The Nasdaq Composite recorded its best showing in four years since the repair work from the financial crisis and weighed in up a remarkable 38 percent. This considerable strength logically led most pundits to believe that 2014 would not be nearly as strong as 2013 and could, in fact, become a bear market at some point.

One of the primary themes around the country in the first quarter of 2014 was the terribly cold weather in much of the country. This cold weather dampened economic activity, and this, in combination with the new Federal Reserve president, Janet Yellen, leading a paring back of its asset purchases, led to some early sluggishness in the stock market. The fact that emerging markets were also under pressure due to rising international interest rates also provided downward momentum after such a great year. In January, the DJIA lopped off 5 percent, the S&P 3 percent, and the Nasdaq Composite 2 percent. The principal trading desk's 2013 strategy of staying long and riding the wave would most likely not be a profitable strategy this year. We got clipped pretty good in January, a timing that I always hated. To start the year in the hole is tough on the psyche and causes upper management to put the trading head on speed dial early and often. This quick market correction wasn't a total surprise, given the prior year performance, but when it happens with such rapidity, it is still a rude awakening.

I personally felt the ramifications of harsh weather at my Hudson Valley weekend home when I walked in the door on January 11 and discovered a three-inch swimming pool all over the first floor, after a pipe had exploded in the kitchen. If I hadn't come home sooner, who knows how deep the "pool" would have been!   Thank goodness for Allstate and their $120,000 check!

As the expectation of a pullback in the equity market began to become a reality, the yield curve continued to flatten, as short-term yields held steady while long-term rates declined. The Russian invasion of the Crimea region of Ukraine in February added to the international nervousness of the world's markets. Just as it seemed like the market would never see a downtick in 2013, it felt like we would never see an uptick in 2014. I recall nursing a bad, long Amazon position for a few days with my Amazon trader and him stating, "I think this stock is just going to go down $2 every day to zero!" (The stock traded down from approximately $400 in the beginning of the year to $304, down 24 percent, by April 30.) The Wall Street expression, stolen from the drug world, was, "Don't get high on your own supply," was also applicable here.

By the end of the first quarter, I was ready for a vacation. The seemingly daily bad news about the Russian invasion, the submerging emerging markets, and worldwide asset uncertainty made me certain that I needed some time away, so my travel partners and I took a look at a world map and decided that the three of us should head to Colombia, South America. As we researched the country and began to put together an itinerary, I consulted a New York-based Colombian friend who said, "You and your buddies have a good time, but don't get scoped!" I initially thought he was referring to us getting shot with a scope rifle by the communist guerilla forces known as FARC (Revolutionary Armed Forces of Colombia) in the woods of Colombia, but he said that scoping is a term for getting drugged by a substance called scopolamine, which is plentiful in Colombia. It's also called devil's breath, and if you get any on you, inhale it, or drink it, it will make you like a zombie. He further explained that you stay awake and conscious under the influence of this drug, but you lose all sense of right and wrong. He told me stories about people getting scoped and willingly emptying their bank accounts while standing with the criminal at the ATM. He said there was one story about a guy getting scoped and him helping criminals empty out his entire apartment and then wondering what happened to his furniture after the drug wore off. Despite these and some of the other horror stories we'd heard about Colombia, we decided that if we stuck together and stayed acutely aware, that we would be safe.

When we landed in Bogota, the first leg of our three-city vacation, we were immediately on the defensive. My Colombian friend had forewarned me about airport taxi drivers taking some sort of antidote and then burning scopolamine as incense, with the air conditioning on and the windows rolled up, and then dropping off "willing tourists" on the side of the road wearing nothing but their birthday suits! It seems our taxi driver was ready to play that game with us, but before he went further, all three of us yelled, "Keep the windows down!" I'm not sure he understood what we said, but he got our message. So much for getting away from the stress of the trading desk.

Our stay in Bogota and Medellin was wonderful and uneventful, which was fine by me. I can't say the same for Cartagena, the last stop of our Colombian tour. We took a taxi from the airport to the famous/infamous Hotel Caribe. This is the hotel where President Obama's Secret Service detail had gotten in trouble with hookers, but I figured if the hotel was good enough for the Secret Service, it was good enough for us, despite the prostitution association.

As I was checking in at the hotel desk, a pretty Colombian lady sidled up to me and caressed my arm. I was a bit startled, but I thought perhaps she worked for the hotel. I was about to sign the bill when I saw an additional charge for the room. When I asked about it, the desk attendant told me it was for the extra towels and sheets. I asked why I needed extra towels and sheets, and he pointed to the pretty Colombian lady who was now nearly stuck to my side. The ensuing exchange I had with the desk clerk made me feel like I was in a Laurel and Hardy Who's on First routine, but in the end, the young lady realized she wasn't a welcome guest as I peeled her off me. I later learned that the Secret Service were publicly exposed by the hotel, not the prostitutes, because the officers refused to pay the additional charge for the extra towels and sheets.

Aside from this incident, the remainder of our trip was pleasant, and we arrived back home unscathed and unscoped.

■ ■ ■

Back at Pershing's headquarters in Jersey City, we continued working on a previously agreed to merger of two broker-dealers within the Bank of New York Mellon. In 2012, two different fixed income divisions within BNY (Pershing's fixed income department and a legacy fixed income business at BNY) were merged, and the combined entity was physically wedged into some existing space at a BNY building on Water Street, in Lower Manhattan. They got there just in time to have their building nearly float away when Hurricane Sandy washed ashore in late October, which crimped operations there for some time.

I was grateful and glad that the fixed income department at Pershing had moved first, allowing the equity division leadership to learn what to do and not do, and perhaps have some of the "trip wires" revealed, which is always inevitable in a merger, whether it is intra-company or two different companies. Aside from the meshing of people and technology in one physical footprint, not surprisingly, the personalities and the differing cultures became the biggest impediment to a smooth transition.

The equity leadership teams on both sides of the Hudson, the BNY compliance and legal staffs, and the FINRA industry regulators, spent many hours nailing down the particulars of the merger, evidenced in a document called a 10-19. The regulators were concerned about many aspects of the physical and structural move, including what the reporting lines and exact responsibilities would be in the combined entity. There was also major concern about the technological aspects of the move, as no one wanted any errant orders or runaway algorithms to surface when we flipped the *unified* switch. We tried to examine every single aspect of the combination of Pershing's equity business with the legacy BNY equity unit, but with so many moving parts, it was inevitable that something would be missed.

The biggest financial asset related theme in the second half of the year was the initially mysterious 40 percent drop in oil prices. In June, a barrel of oil stood around $115, and by December, oil was trading around $70. All sorts of reasons and ramifications of cheap oil were being thrown about, but by year end, it was generally agreed that the downdraft in oil was just a supply and demand equilibrium. OPEC and other oil-producing countries seemingly turned a blind eye to a slowing worldwide economy and the significantly stepped-up drilling and oil production in the United States. Both equity and fixed income traders were paying more attention to oil prices than they had in over a decade, if not longer.

On the personal front, I dedicated the second half of 2014 spending quality time with Kara and Julian. Kara's high school graduation gift request was to travel to London with me for five days, and Julian's desire was to follow one of his passions and attend the U.S. Formula One Grand Prix race in Austin, Texas. Both trips provided interesting racial observations.

I had been to London no less than twenty-five times over the course of my working career and knew the city fairly well from a business perspective; however, I had only been to London as a true tourist a handful of times, and the experiences were markedly different.

We stayed at the same posh hotel we stayed in on the last family vacation in the summer of 2007, before the marital split in 2008. Unlike in 2007, where I mapped out the entire itinerary for the family, this time, Kara handled that duty. She primarily wanted to go shopping and eat at interesting restaurants. I was clueless on the teenage shopping tips, but I did offer a number of dining recommendations, including my favorite Chinese restaurant on the planet, Hunan, in the Belgravia section of London. I had been there so many times that I got to know the owner/father, Pang, and his son, Michael.

As Kara and I walked the streets and shopped on Portobello Road and Spitalfields Market, I noticed a much more diverse city than I had in my twenty-five years of visiting London. When I made my first trip in 1992, every face I saw was paler than mine, and I'm pretty pale. I only started to consistently see people of color on a regular basis in London well into the new millennium. It seemed that London had become a more cosmopolitan city under Prime Minister Tony Blair, who was prime minister from 1997 to 2007. During that time, I noticed an increasing number of people of color each and every visit. Not only did the cuisines of London multiply, but it became a much more exciting and vibrant city from an entertainment and nightlife standpoint. As much as I abhorred visiting London during the nineties, due to its lack of diversity, bad food, in my view, and a lack of sun, it ended up becoming one of my favorite international cities.

■ ■ ■

Back in New York, on Friday, August 15, after the close of the market, we moved the Pershing equity trading operation from Jersey City to 101 Barclay Street, in lower Manhattan, one block away from the West Side Highway, one block away from Goldman Sachs' headquarters, and two blocks from the new World Trade Center complex. The 101 trading floor had been built out in the previous six months in preparation for our move. The combined fixed income division had moved in approximately six months earlier, leaving their dark and cramped trading floor on Water Street. The fourth-floor space was brand spanking new and held a lot of promise, if only from a physical standpoint, because now we had all the trading businesses: fixed income, equity, options, and foreign exchange sitting together with compliance, legal, technology, and support personnel sprinkled in between. The various businesses in close proximity can help immensely from a market intelligence standpoint. For instance, the bond traders can give the equity traders a quick verbal heads up, and vice versa, if something extraordinary

365

happens in their respective market, at times before the event hits the tape for all market participants to see and react.

After the move, which went swimmingly well, we all settled in and got used to our new surroundings. The balance of the summer was slow from a volume standpoint, but market moving events continued to happen all around us, most of them internationally. The timing of our move was excellent, given that there weren't any huge dislocations in the market, and that allowed us to get our physical bearings, work out small technology kinks, and get used to our new surroundings.

Toward the end of August, I proudly dropped Kara off at Duke University. I couldn't have been happier for her, as she had worked her tail off to make this happen. At the other end of the spectrum was my sad bank account. The all-in cost (i.e., tuition, room and board, books, supplies, two trips home a year, etc.) to attend Duke University was roughly $65,000 a year. When my dad dropped me off in August 1975, the all-in cost of attendance was less than $5,000. Thankfully, I was on a full athletic scholarship and my parents didn't have to sell my younger brother to raise the funds for me. (In 2019–2020, the all-in cost is $73,500.)

As I left Kara, I told her to "grab the whole ball of wax." I'm sure she had no idea what the hell I was talking about, but those were the same words my dad said to me when he dropped me off in 1975. It meant, get involved in everything you can and maximize your experience. I knew Kara would excel at doing just that.

At the end of October, I took Julian to the U.S. Formula One Grand Prix. As I mentioned previously, he's had a lifelong passion for cars and racing, and he was really looking forward to attending this race. We had previously been to the Brickyard 400, the 400-mile NASCAR race in Indianapolis, and we laughed at the lack of diversity at the Austin venue, as we counted less than 10 black people in the crowd of approximately 250,000 people who attended the race. I'm sure there were a few more, but clearly car racing, at least NASCAR racing, is not on most black people's bucket list. Julian thought the racial makeup of the Austin crowd would be more diverse, especially since one of the top Formula 1 drivers, Lewis Hamilton, was black, even though he was British.

Over the three-day event, we realized that even Lewis Hamilton didn't bring out more people of color to the event. In fact, when I heard someone yell, "Yee-haw," I told Julian we may as well be deep in Alabama! Julian said that if a race riot broke out, we'd be toast!

We ended our visit with a trip to Driftwood, Texas, about twenty-five miles outside of Austin, where we were told we would find some excellent food at Salt Lick BBQ; maybe we'd even find some black people, given our love of BBQ. Well, at least we scored on great BBQ!

■ ■ ■

The 4th quarter of 2014 warded off the plummeting oil prices, the Russian aggression in Ukraine, ISIS terrorists taking control of three cities in Iraq, the Ebola virus outbreak in West Africa, and a soaring dollar. While international markets swooned, the U.S. equity market became the safest haven for equity investors, and the S&P 500 was up 4 percent in the fourth quarter alone. For the year, the S&P 500 finished up 11.4 percent, its third straight year of double-digit gains. The DOW closed up 7.5 percent for the year, and the tech-based Nasdaq Composite 13.4 percent.

I closed out the year with a trip to Tel Aviv with my friend Owen May; we met another friend there. This was my first time in Israel, and I was quite impressed with Tel Aviv, especially the food, but I was really looking forward to a planned trip to the holy city of Jerusalem. The friend we met in Tel Aviv had a relative who was close to or in the intelligence agency, Mossad, and told us that it wouldn't be wise to visit Jerusalem during our stay. About three weeks prior to our visit, there was a violent massacre at a synagogue in Jerusalem, where five people were slaughtered and seven people injured by two Arabs wielding an axe, a meat cleaver, and a gun.

While in Tel Aviv, there were reports of terrorists running over pedestrians with cars on the street curbs of Jerusalem. There were also spotty reports of stabbings in various areas near the Gaza Strip and Jerusalem, as well as constant conflict between the Palestinians and the Israelis. We were extremely disappointed that Jerusalem was off the itinerary, but our intel had been pretty accurate, so we laid low. Instead of going to see the Wailing Wall, the Holy Mount, the Dead Sea, and other sacred sites, we spent more time in places like Jaffa and the Tel Aviv Port. I had taken a solo trip to Jaffa looking for a nice piece of pottery for my collection of pottery from around the world. The cab driver on the way to Jaffa asked me if I had been to the place with the best hummus in Israel. I told him I hadn't, and he said that if I did nothing else in Jaffa, to make sure I went to Abu Hassan Homos and have some hummus. My friends and I did go to what's actually a little hole-in-the-wall restaurant, but it did have the best hummus I'd ever had.

On my return trip from Jaffa to Tel Aviv, with pottery in hand, the Arab taxi driver asked my nationality. I told him that I was an American black, to which he replied in broken English, "You guys have it almost as bad as us Arabs have it in Israel!" I then asked him why there couldn't be peace in Israel, and he said they just want their own homeland, but the Jews didn't want them to have it. I told him I thought the Palestinians and Jews were working toward a two-state nation, but he said that would never happen, and even if it did, they would get the shitty part of Israel and the Jews would still try to rule them.

I wished the cab driver well as I exited the vehicle, and he said, "If you come back ten years from now or a hundred years from now, it will be the same shit. Have a nice day."

My buddies and I spent one of our last nights in Tel Aviv, at an Israeli sports bar, Mike's Place, next to the American Embassy and about fifty yards from our hotel, which overlooked the Tel Aviv Mediterranean beach. We watched a live televised Duke basketball game in the bar, and I mentioned to my friend that at least we were safe here. He surprised me when he said the bar was the location of a suicide bomber attack a few years prior that killed a few people and wounded many more. I pulled out my phone to verify the incident, and sure enough, in 2003, the bombing killed three people and wounded fifty others. Suddenly, I wasn't feeling so safe, so I dropped some shekels on the table for my food and headed for the door. "Duke is probably going to win this game, so I'll get with you guys in the morning. Not being sent back to New York in pieces!"

24

THE FIRST FULL YEAR AT THE COMBINED PERSHING AND BNY EQUITY SALES AND TRADING ENTITY

The Greek debt crisis and concern about the crisis spreading across Europe, continuing oil price declines, a sharp economic slowdown in China, trepidation about the Fed raising rates after years of artificially low rates, and teetering emerging markets were more than enough to cause almost daily dramatic moves in the 2015 equity market. The trading desks I managed deftly handled the volatility, as we posted good numbers for the first quarter. Sprinkled in between was an active February in which the firm made a valiant effort to celebrate Black History Month with various educational programs and outreach efforts. I participated in one of the events by interviewing a prominent black leader from a competitor Wall Street firm.

Thankfully, by early March, equity trading had posted a solid two months, and given that I had very capable people managing the various businesses for which I was responsible, I was able to take what had become one of my favorite three-day excursions to Las Vegas, for the NCAA college basketball tournament. I stayed at The Palazzo at The Venetian, where I found a home for the next few days in their wonderful sports book facility, Lagasse's Stadium. The plush stadium seating, surrounded by massive television screens and betting boards, as well as the topnotch food, made for a most enjoyable ten hours each day. (Sadly, the pandemic of 2020 has caused my favorite venue in Vegas to permanently close).

Most of the guys were wearing their favorite team's gear, and I was no different, even though my allegiance was a bit understated. During a bathroom break, a guy asked me what the white D on my navy shirt stood for. I told him Duke. I think the guy was a little tipsy, as he next asked if I went to Duke or just cheered for those assholes. I told him I was a Duke grad, to which he replied that he thought the only black people who got into Duke were basketball players. I was a little peeved at this point, so I told him maybe the alcohol had him stuck in the 1950s. Not that he cared, but I told him the only two requirements to get into Duke were to be smart and respectful, and I doubted he'd qualify on either front.

After raking in a few dollars and watching the Duke Blue Devils win a couple games to proceed to the next round of the tournament, I returned back to the trading floor of BNY Mellon.

Two weeks after the Las Vegas trip, I traveled to Indianapolis to watch my Blue Devils win the national championship over the Wisconsin Badgers. I took my son with me this time. At the championship game between Duke and Wisconsin, Julian, being the very observant and race-conscious person that he is, mentioned how few black people were in the stadium. He wasn't surprised at the absence of black people at the Formula 1 races the previous year, but this was basketball, the black people's sport, where most of the players are black! All I could do was shrug my shoulders and offer that maybe it was an economic thing. I was just happy that I'd be taking home a Duke championship hat to display in my office!

■ ■ ■

In late May, my Italian girlfriend and I took off for Istanbul, Turkey, and Athens, Greece. Istanbul is a fascinating place, the Middle East's most populous city, boasting nearly sixteen million people (nearly twice the population of New York City). Over the course of four days, we covered this historic gem, the only major city to span two continents (Europe and Asia), as its 2,063 square miles straddle the Bosporus River, whose strait is the conduit between the Black and Mediterranean Seas. Being the shopper that I am, I first wanted to visit the Grand Bazaar, which has more than 4,000 primarily rug and craft shops, stretching through miles of streets and alleys. One could easily get lost in this maze of passageways. I challenge any newcomer to find his way back to their original starting point.

In addition to shopping, we went to the Hippodrome, the Museum of Turkish and Islamic Art, the Basilica Cistern, and the beautiful Blue Mosque, named so because of its cobalt blue tiles. We also toured the Ayasofya (aka Hagia Sophia) Mosque, one of the world's architectural masterpieces. Our last visit of note was a trip to the sprawling Topkapi Palace, where we came upon the harem complex, where the sultans of the fifteenth and sixteenth centuries kept their harems of women, who were protected by palace guards around the clock. Our guide told us that the guards were castrated so that they wouldn't feel compelled to screw any of the women in the harem, but, apparently, it was discovered that even a eunuch could still impregnate one of the sultan's harem. The sultan further realized that he wouldn't be able to tell if a child was his or one of his guards, since the guards were the same nationality as the royal. As a result, the sultan decided to employ only black men in his stable of guards, who were also castrated, because if a member of his harem yielded a black child, the sultan would definitely know that the child was not of royal sultan blood. I walked away from this exhibit, where the castrating instrument was displayed, with my legs crunched up in a protective position and in somewhat disbelief. I also wondered if those black guards knew what awaited them when they were "promoted."

From Turkey, we took a ninety-minute flight across the Aegean Sea to Athens. This trip was a dual-purpose excursion, as my daughter was in the Greek islands attending an educational summer program studying ancient Greece. We had planned our visit to Athens to coincide with her group's three-day visit to Athens.

The first evening, my girlfriend and I had a lovely dinner at the Tudor Restaurant in the King George Hotel on Syntagma Square, in the heart of Athens. Our early evening view was breathtaking, as we looked out on the lit Parthenon, sitting a few miles away on the Acropolis, which we visited the next day. Some call the Parthenon the most important ancient site in the Western world. We also walked through the Erechtheion Sanctuary, the temple of Athena Nike, and the performing arts area known as Odeon Herodes Atticus while on the Acropolis. We next ventured down the elevation to the Acropolis Museum, which is built over an adjacent city to the Acropolis but has a glass floor throughout so you can see the ancient city beneath. It's an engineering marvel and absolutely stunning.

From the Acropolis, we walked back to the hotel through the Plaka area, full of charming shops and restaurants. The only unfortunate thing about strolling through the shops was that I started to feel like I was back in the States, as more than a few shop owners followed me around. I guess paranoid racism exists everywhere. My girlfriend remarked that if she hadn't seen it for herself, she wouldn't have believed the unfortunate surveillance.

That evening we had dinner with Kara on the rooftop of the famous Hotel Grand Bretagne, a sister hotel to the King George, at the GB Rooftop restaurant. Kara said she was glad to see me and my girlfriend but that she hoped I had some hard currency—in this case euros—for her. Actually, she wasn't out of money; she was just having trouble getting money out of the ATM because there was a run on hard cash in Greece.

We were in Athens when Greece was on the verge of leaving, or getting tossed out, of the eurozone and badly in need of a financial bailout by the European Union before the country went belly up. Unlike a number of other affected countries, Greece was still reeling from the 2008 worldwide financial crisis and was in serious debt and about to be booted out of the eurozone, for starters. If that happened, one of the serious ramifications was that the citizens believed the euros they held would be converted to the old Greek drachmas, and the conversion wouldn't be a one-for-one conversion. Euro holders in Greece would receive something significantly less, so the Greek citizens were taking as many euros out of the banks as quickly as possible, before their accounts were either frozen or they received an unjust conversion. Kara was caught in the middle. Conversely, I was sitting pretty with U.S. dollars in hand, along with my euros, and I also received substantial discounts for everything I paid in dollars rather than euros. The green back was indeed king and sought after by every merchant in Athens. If the merchants recognized me as an American, many times they asked for greenbacks in exchange for a discount on my purchases.

We ended our trip by visiting Athens' Central Market, strolling through the district on Voukourestiou Street, and then taking a cable car/funicular to the top of Lykavittos Hill (Hill of Wolves) to take in the great panoramic views of the city.

■　■　■

Back in the Big Apple, I returned to work and felt the daily push and pull of the Greek financial crisis affecting U.S. capital markets. I felt like I understood the scenario better than most after having seen it up close and personal. I told my traders that I felt that Greece was on the brink of anarchy and that we should have a short bias to the market for the next few weeks until the Greece situation got sorted out or the place went up in flames. As we intently watched what was going on in Greece and the eurozone, a major problem a little further east of Greece began to bubble up. Chinese investors, especially retail investors, had been piling into Chinese equities with reckless abandon for the last twelve to eighteen months. These investors seemingly had no regard for company earnings and prospects. In June, the bubble in China was pricked and the Shanghai Composite Index lost nearly a third of its value before rebounding sharply. This volatility continued through the summer, and each morning, when our traders arrived, we first had to see what China had done overnight. In five days, the Shanghai Composite had lost a teeth-rattling 20 percent. The Chinese market volatility affected worldwide markets and was clearly the dog wagging the tail of every other market. In August, the Shanghai really got clobbered, as it dropped 8.5 percent, its largest one-day implosion since the worldwide financial crisis in 2007. Our traders once again handled the volatility with aplomb.

In October, I once again felt the itch to travel abroad, since everything at the office, at least trading-wise, was under control. The traders, led by the very capable Brian Hayes, were a seasoned and disciplined crew that had been with me for eight years now, and I felt very fortunate to have them.

I decided on traveling to South America again, specifically to Santiago, Chile, and Buenos Aires, Argentina. I planned on traveling with my two friends who went to Columbia with me, but two weeks before we were scheduled to leave, they both had to cancel, for legitimate reasons. I contemplated canceling the now solo trip, but since I had the time and had planned the trip to a T, I kept my plans.

The trip from the airport to my hotel in Santiago traversed extensive slums and shacks adjacent to the Mapocho River, a river that divides North and South Santiago, the capital city that holds nearly a third of Chile's eighteen million total population. The democracy that arose in 1990 after seventeen years of military rule under dictator Augusto Pinochet had obviously served some of Chile's citizens well and others not so well, as I saw pockets of dire poverty along the river, while the mountainous area known as Santa Maria de Manquehue displayed immense wealth.

The city was more modern and hipper than I had anticipated, with upscale shopping and great restaurants. It possessed the largest mall in South America, the Castanera Center, which took up six floors of a seventy-five-story building, the tallest building in South America. My hotel was located in a nearby neighborhood called Sanhattan, named for its international and economic flavor, similar to Manhattan. As usual, on my trips, I enjoyed visiting the local food markets, and Santiago boasted one of the top ten in the world, La Vega Centra, which covers nearly 650,000 square feet. This heavily French-influenced country, whose primary industries are copper mining, fruit, timber, and fishing, is truly a jewel, and at the time of my visit had South America's strongest economy.

During my three-day stay in Argentina, I learned a lot from the local taxi drivers, hotel employees, and various merchants. They saw the government as corrupt; the unemployment rate was staggering; the people didn't vote because they didn't believe it effected change; the country was in debt; and there was no middle class. You are either rich or poor. From my own observations, it's just not a very friendly city, and the food is very expensive, which says a lot coming from a New Yorker.

I spent my last day in Buenos Aires focusing on food and fun, treating myself to a few great meals, visiting some of the local shops, and topping off the day watching an exquisite Tango routine at the hotel. It was a nice way to top off an interesting, albeit eye-opening, vacation, but I was more than ready to get back home.

■ ■ ■

In the last two months of 2015, the markets settled down a bit as the trading community had become somewhat numb to China, Greece, oil, and the eurozone issues. The merger and acquisition departments of Wall Street firms were also busy, setting a record for the value of the deals being consummated at slightly less than $5 trillion; however, the stock market volatility was replaced by internal BNY volatility, as the third leader of the Capital Markets division arrived in a span of less than eighteen months.

My last hurrah in 2015 away from the BNY trading desk involved the trading of a Pershing client. I was asked to testify on behalf of Pershing regarding a trader at Rochdale Securities, a client of ours, who bought 1.625 million shares of Apple stock when he was supposed to only buy 1,625 shares, an obvious substantial difference. It was later reported that the trader intentionally bought the exaggerated amount and was intending to share in the profits with his client if the stock appreciated and would claim an honest purchase mistake if the stock depreciated. The purchases took place right before Apple reported earnings after the close that particular day, and the stock cratered immediately after the unauthorized purchase, as Apple's earnings report was below expectations. Pershing, being the clearing firm for Rochdale Securities, would have significant financial exposure if Rochdale went under with the $1 billion dollar stock purchase. Senior Pershing management ordered the Rochdale superiors to immediately unwind the trade after it was discovered. The client claimed that the immediate and forced liquidation of the Apple position, at the behest of Pershing, rather than an allowance to finesse and trade the position, led to Rochdale violating regulatory capital limits and subsequently being forced out of business. I was asked to provide some technical information to a FINRA (the securities industry regulatory body) arbitration panel regarding what trading information was communicated by Pershing in the aftermath of the unauthorized, speculative trade. I also testified that if Rochdale had acted when Pershing instructed them to and traded the bad position aggressively, their "hit" would have been substantially less than the $5.3 million loss it turned out to be. I testified once more in December and firmly believed that Rochdale had a very weak case in its attempt to recover financial damages from Pershing. (In October 2016, a judge ruled that Rochdale was due $8 million in damages from Pershing.)

■ ■ ■

Despite the tumultuous and highly volatile year with China, Greece, plummeting oil prices, and the Federal Reserve's first interest rate increase in nearly a decade the DJIA only closed down 2.2 percent, the S&P closed down less than 1 percent, and the Nasdaq Composite ended up 5.7 percent. What a boring year it was. Not!

25

TOUGH MARKET

Twenty-sixteen started off with a very loud, negative bang, as the continually weakening Chinese economy and plunging oil prices depressed world equity markets and helped to take a quick 6 percent off the DJIA in the first week. The velocity and depth of this sell-off caught many of our traders by surprise, as they had never witnessed this before this early in the year. Quite frankly, no other traders on the Street had witnessed this type of action right out of the chute in the history of the market either, as this was the first time this had happened to start a year.

While we got clipped a bit at the close of the first day of trading, it could have been much worse. At least that's what I told one of the members of the senior management team when he called at the close of the market and asked if we had any money left. I sarcastically told him that I thought we could open for business the next day, but I may have to hit a Brink's truck on the way in to work!

As an aside, I went by myself to see the Broadway hit *Hamilton* on a night I would have been better off going home and collapsing, as I had an aisle seat in one of the upper tiers, and my knees were scrunched up into my chest and my posterior wedged into a matchbox seat. *Hamilton* is a play that requires paying close attention or you'll will miss essential dialogue, and I was struggling to follow the quick dialogue and rapping from the outset. It didn't help that the wife sitting next to me kept asking her husband what was said every other passage, and they got into a small argument as he became annoyed. I was annoyed as well, as their back and forth prevented me from hearing the play. One thing she said, however, caused me to turn and look her squarely in the face, while throwing a disgusted nod to her husband, in a "You'd better get your wife under control" manner. During one of the scenes she said, "Why did they get nothing but niggers and spics to do this play? There were lots of white people during that time. This is not realistic." I couldn't hear the husband's response to his wife as he whispered in her ear, but I think the woman had no idea that I was black, not that a white person wouldn't have also been offended by the racist remark. I missed at least the next twenty minutes of the play as my mind raced and I looked for a non-existent empty seat in which to move.

At work the next day, a number of people asked what I thought about the play, saying, "Wasn't it great?" They were a bit perplexed that I said it was just alright. I only told a few friends what had happened at the play, and, in all fairness, I couldn't really judge how good it was because I had heard very little of it, primarily due to that woman's racist comments and how they affected me.

■ ■ ■

By mid-February, oil had bottomed around $26 a barrel and the U.S. equity market bottomed with it. By mid-March, the DJIA was positive for the year and the next few months were choppy, but nothing like the previous volatility. One of the bigger stories of the spring was the corporate scandal and subsequent unwinding of a $90 billion drug company called Valeant Pharmaceuticals. I served on the Fuqua Board of Visitors with the pharmaceutical concern's CEO, Michael Pearson, and for a few years had followed the building of his company since he became CEO in 2008. Pearson's apparent business model was to buy other drug companies with promising products rather than grow organically, and not have to spend millions on research and development. Once a new company was under his umbrella, he squeezed costs out of the company and raised the prices on its drugs. Pearson bought over a hundred companies in a little under seven years, and he did everything with his shareholders and the tax code in mind. His reported motto was "Bet on management, not on science."

In the spring of 2016, Valeant's house of cards came tumbling down, as its accounting methodology was called into question, as well as its ethics in raising drug prices to exorbitant levels. In our Fuqua School of Business board meetings, I had mentally noted that Pearson wasn't anything like the typical CEO, certainly not like any that had come and gone since my joining the board in 2004. He didn't remotely mirror other board member CEOs like Robert McDonald and David Taylor of Proctor & Gamble, Gerald Hassell of BNY Mellon, Joe Swedish of health care company Anthem, or Rick Wagoner of GM, not that him being different was a negative. He just appeared to me to be very seat-of-the-pants reactive, rather than the typical pensive CEO, but I guess that approach worked well for him and his firm until it didn't. Pearson unsurprisingly had bold ideas and some of them I thought were very good. However, at one meeting he suggested that in order to instantly prop up the Fuqua School's endowment during one of its capital campaigns, everyone on the roughly 40- to 50-person board should give a million dollars, and that would get us to our goal. I remember looking around the room after this comment and catching the eye of B-School friend and fellow board member Owen May and both of us silently mouthing, "This dude is crazy," certainly given my previous soliloquy about the average black person and their charitable priorities and financial wherewithal.

■ ■ ■

Back at BNY Mellon, the possibility of the United Kingdom breaking away from the European Union was brewing. A rise of nationalism, selfish economics, and a distrust of the British elite led the Brits to insist on a referendum for mid-year. Most people on this side of the Atlantic felt there was no way that the citizens of the UK would vote to leave the EU. I was so certain that the Brits would vote to stay in the EU and that the markets would remain calm that I booked a trip to Montreal with my girlfriend right around that time; however, that trip was quickly nixed. On the morning of June 24, 2016, in a public vote the previous day, British citizens, by a margin of 52 to 48 percent, elected to leave the European Union, an economic and political entity of which they had been a part since 1973. Many people, including me, found it hysterical that the most active search on Google in the UK after the vote was, *what is Brexit?*

The British pound fell sharply, and the UK's primary stock market index, the FTSE, immediately imploded about 9 percent on the opening, even though it recovered to close down only 3 percent. Other European markets fell as sharply but stayed there, as the feeling was that Europe, in general, would fare worse than the UK, with the UK's so-called Brexit decision. The two major equity markets in France and Germany closed down a bit below 7 and 8 percent, respectively. This weakness spilled over into the U.S. market, to complete the global rout, as the DJIA closed down 611 points, or 3.4 percent, and all the U.S. equity indices went into negative territory for the year. Our trading desk was luckier than smart, as we heavily bought the opening as investors panicked out of equities, and, thankfully, we were able to sell in the first significant uptick that day and escape financial danger. If the market had continued south, we would have had more than the usual headache.

That Friday evening, I attended a memorial service for a fellow Fuqua alum and fellow Fuqua Board of Visitors member, Sanjay Valvani. Sanjay was only forty-four years old, a family man, and very personable. He worked at a New York City-based, $8 billion hedge fund as a portfolio manager and had recently been indicted for insider trading, related to an apparent conspiracy with an FDA official, where he was reportedly getting non-public information on drug applications. Sanjay claimed he was innocent of the $32 million scheme and that the Feds didn't have a real case against him. Although he didn't discuss the details of the case with me, he said he expected to be exonerated at trial. On Father's Day, he celebrated the day with his lovely wife and two young daughters. The next day, Monday evening, he was found dead in the kitchen of his Brooklyn Heights townhouse, where he had slashed his own throat. Obviously, his death at such a young age, and over such a bad situation, was tragic for his family and friends alike.

■ ■ ■

In July, I had an opportunity to put another data point on the board regarding black people's attendance at sporting events when I attended the PGA Championship at the famous Baltusrol Golf Club in New Jersey, at the invitation of the Duke University Athletic Department. Sadly, I think Shane Battier, one of the Duke alums, and I represented about 25 percent of the black people in attendance.

■ ■ ■

The U.S. equity market climbed from the Brexit-related abyss through the summer and traded in a fairly tight range into the fall. Our trading desk was slightly below our revenue budget at this point, and we were hopeful that a volatile fall would help us close the gap. We were also upgrading our market-making technology, specifically our quantitative trading platform, while also building strategies and algorithms to quickly respond to changing market dynamics.

Back at 101 Barclay, the new head of Capital Markets brought in a consultant in mid-September to analyze the equity business, among others, and detail the state of the business and potentially make recommendations regarding how to improve the operation.

I expected the fourth quarter to be a humdinger, internally and externally. Internally, we all awaited the consultant's report on the various businesses. Externally, the November presidential election between Hillary Clinton and Donald Trump was certain to roil securities markets one way or the the other, as the division in the country between the Democratic candidate and the Republican candidate was as stark as ever. The market was expecting a Democratic victory, given the Trump pre-election campaign.

I decided to spend my last week left of my vacation time bouncing around Europe, with my daughter as the primary incentive, as she was spending the fall semester of her junior year at Duke studying in Barcelona.

It was great to experience this vibrant city through her eyes, and it turned out to be one of my more memorable trips anywhere, as she was the perfect tour guide.

I really enjoyed my time with my daughter as we explored the city's treasures, like the stunning Sagrada Familia Basilica, and we capped off our last evening together at perhaps the world's most fascinating food market, La Boqueria, on the Las Ramblas. A perfect way to end our trip.

From Barcelona, I traveled alone to Palma, Mallorca, a small Mediterranean island I had always wanted to visit, known for its laid-back reputation and outstanding craft venues. At dinner one evening, a European couple seated next to me asked if I was American. I affirmed I was. They said they had watched the U.S. presidential debate between Hillary Clinton and Donald Trump and asked if I had seen it, which I did. The gentleman then said, "Trump is an outrage machine! Why do Americans like him?" I just raised my hands in agreeing disbelief and told him that, hopefully, we'd only have to deal with him for another few weeks.

I ended my trip in Lisbon, Portugal, where I spent three days roaming through the Chiado, Baixa, Bairro Alto, and Alfama neighborhoods and enjoying the local cuisine at each stop. Note to travelers to Lisbon: wear comfortable shoes to traverse the cobblestone streets and spend some time upping your cardio fitness, as the land of the seven hills will definitely challenge you!

■ ■ ■

In the early morning hours of Wednesday, November 9, the country, and perhaps the world, was coming to terms with the fact that Donald Trump would be the 45th president of the United States. To say his victory was shocking, regardless of one's political affiliation, would be an understatement. Like most Americans, I watched the election returns Tuesday night and into early Wednesday morning with my mouth agape. Throughout the night, as the state-by-state returns came in, I received calls and texts from my Democratic friends who shared their utter disbelief and shock at the election results. The stock market was in shock too and reacted very quickly, as the DJIA futures that evening plummeted 900 points as it became clear that Trump was going to win.

While I wanted to get some sleep before sitting in the hot seat at work the next morning, I spent a bit of time responding to texts from friends around the world. But the most important texts came from my two children, Julian and Kara. Julian was one of the few people who thought Trump was going to win, and his text simply said, *I told you, Dad. The writing was on the wall.* He obviously saw something very few others did, including me. Kara's text was more emotional, starting with a *Dad, WTF???* She said the people in Barcelona were walking around in a trance and shaking their heads, and that was just the Spanish people. She couldn't imagine how Americans were feeling, probably hiding in their closets with a loaded gun. I told her that I was in a state of shock too, and although the results were tragic, I told her to just hang in there. I didn't know what else to say.

The DJIA futures climbed bit by bit throughout the morning hours on Wednesday as we got closer and closer to the New York opening at nine-thirty. I sat on the desk and instructed the traders to be nimble and not to outsize themselves. Essentially, I told them to keep turning over their positions and to not get stuck holding a lot of capital. Volume was likely to be heavy, and liquidity would be substantial, but most of that liquidity would be one way: selling volume. We opened down hard but not nearly as hard as was indicated overnight by the futures market. Market talking heads had attributed the rising strength overnight to Trump's victory speech and to something the market always appreciates, certainty. By midday, the trading desk was in good shape and had a pretty profitable morning, as we were able to shed long positions into the rising market. The market continued to rally into the close as three sectors led the comeback. The financials were strong, as the expectation that Trump would undue financial regulations came to the forefront. The health care sector had been weak for months, as the expectation of a Hillary Clinton victory and a focus on health care costs by Democrats weighed on them. With Trump and his strong desire to undue Obamacare, the health care sector was back in vogue overnight. Last, the defense sector rose, as there was an expectation that Trump would spend heavily on the military.

The last hour of the U.S. equity market saw the DJIA rapidly rise 312 points, as the index closed up 1 percent, 257 points. The turnaround from potentially being down 3 to 4 percent as the early futures indicated, to the market closing up 1 percent, was truly remarkable. The only time I had seen sentiment change so dramatically in so little time was during the crash of 1987, twenty-nine years beforehand.

As things settled down a bit someone in BNY's Pittsburgh office, and part of the internal communications team, called to ask me if they could interview me for the firm's intranet web page called Newsroom. They wanted to do a profile on me, something that regularly appears in this monthly internal publication. I was reluctant to do the profile at first because I had more than a few experiences in my Wall Street career where there was some jealousy, if not just low-level negativity, amongst my peers if I got any publicity for anything; however, the interviewer appealed to me that he knew a bit about my background, thought it would be interesting to many of the 50,000 strong BNY employees, and could be really helpful and inspirational to other minorities hopeful of climbing the ladder at BNY. The profile hit the intranet in late November, and I was pleased that the majority of my peers liked the piece and the message.

26

TOTAL ECLIPSE
OF THE SUN

The bull market in U.S. equities was in its eighth year now, and the DJIA closed at 19,827 on Trump's Inauguration Day on January 20, 2017. The market had struggled to pierce the psychologically 20,000 barriers since the November election, but by late January, the market began to heat up, being led by technology stocks. The Trump administration's reported pro-growth policies, talk of a corporate tax cut, and the campaign promise to address what the Republicans felt was a broken health care system, helped to propel a 4.6 percent rise in the DJIA in the first quarter, a 5.5 percent rise in the S&P 500, and a whopping 9.8 percent rise in the Nasdaq Composite.

Despite the strongest first quarter rise for equities in a few years, one of the two primary components of a profitable trading operation was missing: volatility. If you have volume with no volatility, you can't capitalize on most of the strategies, or if you're a market maker (i.e., providing capital to execute customer trades), you just increase your execution expenses, as the volume flows through your trading book. As a result of this record lack of volatility, the second lowest level of volatility in twenty-seven years, our trading desk had an abysmal first quarter. It wasn't that we lost so much money, we just didn't make much. It should be noted that volatility without adequate volume is also a recipe for disaster, and in my view is even worse than volume and no volatility.

A writer at a major financial publication called me in late 2017 and told me he wanted my thoughts on whether I thought the number of blacks on Wall Street may have been less in 2017 than in the eighties and nineties and, if so, what were some of the reasons. Neither one of us knew at that point if that was indeed true, but I surmised that I wouldn't be surprised if there were fewer now, certainly as a percentage of the industry. I told him that shortly before coming to Wall Street in 1984, and for a time thereafter, there was a hiring boom of black people on the Street, as many of America's major cities, such as Los Angeles, Washington, DC, Chicago, Philadelphia, Atlanta, and later New York, either had or elected black mayors. Wall Street correctly surmised that these black mayoral administrations would desire and welcome some black and brown faces in their meetings to discuss municipal offerings in a very needy financial time for America's major cities. At Morgan Stanley, I remember seeing an increase in blacks riding the elevators at the Exxon building and getting off on the public finance floor. That boom probably brought more blacks to the Street than at any other time; however, this was somewhat short-lived, because around the crash of 1987, I remember Salomon Brothers shocking the Street by closing their entire municipal finance department, and I believe they had the number one public finance operation on the

Street. Their reasoning was, that despite them being number one, the revenue wasn't really there given the competition, margins, and tight spreads. Whatever the reason, them getting out of the business caused heavy black job loss not only at Salomon Brothers, but around the Street, as other firms shrunk their municipal footprint as well. So, as quickly as blacks were hired in public finance, they were fired three to seven years later, certainly if the LIFO (last in, first out) method of termination was followed. Furthermore, when Wall Street goes through its sometimes inevitable, periodic heavy layoffs, municipal department or not, the LIFO method tends to hit minorities harder because of our short tenure. Also, given the absolute small representation of women on the Street, the focus in diversity switched, in my opinion, from racial diversity to gender diversity. Black and brown diversity was pushed to the back of the bus in favor of women entering the Street. I would have hoped that a dual strategy could have been utilized, but I think the pressure to bring on more women outweighed the pressure to bring some color to the Street. As the numbers declined, few black and brown young people in business schools had role models on the Street, and what you don't see is hard to aspire to be. In fact, I could probably name 50 percent of the blacks in senior positions in equities on the Street on one hand. I also told the interviewer that I believed the major reason I thought our numbers were worse now than in the eighties was that there were more high paying options not only for blacks, but for all races. Google, Apple, Facebook, and other Silicon Valley firms offered many more choices to all business undergrads and grad school people. These options were nearly non-existent twenty to thirty years ago, and in many cases, ten to twenty years ago. Plus, those jobs were considered sexier, hipper, and less structured.

The article ran a few weeks later and, rightly, focused more on the racial angle than the gender angle. Neither my name nor BNY were mentioned in the article.

■ ■ ■

Back on the trading desk, we were still struggling with the lack of volatility. We toyed with our quantitative trading engine nearly daily to see if we could discern some way to better trade a market that didn't move, and when it did, it went one way: up. Our sales organization was bringing in significant order flow, and there was adequate volume in the marketplace, but without volatility, we were dead in the water unless we became portfolio managers and tied up capital and balance sheet mid- to long-term. That wasn't our business model, nor our mandate, so we were somewhat stuck. The technology enhancements that a group of quants, outside of my business unit, were working on did nothing to help our cause either. We could only hope that the second half of the year would be half as volatile as we expected it to be, given the stark bipartisan politics in Washington and the daily divisive rhetoric that came out of Donald Trump's mouth.

At the end of March, I attended a Duke University-sponsored event at the National Museum of African American History and Culture, in Washington, DC. Prior to the event, we met with three members of the Congressional Black Caucus at the Capitol Building. It was a short distance from my hotel, so I walked to the meeting. I decided to take a shortcut to the back door by walking on the grass, and when I got halfway across the lawn, I heard a series of what sounded like gunshots. Immediately, a door flew open at the back of Capitol and about ten armed officers in full riot gear, with what looked like assault rifles, piled out of the building and ran directly toward me. I went to my knees and put my hands high up in the air. I thought I had tripped some detector or trespassed in a forbidden area, but the armed guards ran right past me and turned up the hill, to the side of the Capitol Building, where the chaos had ensued. Reportedly, a woman was on the upper level driving a car erratically and rammed a police car, nearly hit an officer, and drew gunfire from the officers. After I realized that the officers weren't going to blow me away, I got up, brushed off my knees, and got myself together. Unfortunately, some of my Duke alum friends witnessed my "surrender" as they were waiting in line at the back door, laughing hysterically after they figured out what had transpired. To this day, I get, "Penn, hit the ground before you get shot!' I know they are just joking, but I didn't find it particularly funny, given the number of black men being shot and killed by police far too often for head-shaking reasons.

The primary discussion with the congressmen surrounded, not surprisingly, Donald Trump and his unpresidential behavior, racist comments, and divisive activity. One of the congressmen stated that Trump had been in office for less than three months and had already told more lies, or mistruths, in that time (roughly 1,500 lies) than Barack Obama had in eight years in office. The congressmen went on to say that Obama had told three lies, apologized for two of them, and corrected the third on his own.

The session with the members of the Black Caucus was informative and gave the Duke alums some insight regarding how the government works, or doesn't work, and how they were addressing the issues at hand.

The trip to the African American Museum that evening left me numb. It is a fascinating museum filled with the stories, artifacts, and souls of the black experience, from the beginning of our existence in America. I walked through the exhibits with my mouth agape at the horrors black people had endured, yet I was mesmerized by their strength and endurance in overcoming what befell them. One particular exhibit really struck me, and I had to sit down and reflect on it for a few minutes. There is an old train car in the museum that looks like a normal passenger car. If you look in the car, you see the first several rows of seats are padded to provide for a reasonably comfortable trip for its passengers. The last few rows of the car were just wooden benches. At first, I just thought that perhaps this was where luggage was stored or cargo was carried. I don't remember if I read about it or someone in the museum told me, but I learned that those unpadded seats were where black people had to sit. I struggled with the abject cruelty and unnecessary hate on behalf of white people to make such rules. I was quickly brought back to a better place when I overheard a white woman tell her husband that whites in those days should have gone straight to the devil.

The other exhibits displayed even more abhorrent examples of how black people were treated in the times of slavery and segregation, but for some reason, that train exhibit got to me the most, maybe because it was a situation where common decency and respect could have prevailed without much effort, but people went out of their way to be hateful.

I left the museum angry and ready to strike if a white person so much as looked at me the wrong way, but the walk back to my hotel room allowed me to cool down a bit. Some detestable moments in black history always have a way of rearing their ugly heads in the present day when you least expect it.

■ ■ ■

In the second quarter, the U.S. equity market was propelled higher due to strong economic reports and solid corporate earnings, but the debate over health care and the Republican effort to repeal the Affordable Care Act continued to command the front pages. The daily political infighting over Obamacare failed to slow down the overall market's appreciation. As traders, we were hopeful that the heated congressional battle over Obamacare and the daily rhetoric from the Trump administration would provide some much-needed market volatility, but it never did.

■　■　■

Stocks grinded higher in the third quarter, and the S&P rose a record 4 percent, while the Nasdaq Composite jumped over 5 percent. The market dealt with a deadly and politically divisive racial protest in Charlottesville, Virginia, a devastating hurricane in the Caribbean, especially in Puerto Rico, and continued hostility between North Korea and the United States. All this and still no stock trading volatility. Our trading desk and all equity trading desks on the Street were struggling mightily. To add insult to injury, trading volume also decreased in the third quarter, which was not a huge surprise, as the summer months were typically slower.

In late August, I headed to Charleston, South Carolina, to see the total eclipse of the sun. I had only been to Charleston once before, many years ago, but absolutely fell in love with the charming town. The restaurants were outstanding, the shopping was interesting and eclectic, and the scenery was something out of a storybook. I also visited the Emanuel African Methodist Episcopal Church, where the white supremacist Dylan Roof killed nine black people, in one of the most horrific mass shootings on record. The morning I visited the church, the sun was shining and the birds were chirping. It was hard to believe that something so heinous and hateful could have happened in such a beautiful place.

On Monday, August 21, I walked over to the Charleston waterfront to set up camp for the eclipse that was due to start around one p.m. About fifteen minutes later, the area went stark black, the temperature instantly dropped fifteen to twenty degrees, the winds kicked up, and some of the dogs in the area started running in circles and barking madly. As the eclipse broke through the clouds, there was thunder and lightning. It was one of the most awesome sights I had ever witnessed. Nature ruled again. Nothing could match the sight of the corona, which is when the moon is totally in front of the sun and the sun barely outlines the outside of the moon. The total eclipse itself lasted for one minute and thirty-eight seconds, but the whole process lasted an hour and forty-five minutes. By three p.m., the sun was back out, the temperature soared back into the eighties, and all was back to normal again.

■ ■ ■

The beginning of the fourth quarter began with U.S. equities at record highs. The anticipation of lower taxes for corporations combined with an already strong economy led equities to continue their northerly move. It was an unusual year for people sitting at equity trading desks for a number of reasons: no volatility of which to speak, no pullbacks intra-year of any significance, and a market that totally ignored any bad news.

In December, I received a gut punch when I learned that one of my dear first cousins, Keith Penn, with whom I was very close, died at the age of sixty-one from diabetes-related complications. Keith lived in my hometown of Youngstown, Ohio, and was a character unlike any other. His lifestyle wasn't one that I necessarily aligned with, but he had a great sense of humor and a heart of gold. To this day, I miss him, especially our fun banter, as I was always busting his chops about something he had said or done, and he would end the conversation poking fun, with a "F*** you, Derek!" I loved it and miss it.

The year ended with the DJIA up a remarkable 25 percent, its best year since 2013. The S&P 500 and Nasdaq Composite also had their best years since 2013, with them rising 19 percent and 28 percent, respectively. Trump's tax reform package was passed in late December and lowered the corporate tax rate from 35 percent to 21 percent, and 2018 was set up to further explode on the economic and securities market front. The equity market was set up for further impressive gains in 2018, while I, on the other hand, was anticipating an eclipse similar to the one I had witnessed in Charleston, but I doubted whether mine would be as beautiful and fulfilling.

27

AN ERA ENDS

As expected, January 2018 continued the strong momentum in equities that closed out 2017. Oil prices continued their upward trajectory, retail sales got the wind behind its back, and the economy continued to gain strength while unemployment ticked lower. The DJIA and S&P 500 were both up over 5 percent in the first month, and the Nasdaq Composite was even stronger, as it appreciated 7.3 percent.

In the category of be careful what you ask for, Monday, February 5, brought the volatility that us equity traders had been asking for, for over a year, if not longer; however, we didn't want outrageous volatility that seemed to be without bounds. Some concern about an overheated economy began to seep into investors' minds the previous week, which prompted thoughts of inflation and, subsequently, a fear that the Fed would put its foot on the accelerator to raise interest rates quicker than previously expected. The DJIA went into free fall at the opening bell and caught most people off guard, including my troops. I came out to the market-making desk and told the traders, "No heroes. Let's go with the flow, no fighting the tape, be nimble, and don't try and pick the bottom, assuming there is a bottom." At its lowest point, the DJIA was down 1,600 points, easily its biggest point decline ever up to that point. Late in the session, the market rallied a couple hundred points, but by the closing mark, it was still down 1,175 points (4.6 percent), the worst one-day point decline in history up to that point. We came out of it relatively unscathed, but we missed some great opportunities toward the close. In an effort to be nimble, as I had directed, we bailed out of our longs just as the market started its march back up in the last few minutes of trading. Missed opportunity, but then again, we were in shape to fight another day—my mantra.

By the end of that week, the equity market was down 10 percent, and Street traders had to put their helmets on. Despite the accepted themes of inflation concerns, dollar strength analysis, and interest rate movement, I personally just thought the market was overbought, overextended, and investors were looking for an excuse to sell. Ironically, the Monday of the crash was also the new Fed chair (Jerome Powell)'s, first day on the job. In a sick, Wall Street sort of way, I also thought that traders may have been testing the wit and backbone of the new player. In any event, volatility was back, and this was hopefully going to be the revenue opportunity year we had wished for, for almost two years.

On February 12, I attended an event sponsored by *Black Enterprise* magazine at J.P. Morgan's headquarters. The event was to celebrate the magazine's 100 Most Powerful Black Executives in Corporate America. The list was different than the magazine's previous lists of top blacks on Wall Street, but, nonetheless, I was included on this list, as I had been on every other list the magazine had published since the eighties.

J.P. Morgan's highly touted industry mogul/CEO Jamie Dimon addressed the one hundred honorees and talked about his firm's efforts to improve their diversity numbers and how he hoped the industry's poor numbers would improve soon, with perhaps J.P. Morgan providing the prescription for improvement. He spoke about some of the things J. P. Morgan was doing, but he made a statement that caused everyone in the room to chuckle, then bristle a bit when he said, "I've told our people that when they see a black person on the street, take that person to lunch. Get to know them. See how you can help. See how they might be able to help us." Nearly every black person in the room, including me, couldn't believe what he'd just said. He may have meant well, but it sure came across awkwardly. To top it off, someone then said, "I don't need anyone to take me to lunch, but ..." We all laughed nervously, and Jamie laughed as well. I think the woman who put the event together was trying to figure out how she could quietly leave the room to save face.

February being Black History Month, I was also asked to participate in an event at Société Générale, the French multinational banking and financial services company, to publicize an effort by some private individuals to tell the story of blacks on Wall Street and to have some black industry veterans, like me, discuss their careers. A video was also in the works that would hopefully become a full-blown documentary on the history of blacks on Wall Street.

During the panel session I was asked how I managed to stay on Wall Street for thirty-three years. I told the group that, first, I was lucky. I realized that not a lot of black people had thirty-plus-year careers on the Street. Part of my luck came because I knew my craft well and had a thorough understanding of how to trade. I had also worked for five different firms and had been through massive layoffs at each one. I'm sure my name had come up a few times for termination; however, the fact that I could trade numerous other equity products like converts, options, and foreign exchange, besides the bread-and-butter Nasdaq, NYSE, and foreign equities, I was more valuable than the next guy. I certainly wasn't an expert in all of these asset classes, but I knew enough to be dangerous. I also think having an MBA gave me an edge in my career, even though, at the end of the day, it comes down to know-how, not credentials. Still, I think it helped.

The event was informative, and I publicly applauded the French firm for sponsoring it, in an effort to further promote black history, which was more than some American firms had done.

■ ■ ■

The equity market in the second quarter was consistently the most volatile I had encountered in my career. In 2017, during roughly 252 trading days, the S & P moved 1 percent in either direction for 11 days. Thru mid-April 2018, the index had already moved 1 percent or more for 28 days. That extreme volatility helped the trading desk stay close to budget through the second quarter. Once again, in a presentation to senior management, I showed a chart detailing the direct correlation between volatility and trading revenue for not only our trading desk, but for the Street in general.

In early June, I moderated a panel at Pershing's client conference, INSITE, in Orlando, Florida, where I had the opportunity to interview industry expert Larry Tabb on the trends and future of equity sales and trading. When I got back to my hotel room after my session, I checked my emails and saw that I had a calendar invite back at the job on Tuesday, June 12. The subject line read HR Follow-up, and it was for a meeting on the twelfth floor. I knew immediately that this was my termination event.

On Monday, June 11, my workday was a normal one, but after the market closed, I packed up my basic essentials and left the building, knowing that once you were severed, you weren't allowed to go back to your desk or your office to retrieve anything; your belongings would be sent to you a few weeks later. That evening I went to the gym and then had dinner at one of my favorite local restaurants with my lovely Latina girlfriend. I never mentioned to her what I suspected was going to happen the next morning.

The next day, I got to work early and packed my briefcase with a few more personal items that I thought I might need in the short term. At 7:25 a.m., I grabbed my briefcase and jacket and headed over to the elevator for my 7:30 a.m. meeting on the twelfth floor. The human resource person, whom I had utilized to sever other people on occasion, and my direct manager and the COO of Capital Markets were in the room. As the human resource person began her oration, I politely interrupted and told her I was quite familiar with how this discussion went, having delivered the unfortunate news many times in reduction-in-force situations myself. She said the firm was shutting down the equity market-making unit and the associated technology and support staff as well. She said the traders and staff were being terminated because the group's profitability wasn't up to snuff. They would be given notice individually, but I told her I wanted to speak to the group as a whole, to make sure they left with some level of dignity and reassurance that they were not failures. She wasn't keen on the idea, but I insisted, as I had pledged after the Fidelity firing fiasco after 9-11 that I would always be in the room when anyone who worked for me was terminated. I closed my conversation with the traders by saying, "Walk out of here proud and with your head up. Nobody here is a failure."

I walked out of BNY Mellon around ten that morning.

28

MY TOP 20 OBSERVATIONS OF LIFE AS A BLACK MAN ON WALL STREET

1. There is ample room for both genders, all races, all religions, all ethnicities, all sexual orientations, and any other people category one can think of. The trick is matching a particular person's strengths with whatever the role is, and providing a platform that will ultimately allow that person to flourish as they grow.

2. Men, if you're thinking about starting a romantic or sexual relationship with a woman at work, don't do it! As the saying goes, "Don't s*** where you eat!" I've seen more than a handful of men's careers, and their marriages, blow up due to affairs on the job.

3. Never leave a production position for a support role if you're looking for longevity on the Street. In a downturn or layoff scenario, support people are the first to go.

4. The advancement of women in the ranks of Wall Street, especially white women, has superseded and displaced the advancement of people of color on the Street over the last thirty years.

5. Many people of color on Wall Street are reluctant to help another person of color with employment assistance within their firm. One of the reasons is a belief that the firm has a quota, and if another person of color comes in, a person of color is likely to be dismissed at some point in the near future to keep the "color" numbers in line.

6. If you don't network internally and externally and respectfully toot your own horn, you become invisible over time.

7. One of the keys to longevity on the Street is having multiple skill sets and a knowledge of multiple products. The era of having a unilateral perspective is over.

8. Possessing quantitative and technical skills are an absolute must now.

9. White folks don't need the same level of credentials to get an entry-level job on the Street as people of color. A senior-level white person's golf caddie at the country club often has as good a chance, if not better, of obtaining an entry-level position than a person of color with an undergraduate degree from a top ten university due to connections and familiarity.

10. Most Wall Street diversity programs need signifiant enhancement, but I've recently become encouraged that the current industry effort has teeth. I feel the commitment is at the very senior levels, but historically has dissipated as it funnels down through the organization. I also feel there needs to be a more focused effort to genuinely tie compensation to diversity to really effect change.

11. Keep your compensation to yourself. In an industry where money is your personal currency and you're measured to some degree by your W-2, compensation jealously is at an extremely high level.

12. Fly under the radar with your material possessions. Many individuals on the organizational chart who are aligned with you or are above you get attitudes if you exhibit more bling than they do. I'll never forget the young Goldman Sachs employee who drove a Porsche to work, and when he was terminated, the manager said, "Now you have plenty of time to drive your Porsche!"

13. Avoid publicity, both positively and obviously negatively. Many senior people harbor jealousy toward those who get more press internally and externally. This is tricky when there is also a need to toot your own horn a bit to not get lost in the mix.

14. In a layoff, people of color are generally the first to go. While layoffs are generally, and hopefully, not racially motivated these days, it often comes down to the last in, first out, and that primarily falls on people of color.

15. It is said—and is oh so true—that bad news takes the elevator to the upstairs corner office and good news takes the fire escape stairs.

16. Handsome, tall white men are more highly regarded for leadership roles than any other category of people on the Street. Tall black men are many times looked at as threatening to the majority. A white executive once told me that I was too serious and as a result too scary to be a senior manager.

17. A black man on the Street is rarely given the benefit of the doubt. He must always prove and reprove himself, over and over.

18. Forget what you know about the market. If there are more buyers than sellers, the market/stock is going higher. Don't *fight the tape* or the Fed, regardless of what you think the market or a stock should do.

19. Age and racial discrimination are alive and well, and I suspect this will still be the case going forward, even though I'm more encouraged now for positive change than I have been in my entire thirty four year career. There is positive momentum from a number of angles that heretofore were largely ignored or toothless in my view.

20. Always have an exit strategy!

29

MY TOP 20 OBSERVATIONS OF LIFE AS A BLACK MAN

1. A country founded on racism will always be racist, despite the efforts, actions, and good intentions of good people of all races. Some people of color understand this and navigate it well, while others don't. Racism is part of this country's DNA, and people of color have to understand this and maneuver accordingly. Having said this, the racist events and the subsequent reactions of *woke* white people in 2020 have given me hope that things will gradually change for the better for people of color.

2. Education is the *partial* equalizer; nevertheless, a person of color generally needs to have a more impressive degree, or

at least one degree more than a majority person, to attain the same level of accomplishment.

3.   Many white people have some sort of financial backstop in the event things go south, whether that be a wealthy, charitable relative, a trust fund, or an inheritance. Most people of color can't go beyond their own checkbook. This comes from a four-hundred-year head start that the majority had, that my dad always referenced in discussions about equality and a level playing field. Of the twenty wealthiest Americans, not one is a person of color.

4.   Every black family has at least one family member or relative who is stone-cold ghetto. I've been told by my white friends that every white person similarly has a hillbilly in their family as well.

5.   Don't lend money to family unless you call them Mom or Dad. Family is more prone to screw you financially than non-family when it comes to money.

6.   A person is 90 percent baked when they come out of the womb. Afterwards, Mom and Dad mold 5 percent and the child's environment molds the last 5 percent.

7.   A child that disrespects his or her parents will probably grow up to disrespect everything else in life.

8.   Good health is the most important thing in life. Without it, you can't enjoy much else.

9. White folks get multiple chances to fail and, perhaps, subsequently succeed. People of color get one or two chances if they're lucky.

10. The likelihood of a white person recovering from a financial, health, legal, or social calamity is significantly higher than a person of color. The pandemic of 2020 has proven that the majority of minorities are a paycheck or two away from financial collapse.

11. Prepare for the bad times in the good times.

12. How you take care of yourself health-wise between the ages of 20 and 40 will generally determine your level of health and related happiness between the ages of 40 and 70. After 70, I suspect nature largely takes over and dictates your forward health.

13. Everyone is responsible for their own happiness. If you're in a job you can't stand, or a marriage that makes you unhappy, or any other situation that you have the power to change, then it's on you to effect the change.

14. What a better, more efficient world we would have if people actually did what they said they were going to do.

15. I believe there are five major decisions you make in life that determine much about the quality of your life as an adult, which are where you go to college and what you study; who you marry, if that's the path you take; where you decide to live; how many kids you have, if you decide to have children;

and what career you pursue. If you make a poor decision on one of these, you can recover. If you make a poor decision on two of them, life gets tricky. If you blow more than two, especially if one of them is your significant other choice, cancel Christmas!

16. Bet on yourself. You know the inputs better than anyone else, and you have a better chance of controlling and maximizing the outcome.

17. Family is the true constant. Friends come and go, outside of maybe two or three lifelong, ride or die friends. Family is there through thick and thin, for better or for worse. Just don't lend them any money! Gift it instead, and you'll relieve yourself of long-term regret.

18. Rely on those closest to you for advice and for help in making important decisions in your life.

19. I endorse the old adages *enjoy life to the fullest* and *don't put off till tomorrow what you can do today*. I think of my friend Calvin Gooding, who perished at the World Trade Center on 9-11. Calvin was preparing for a wonderful post-40 life that never came.

20. If an attorney who is representing you talks about a financial settlement early on in your claim for damages against another person or entity, get another attorney. Your attorney should righteously fight for you until a settlement makes tactical and financial sense.

EPILOGUE

Since leaving BNY Mellon in June 2018, I have done what one would expect of someone ending a thirty-four-year career. I started watching all the late night talk shows; I got up at eight a.m. rather than five-thirty a.m., as I did during my professional Street life; I made leisurely afternoon workouts at the gym the norm rather than rushed workouts after work, followed by a hurried dinner while opening mail, watching a sporting event, or answering emails and texts before my ten o'clock bedtime; and I finally had the time to focus on all the small projects that needed to be done at my Hudson Valley home that I had neglected over the years due to lack of time or a desire to tackle them on the weekend.

Aside from my new routines and the small house enhancement jobs I've tackled, I was eager to find a new outlet, one that was relevant and meaningful to me, and that became writing my story, which I lightly started at the beginning of 2018. The thought of writing a book about my life, especially about my Wall Street career, had crossed my mind often, but my initial intent was to write a book for my family and friends only. The world of Wall Street was fascinating to them, and they had asked questions over the years about the inner workings of the Street and how it was for a black man working in the canyons of lower Manhattan. The prospect of writing a book was made easier because I began keeping detailed, written calendars early on in my life, especially during my Wall Street days, which began in 1984. By looking at my calendars, I could pretty much determine, with considerable precision, what was going on in my life professionally and personally. I used these calendars to create an outline, and then consulted a number of major newspapers, such as the *Wall Street Journal*, the *New York Times*, the *Washington Post*, *USA Today*, *Barron's*, and the *New York Post*, to fill in the blanks about market conditions and details of certain occurrences. My surprisingly still solid memory and discussions with friends about certain events also served me well.

Once I started writing my book, I realized that I wanted to continue working, preferably back on Wall Street, if I could find a situation in which I could leverage my considerable experience and add some value to a solid, reputable organization and work with some decent, respectful colleagues. Fairly early, I received a few Wall Street offers, but they were offers with firms in desperate straits, either in regulatory trouble or with people I considered undesirable. One firm wanted my first order of business to be to travel to their European headquarters and fire a hundred or so employees. No thanks; bad karma right out of the chute. Another firm had MAGA hats all over the floor, and the managing partner said, "I love Donald Trump, don't you?" Next. I also had an offer or two in other cities, but I thought I'd give staying in the New York City area a chance.

If I don't ever return to the Street I am extremely thankful and grateful for my past thirty-four year career. My participation in this fantastic industry has allowed me to stretch my mental capacity, make a ton of friends and acquaintances, be a tiny cog in the circulatory system of the economy and see how a segment of it works from the inside, and provide financial rewards for me and my immediate and extended family. My earnings, and being on the team at five great firms has also allowed me to financially and intellectually contribute to various institutions, like my absolutely beloved Duke University, and also contribute in different ways to a wide range of charitable causes and platforms that are important to me and my loved ones.

Each of the industry significant firms that employed me had their own considerable merits, despite the flaws and issues that I have mentioned throughout this book; there is no perfect firm in this industry, and probably not one in any industry for that matter. Morgan Stanley, from top to bottom, had the strongest and most consistent brainpower of any firm that I worked for during my career. I thank John Mack and Dick Fisher of Morgan Stanley for initially extending that first offer to come to the Street. The strength and world-wide reach of Merrill Lynch was phenomenal, and I thank Kelly Martin and Anne O'Connor Mills for their reach to bring me to the "thundering herd" and introduce me to the world of international equities. I thank Donald Crooks, my first manager at Morgan Stanley, who brought me to his new home, Lehman Brothers, when I left Merrill Lynch. I had perhaps the most fun of my career at Lehman Brothers, and much of it was due to the eclectic bunch of employees that Lehman assembled, as Lehman was the firm that in my eyes was the home for all the really smart, misfits that couldn't or didn't want to cope at the other traditional firms. Fidelity, the most technologically creative, innovative, and outstanding customer service firm I received a paycheck from was also very rewarding. People like my human resource manager, Jim Boland, and senior leaders like Bob Mazzarella, Tim McKenna, and Frank Driscoll couldn't have been better people to work for and with. I thank Craig Messinger for bringing me to Pershing after my Fidelity stint, as both Craig and I both also worked together at Fidelity beforehand. Pershing was the most hospitable, ego-less, family oriented firm, full of the most decent people that I've ever had the pleasure of working with on a large scale. The overall BNY Mellon enterprise, which Pershing is a part of, has the capability of being the most powerful firm on the planet if they get all the various channels, divisions, and global strengths going in the same direction.

In the two years since I left the world of bids and offers, I've done some lightweight consulting, a little traveling primarily around North America, and attended various sporting events near and far. I've gotten much gratification from the many individuals on Wall Street that I've helped to get into the business, given career advice to, mentored, and trained that have reached out to chat and check on me. I also made my Upstate home in the Hudson Valley my primary residence, which turned out to be a boss move when the Coronavirus took over New York City in early 2020. The Manhattan building in which I lived, and still have an outpost, reportedly had an incidence of COVID-19 on, ironically, nineteen floors of a thirty-five story building.

I recently served as co-chair of the Fuqua School of Business's eighteen-member Racial Equity Working Group, which was put together by the outstanding and socially conscious dean of the Fuqua School, Bill Boulding, in an effort to create better racial equity at Fuqua by looking at it from a student, alumni, faculty, and staff perspective. This effort was prompted after the George Floyd murder and the uprising across the nation by not only black and brown people, but by whites and people of all ethnic backgrounds who were just as fed up with racial injustice. I also served on a panel at a J. P Morgan-sponsored event to discuss how to increase the number of black and brown people at J P. Morgan specifically and on Wall Street in general. From my standpoint, if a firm wanted to increase their number of black and brown people, they needed to have black and brown people in the current seats. If people of color don't see people who look like them in various positions, it's hard to envision themselves in that same position. If you can't envision yourself in that position, you'll most likely not pursue a career at that firm or in that industry.

My many white friends and former white colleagues and I have often talked about the state of race in America. One friend asked me to explain systemic racism, as he had no idea what it truly was. In the most simplistic of terms, I told him that systemic racism is being disadvantaged in at least five major ways: health care, housing, education, economics, and justice. I then gave him examples of each, and I further told him that if the economic disadvantage was eliminated that would go a long way to reducing the other disadvantages. If people of color had economic equality, despite the still egregious obstacles, they could probably afford a better attorney, go to a better school, have access to better medical care, and be able to find a dwelling in a neighborhood that only cared about your ability to pay. He was appreciative of the explanation.

I've also been asked to explain the Black Lives Matter (BLM) movement to a number of my white friends, whose typical assertion was, "Don't *all* lives matter?" I explained that the slogan might have been better served if it read Black Lives Matter Too, but black lives haven't mattered anywhere close to the degree that white lives have mattered, and that's evident in nearly every aspect of society. I believe those behind the movement were more concerned about putting the emphasis on black lives, not on all of society, as, clearly, equality is highly disproportionate. When my explanation finally sunk in, they let out a collective "Oh, now I get it."

If only I could spread that wisdom, or education, or luminance across the nation and have all of white America respond with an "Oh, now I get it." I think we'd be on our way to a better, more equitable, more prosperous nation.

Personally, I've struggled with the notion, as has been stated, that *none of us are free, until we all are free.* I didn't believe any of my white friends were oppressed at all, at least not in the five ways I mentioned earlier. I sought my younger brother Karl's advice on what that statement meant. He's a knock 'em dead minister and a very *woke* individual. His take is that white America can't be free if they have to spend time suppressing us, keeping us down, and continually falsely reassuring themselves that they are superior. He said they know it's a lie, and if you live every day with a lie, how can you truly be free? I thought his insight was brilliant, and it helped me to better understand two related quotes from two icons my dad truly admired: basketball great Bill Russell and Martin Luther King, Jr. Russell said, "Without justice for all, none of us are free"; and King said, "We are tied together in a single garment of destiny. Whatever affects one directly, affects all indirectly."

I am hoping to return to the working world in some capacity, perhaps even on a corporate board or two, sometime in 2021. All the trees that could currently fall on my house have been cut down. All the walls inside and out are painted. The lawn has been reseeded and will hopefully produce a lush green lawn in the spring of 2021. And my book is obviously out, hopefully inspiring some young person of color to charge on, despite any obstacles, to pursue his or her dreams, and to rise like the kid from Youngstown, Ohio, did. I also hope that the majority people reading this book will better understand the life and struggles that a person of color must endure on a daily basis. I'm what some consider to be a successful black man, yet I'm many times exhausted from dealing with the daily trials and tribulations that come with being a black man in America. One can only imagine what level of daily exhaustion and angst that a black man who hasn't had the assistance, opportunities, and luck I've had, must endure. Last, if you just wanted to read a good narrative, learn or recall a little financial history, shake your head a few times in disgust, or just have a few laughs, hopefully I delivered.

Keep hope alive.

ACKNOWLEDGMENTS

First, I would like to thank the Reverend Solomon Hill, of Youngstown, Ohio, who told me I should write a book after I spoke at a church event fifteen years ago.

Additionally, I owe a special debt of gratitude to William Cohan, prolific financial author and fellow Duke alumni, for his guidance in helping me launch my writing effort.

I want to acknowledge Duke University pal Johnny Moore and fellow Duke alum Reggie Love, both authors of a book or two, for their helpful tips on how to write a book.

Another Duke alum I want to thank is friend, author, and legal expert Richard Bell for introducing me to his publisher, Word Association.

I'm grateful to Simon & Schuster editor Jofie Ferrari-Adler for offering his positive comments when I discussed aspects of my book with him.

Last, but not least, a special thank you to writer and consultant Asha Bandele for her late-stage guidance in getting my book published.

WA

Made in United States
North Haven, CT
08 June 2023

37516729R00239